BUILDING A SECURE COMPUTER SYSTEM

Morrie Gasser

 VAN NOSTRAND REINHOLD COMPANY
_____NEW YORK

Copyright © 1988 by Van Nostrand Reinhold Company Inc.
Library of Congress Catalog Card Number 87-27838
ISBN 0-442-23022-2

Printed in the United States of America
Designed by Beth Tondreau

Van Nostrand Reinhold Company Inc.
115 Fifth Avenue
New York, New York 10003

Van Nostrand Reinhold Company Limited
Molly Millars Lane
Wokingham, Berkshire RG11 2PY, England

Van Nostrand Reinhold
480 La Trobe Street
Melbourne, Victoria 3000, Australia

Macmillan of Canada
Division of Canada Publishing Corporation
164 Commander Boulevard
Agincourt, Ontario M1S 3C7, Canada

16 15 14 13 12 11 10 9 8 7 6 5 4 3 2 1

Library of Congress Cataloging-in-Publication Data
Gasser, Morrie, 1947–
    Building a secure computer system.
    Bibliography: p.
    Includes index.
    1. Computers—Access control. 2. System design.
I. Title.
QA76.9.A25G37   1988   005.8   87-27838
ISBN 0-442-23022-2

TO MY WIFE,
KATE,
AND MY CHILDREN,
BECKY AND DANNY.

CONTENTS

FOREWORD

The lack of a technical reference work on computer security has for years been a serious impediment to the growth of the field. Removing this obstacle required an author thoroughly conversant with the technology, skilled in writing, and fully dedicated to completion of a most difficult undertaking. Mr. Gasser has accepted this formidable challenge and has succeeded beyond what even we optimists would expect. Although I recognized that Mr. Gasser was unquestionably qualified, I was frankly skeptical about whether or not it was possible to produce a practical, understandable, and thoroughly accurate first book on the subject. As I started to read the book for the first time I found myself engrossed into the wee hours of the morning, and came away impressed that this singular effort had at long last given the field a definitive reference work for technical solutions to computer security problems.

The field of computer security did not begin to emerge until the late 1960s, with the growing recognition by several groups in the government and private sector that computers were highly vulnerable. The landmark report by Willis Ware of RAND in 1969 alerted those within the Department of Defense to many of the technical weaknesses of computer security. The publicity associated with IBM's commitment of forty million dollars to address computer security in the early 1970s brought the problem to the public's attention as well. Unfortunately, many of those building computer systems took the position that internal computer controls (those that are embodied in software within the operating system) could effectively limit the access of users to authorized information only. For a number of years many were lulled into the belief that computer security was a "people problem" that could be addressed by encouraging people to follow the "rules of the road". A few organizations, especially in the military, formed "tiger teams" to simulate adversaries trying to obtain unauthorized access to information.

These tiger teams consistently found that circumventing the internal computer controls was an easy way to compromise security. Even when the system builder made a major and concerted effort to find and patch all the holes, the technical controls were usually penetrated with ease. In recent years the media coverage of the exploits of "hackers" have increased general awareness of such computer vulnerabilities. However, awareness that a problem existed did little to help the designers and builders of systems understand the underlying issues needing to be addressed in order to respond to the problem. This book brings together the problems and technical solutions in a balanced perspective that pinpoints constructive responses to some of the most significant aspects of the problem of computer security.

Any computer system can only be secure with respect to some specific policy that defines what information people are authorized to read or modify. This book presents the two major classes of policies—discretionary and mandatory—and shows how the informal policies contained in rules and regulations can be fine-tuned for use in building a specific computer system to meet a desired policy. This is the first design step. Fortunately it is now understood that policy can be mathematically modeled abstractly, so that a wide range of end-user policies are represented by a single model. This means that a single system design can be used effectively for private and commercial as well as civil and military uses.

The nub of the problem of secure computers is how to determine if a computer is in fact secure. In fact, in practical terms, one of the most serious and difficult impediments to widespread introduction of highly secure systems is the limited number of evaluators who can accurately and consistently judge the security of a computer. The key to this problem lies in specifying a chain of objective evidence that bridges the gap from policy to implemented system. Although the steps identified in this book fully support the *Trusted Computer System Evaluation Criteria* produced by the National Computer Security Center, the technical elements of an objective evaluation are not tied to any particular organization or class of users. Reproducible design steps that are carefully documented make it possible for a third party to objectively judge the efficacy of the builder's use of the technology. Understanding and using these steps make it possible not only to build a secure computer, but also to have an evaluator confirm that you have succeeded.

There can be little doubt that it is unusually difficult to build and understand a highly secure computer system. One of the most delightful aspects of this book is its readable style that presents difficult and subtle topics clearly, without excessive jargon or superficiality, while achieving the needed breadth of coverage. This book distinguishes the technical aspects of computer security, and identifies the significance of the vulnerabilities being addressed. If I had but one book that I could recommend to the computer professional on computer security, *Building a Secure Computer System* would be my unqualified choice.

Dr. Roger Schell
Vice President for Engineering
Gemini Computers, Inc.
Carmel, California

PREFACE

This book is for the practicing computer professional who wants to understand—and perhaps implement—technical solutions to computer security problems. It covers the state of the art of applied computer security technology developed over the last fifteen or twenty years. It is a guide to building systems, not an exhaustive academic study, and provides enough information about selected techniques to give you a well-rounded understanding of the problems and solutions.

It is not possible in one book to treat all applications of security while retaining the technical depth needed to cover each topic adequately. I have concentrated on applications for which prevailing literature is weak: operating systems, hardware architecture, networks, and practical verification. Subjects about which books are already available, such as database security and cryptographic algorithms, receive less discussion here.

In selecting techniques for discussion, I have given primary attention to demonstrable practicality. Many interesting techniques have been implemented in experimental systems but have never seen production use. Some sophisticated features appear in research systems that are used daily at universities, proving that the concepts are viable, but for various reasons (not the fault of the researchers) the systems remain one-of-a-kind.

Important technological advances in computer security are only now beginning to see the light of day, as interest in security grows among computer system vendors and users. Experience with many sophisticated techniques is in its infancy, and examples are few and far between. Therefore, despite my attempt to stick to practical techniques, I have included some advanced concepts that are not quite ready for production use but follow logically from today's technology and show reasonable promise.

The technology of computer security is controversial. While everyone agrees that we have a serious computer security problem, few agree on the best response. Many would address the problem through better control of personnel, better administrative procedures, and more suitable laws; others believe that technical solutions are most appropriate. While this book concentrates solely on the technical approach, the ultimate answer will surely be a combination of many approaches.

Even among those who agree that technology is the answer, there is some disagreement on the value of different techniques. While I wish to be fair to all points of view, I emphasize approaches in this book that I believe work, and I make only token mention of others. This manner of selection is not meant to discredit alternatives: there simply is not room to go into adequate detail about all reasonable approaches. In addition, some good techniques may have been omitted because I am not aware of them; I apologize to any researchers and developers whose work may be shortchanged.

Please note: this book does not teach you how to break into systems. If you are looking for a "hacker's guide," this is the wrong place.

Part I of this book provides an overview of elementary concepts and serves as an introduction to the chapters in parts II and III that will enable you to read only the chapters of interest, without getting lost.

I would like to express my sincere appreciation to those who have taken the time out of their busy schedules to review and comment on drafts of this book: Martha Branstad, Paul Karger, Richard Kemmerer, Steven Lipner, Jonathan Millen, John Parodi, Marvin Schaefer, Roger Schell, Joe Tardo, and John Woodward. I am especially grateful to my most critical reviewer: my wife, Kate, without whom this book would never have left the word processor.

PART I

OVERVIEW

Chapter 1

What Is Computer Security?

The meaning of the term *computer security* has evolved in recent years. Before the problem of data security became widely publicized in the media, most people's idea of computer security focused on the physical machine. Traditionally, computer facilities have been physically protected for three reasons:

- To prevent theft of or damage to the hardware
- To prevent theft of or damage to the information
- To prevent disruption of service

Strict procedures for access to the machine room are used by most organizations, and these procedures are often an organization's only obvious computer security measures. Today, however, with pervasive remote terminal access, communications, and networking, physical measures rarely provide meaningful protection for either the information or the service; only the hardware is secure. Nonetheless, most computer facilities continue to protect their physical machine far better than they do their data, even when the value of the data is several times greater than the value of the hardware.

You probably are not reading this book to learn how to padlock your PC. *Information security* is the subject of this book. Furthermore, we are limiting our study to the insider problem: the security violations perpetrated (perhaps inadvertently) by legitimate users whom padlocks and passwords cannot deter. Most computer crimes are in fact committed by insiders, and most of the research in computer security since 1970 has been directed at the insider problem.

1.1 SECRECY, INTEGRITY, AND DENIAL OF SERVICE

Throughout this book, the discussion of computer security emphasizes the problem of protecting information from unauthorized disclosure, or information secrecy. You may find it disconcerting, as you read this book, that information integrity—protecting information from unauthorized modification or destruction—seems to be receiving no sustained attention.

There are two reasons for this seemingly one-sided point of view, one historic and one technical. First, having been funded primarily by the United States government, most computer security endeavors have concentrated on maintaining the secrecy of classified information. This tradition has persisted even in commercial applications, where classified information is not the concern and where integrity, not secrecy, is often the primary goal. And second, the information disclosure problem is technically more interesting to computer security researchers, and the literature reflects this bias.

Fortunately, techniques to protect against information modification are almost always the same as (or a subset of) techniques to protect against information disclosure. This fact is consistently borne out in the technical measures we will discuss. In the rare cases where the techniques differ, that fact will be pointed out explicitly.

While the definition of *computer security* used in this book does, therefore, include both secrecy and integrity, the closely related area termed *denial of service* is rarely discussed here. Denial of service can be defined as a temporary reduction in system performance, a system crash requiring manual restart, or a major crash with permanent loss of data. Although reliable operation of the computer is a serious concern in most cases, denial of service has not traditionally been a topic of computer security research. As in the case of data integrity, one reason for the lack of concern is historic: secrecy has been the primary goal of government-funded security programs. But there is also an important technical reason. While great strides have been made since the early 1970s toward ensuring secrecy and integrity, little progress has been made in solving denial of service because the problem is fundamentally much harder: preventing denial of service requires ensuring the complete functional correctness of a system—something unlikely to be done in the foreseeable future.

If denial of service is your only concern, you should refer to such topics as structured development, fault tolerance, and software reliability. Most of the techniques for building secure systems, however, also help you build more robust and reliable systems. In addition, some security techniques do address certain denial-of-service problems, especially problems related to data integrity. This book will indicate when those techniques apply.

To sum up, *security* relates to secrecy first, integrity second, and denial of service a distant third. To help you remember this, memorize the computer security researcher's favorite (tongue-in-cheek) phrase: "I don't care if it works, as long as it is secure."

1.2 TRUSTED SYSTEM EVALUATION CRITERIA

The U.S. Department of Defense has developed its own definition of computer security, documented in *Trusted Computer System Evaluation Criteria* (Department of Defense 1985), also called "the Orange Book" after the color of its cover (and hereafter shortened to "the *Criteria*"). The document employs the concept of a *trusted computing base*, a combination of computer hardware and an operating system that supports untrusted applications and users. The seven levels of trust identified by the *Criteria* range from systems that have minimal protection features to those that provide the highest level of security modern technology can produce (table 1-1). The *Criteria* attempts to define objective guidelines on which to base evaluations of both commercial systems and those developed for military applications. The National Computer Security Center, the official evaluator for the Defense Department, maintains an Evaluated Products List of commercial systems that it has rated according to the *Criteria*.

The *Criteria* is a technical document that defines many computer security concepts and provides guidelines for their implementation. It focuses primarily on general-purpose operating systems. To assist in the evaluation of networks, the National Computer Security Center has published the *Trusted Network Interpretation* (National Computer Security Center 1987), that interprets the *Criteria* from the point of view of network security. The *Trusted Network Interpretation* identifies security features not mentioned in the *Criteria* that apply to networks and individual components within networks, and shows how they fit into the *Criteria* ratings.

Class	Title	Key Features
A1	Verified Design	Formal top-level specification and verification, formal covert channel analysis, informal code correspondence demonstration
B3	Security Domains	Reference monitor (security kernel), "highly resistant to penetration"
B2	Structured Protection	Formal model, covert channels constrained, security-oriented architecture, "relatively resistant to penetration"
B1	Labeled Security Protection	Mandatory access controls, security labeling, removal of security-related flaws
C2	Controlled Access Protection	Individual accountability, extensive auditing, add-on packages
C1	Discretionary Security Protection	Discretionary access controls, protection against accidents among cooperating users
D	Minimal Protection	Unrated

Table 1-1. Trusted System Evaluation Criteria Ratings. *In order for a system to be assigned a rating, it must meet all the technical requirements for its class in the four areas of security policy, accountability, assurance, and documentation. The requirements are cumulative, moving from class D to class A1.*

You can be sure that a system rated high according to the *Criteria* (that is, at class A1 or B3) has been subject to intense scrutiny, because such systems are intended to protect classified military information. In order to attain such a high rating, a system has to be designed with security as its most important goal. While systems rarely qualify for any rating without some changes, most commercial operating systems can achieve a C1 or C2 level with a few enhancements or add-on packages. The Evaluated Products List is short because the *Criteria* is relatively new and evaluations take a long time. Also, many vendors have not yet shown an interest in submitting their products for evaluation.

While most of the technical concepts in the *Criteria* are covered in this book, we will pay little attention to its rating scale. If your interest is in developing a system for United States government use, the scale is important; for other applications, you will be more interested in specific features than in the ratings.

REFERENCES

Department of Defense. 1985a. *DoD Trusted Computer System Evaluation Criteria.* DOD 5200.28-STD. Washington, D.C.: Department of Defense. (U.S. Government Printing Office number 008-000-00461-7.)

The DoD criteria for evaluating and rating operating systems according to a scale based on security features and assurance. This document discusses many of the computer security concepts covered in this book.

National Computer Security Center. 1987. *Trusted Network Interpretation.* NCSC-TG-005. Ft. George G. Meade, Md.: National Computer Security Center.

An interpretation of the Trusted Computer System Evaluation Criteria *for networks and network components.*

Chapter 2

Why Systems Are Not Secure

Despite significant advances in the state of the art of computer security in recent years, information in computers is more vulnerable than ever. Each major technological advance in computing raises new security threats that require new security solutions, and technology moves faster than the rate at which such solutions can be developed. We would be fighting a losing battle, except that security need not be an isolated effort: there is no reason why a new technology cannot be accompanied by an integrated security strategy, where the effort to protect against new threats only requires filling in a logical piece of a well-defined architecture.

We probably cannot change the way the world works, but understanding why it works the way it does can help us avoid the typical pitfalls and choose acceptable security solutions. This chapter explores some of the classic reasons why the implementation of security lags behind its theory.

2.1 SECURITY IS FUNDAMENTALLY DIFFICULT

Why are computer systems so bad at protecting information? After all, if it is possible to build a system containing millions of lines of software (as evidenced by today's large operating systems), why is it so hard to make that software operate securely? The task of keeping one user from getting to another user's files seems simple enough—especially when the system is already able to keep track of each user and each file.

In fact, it is far easier to build a secure system than to build a correct system. But how many large operating systems are correct and bug-free? For all large systems, vendors must periodically issue new releases, each containing thousands of lines of revised code, much of which are bug fixes. No major operating system has ever worked perfectly, and no vendor of an operating system has dared offer a warranty against malfunctions. The industry seems resigned to the fact that systems will always have bugs. Yet most systems are reasonably dependable, and most of them adequately (but not perfectly) do the job for which they were designed.

What is adequate for most functions, however, is not sufficient for security. If you find an isolated bug in one function of an operating system, you can usually circumvent it, and the bug will have little effect on the other functions of the system: few bugs are fatal. But a single security "hole" can render all of the system's security controls worthless, especially if the bug is discovered by a determined penetrator. You might be able to live in a house with a few holes in the walls, but you will not be able to keep burglars out.

As a result, securing a system has traditionally been a battle of wits: the penetrator tries to find holes, and the designer tries to close them. The designer can never be confident of having found all the holes, and the penetrator need not reveal any discoveries. Anyone entrusting sensitive information to a large operating system or to a computer on a network has reason to be concerned about the privacy of that information. If the information is valuable enough to a penetrator to warrant the effort, there is little reason to assume that the penetrator will not succeed.

But of course there is hope: with appropriate techniques, a system can be built that provides reasonably high assurance of the effectiveness of its security controls—a level of assurance much higher than that of the system's overall correctness. The important factor is not the likelihood of a flaw (which is high), but the likelihood that a penetrator will find one (which we hope is very low). While we never can know whether a system is perfectly secure, we can build a system in a way that will make the penetrator's job so difficult, risky, and costly that the value to the penetrator of successful penetration will not be worth the effort.

The key to achieving an acceptable degree of security is the systematic use of proper techniques. Ad hoc security measures provide, at best, insignificantly increased protection that rarely justifies their expense. At worst, they provide a false sense of security that renders the users more susceptible than ever to the real threats.

2.2 SECURITY IS AN AFTERTHOUGHT

Despite the publicity about computer security in the press, computer and software vendors have rarely taken the trouble to incorporate meaningful security measures into their systems. Security, if considered at all, usually comes at the bottom of a list that looks something like this:

Functions: What does it do?
Price: What does it cost?
Performance: How fast does it run?
Compatibility: Does it work with earlier products?
Reliability: Will it perform its intended function?
Human Interface: How easy is it to use?
Availability: How often will it break?

- •
- •
- •

Security Functions: What protection features does it provide?
Security Assurance: How foolproof are the protection features?

Based on past and current practice, you might say that this entire book is about two of the least important factors in the design of computer systems.

It is unfair to fault vendors entirely for this lack of attention to security. While customers may want improved security, they usually have second thoughts when security features adversely affect other, "more important" features. Since few customers are willing to pay extra for security, vendors have had little incentive to invest in extensive security enhancements.

A few vendors have taken steps to help the few security-conscious customers who are willing to invest in additional protection. These customers include not only the government but some banks, manufacturers, and universities. Several add-on security packages for major operating systems have been on the market for some time. The most notable of these are CGA Software Products Group's TOP SECRET, Uccel Corporation's ACF2, and IBM's RACF, all for IBM's MVS operating system. Stronger mandatory controls (a subject of chapter 6) designed to be integrated into the operating system appear in SES/VMS, an enhancement to VMS offered by Digital Equipment (Blotcky, Lynch, and Lipner 1986), and are under development in the Sperry (now Unisys) 1100 operating system (Ashland 1985). These packages and enhancements are commercially viable despite their significant purchase and administrative costs. Several vendors have made a considerable investment in internal security enhancements to their operating systems without cost add-ons. These systems include DEC's VMS and Honeywell's Multics (Organick 1972; Whitmore et al. 1973). Control Data has also incorporated security enhancements into its NOS operating system. Honeywell was the first to offer commercially a highly secure minicomputer, the SCOMP (Fraim 1983), based on a security kernel, (a subject of chapter 10). Gemini Computers offers the GEMSOS operating system, also based on a security kernel (Schell, Tao, and Heckman 1985).

These and several other examples show that there has always been a certain demand for security features in the user community. But the examples also show that demand is fairly weak and can easily evaporate if the features should have an adverse impact on cost or any other functions.

2.3 SECURITY IS AN IMPEDIMENT

A common perception among users is that security is a nuisance. Security measures are supposed to thwart someone who tries to break the rules; but because of poorly integrated ad hoc solutions, security measures often interfere with an honest user's normal job.

Vendors often implement security enhancements in response to specific customer demands. Such enhancements, made to existing systems at minimal cost, often result in reduced convenience or poor performance. Vendors commonly adopt the attitude that a customer who wants security badly enough should be willing to live with the inconvenience.

Many customers take it upon themselves to fix security problems at their own sites. Because of inherent limitations in the system, fixing security problems often requires restrictive procedural controls: limited access from remote terminals; restricted physical access to local terminals and printers; multiple passwords or logins; frequent password changes; automatic disconnect after periods of inactivity; and call-back devices. Many of these controls do not substantially increase the security of the system, but they do foster the notion that security is painful. Because users and managers do not see a way around the inconveniences, security is often employed only as a last resort, when a problem has already occurred or a clear threat exists.

2.4 FALSE SOLUTIONS IMPEDE PROGRESS

The computer industry, like other industries, is subject to fads. Fads in the computer security area can have a serious negative effect on the overall progress toward achieving good security, because progress stops when people think they have the answer. Since few people have a good understanding of security, security fixes are particularly subject to snake-oil salesmanship.

One misconception (fortunately short-lived) involved *data encryption;* that is, encoding information using a password or secret key so that it cannot be deciphered by unauthorized individuals. Data encryption is indispensable for communications and is useful for protecting the media used to store files, but it does not address the general computer security problem. Few of the penetration techniques used by various "tiger teams" charged with finding security holes in systems would be thwarted by encryption. The primary problem with file encryption is that it does nothing to increase the level of trust in the operating system; and if you do not trust your operating system to protect your files, you cannot trust it to encrypt your files at all the right times or to protect the encryption keys properly. Nonetheless, simplistic statements are still occasionally encountered that claim that securing an operating system is unnecessary if all the files are encrypted. Section 13.2 discusses the legitimate role of encryption in communications and the relationship of encryption to computer security.

A popular security device is the *call-back modem.* The idea is that you telephone a computer from your home or office terminal and identify yourself (via a password) to the modem on the remote computer through your terminal. The computer's modem verifies that the password is correct and tells you to hang up. The modem then looks up your home telephone number in a list, and calls you back. Nobody can dial into the system and masquerade as you, even if that person knows your password, unless that person also uses your phone. Call-back devices are attractive because they do not require any modification to the system being protected—a classic example of add-on security. The danger in these devices is the risk of being lulled into complacency because you feel that only "good guys" can get to your system. You may decide that it is never necessary to change passwords or to enforce any control over the types of passwords people use. You may become lax about access control within your system, allowing too many of your users access to too much information. You may forget that half of your security problem is a matter of keeping your users isolated from each other—not keeping outsiders out.

The worst problem with call-back modems, however, is that they may cause you to forget that there are other ways people can get into your system. Does your system have a connection to a commercial network from which users can log in? Can you trust all other systems with which your system communicates? If one of your users accesses your system via a modem on a personal computer, how do you ensure that the personal computer has not been penetrated by an outsider via that modem? Considering the problems that call-back modems cannot solve and weighing the cost of these devices against simple measures such as better password control, it is hard to see their value.[1]

An example involving the use of passwords shows how a security feature intended for one application can be applied inappropriately to another. Because passwords are so good at controlling a user's access to the system, they are often used for other types of access control— access to certain applications in a system, access to certain files, or freedom to carry out certain operations. Password schemes are attractive because they are so easy to implement and to add onto existing systems.

But passwords are inappropriate for many of these applications, especially when a single password is issued to several people (for access to a common file, for example). When one person in the group leaves the company, the password must be changed and the new password manually distributed. If a break-in by an insider occurs, it is impossible to tell who is at fault. And the greater the number of people who know the password, the greater the chance that it will be revealed accidentally.

Another misuse of passwords involves the requirement on some systems that the user at a terminal reenter the password periodically— supposedly to ensure that the intended user and not an intruder is at the terminal. This feature is dangerous for two reasons. First, repeated entry of the password greatly increases the risk that someone will be looking over the user's shoulder when the password is entered. Second, the prompt for a password, appearing at unexpected times during a session, is highly susceptible to spoofing by a Trojan horse (see chapter 7). Section 6.2.1 lists additional ways in which passwords may be misused.

The false sense of security created by inappropriate use of passwords

---

1. The idiosyncrasies of the telephone system provide a number of additional ways to defeat most call-back devices, but that is another story.

weakens the impetus to seek better controls. The danger of using such ad hoc solutions to address isolated problems is that one can lose sight of the fundamental problems.

2.5 THE PROBLEM IS PEOPLE, NOT COMPUTERS

Many organizations believe that computer security technology is irrelevant to real-world problems because nearly all recorded cases of computer abuse and fraud are nontechnical. Computer crime usually involves exploitation of weaknesses in procedural or personnel controls, not weaknesses in internal controls. Hence, as long as relatively easy, nontechnical ways exist to commit a crime, technical controls will be viewed as superfluous.

But these organizations often fail to recognize that the computer can protect against flawed procedural controls. As we shall discuss in section 3.1, technical controls can often be used to ease the burden of procedural controls. It is distressing, for example, to hear claims that attacks by former employees represent personnel problems that the computer cannot solve, when the system can easily be instrumented to defend itself against this threat.

Consider, too, what will happen when procedural controls are strengthened to the point that technical penetration becomes the path of least resistance. Since many years are needed to make major security improvements to existing systems, a sudden explosion of technical crimes will be very difficult to counter.

Probably because the computer industry is still in its infancy, sufficient knowledge of computers to exploit technical flaws seems to be rare among the dishonest. (On the other hand, perhaps they are so clever that they are not detected.) But as knowledge of computers becomes more common, we cannot assume that only a few honest citizens will possess the requisite skills to commit a major crime. Given the low risk of getting caught and the potentially high payoff, sophisticated computer crime is likely to become more attractive in the future, especially if the nontechnical avenues to crime are sufficiently restricted.

One of the primary arguments that computers cannot prevent most cases of abuse is based on the observation that computer crimes committed by insiders usually do not involve a violation of internal security controls: the perpetrator simply misuses information to which he or she normally has access during the course of normal work responsibilities. Something akin to artificial intelligence would be required to detect such abuse automatically. But on closer inspection, we often find that people routinely gain access to more information than they need, either because the system's security controls do not provide adequately fine-grained protection or because implementing such protection within the architectural constraints of the system is too inconvenient or costly. The problem appears to be solely one of people, but it is exacerbated by a technical deficiency of the system. The technical solutions are not apparent because an organization's way of doing business is often influenced by the design (and limitations) of its computer system.

2.6 TECHNOLOGY IS OVERSOLD

There has long been the perception that true computer security can never be achieved in practice, so any effort is doomed to failure. This perception is due, in large part, to the bad press that a number of prominent government-funded secure computer development programs have received. The reasons for the supposed failure of these developments are varied:

- Programs originally intended for research have been wrongly criticized for not fulfilling needs of production systems.
- Vying for scarce funding, researchers and developers often promise more than they can deliver.
- Funding for the programs has been unpredictable, and requirements may change as the programs are shuffled among agencies. Often the requirements ultimately expressed are inconsistent with the original goals of the program, leading to unfortunate design compromises.
- Developments are often targeted to a specific model of computer or operating system, and inconsistent levels of funding have stretched out programs to the point where the original target system is technologically obsolete by the time the program is ready for implementation.
- The public does not realize that the first version of an operating system always performs poorly, requiring significant additional design and tuning before becoming acceptable. Vendors do not release such preliminary systems, postponing their "Version 1.0" announcement until the performance problems have been addressed. Government programs are highly visible, and any problems (even in early versions) tend to be viewed by critics as inherent characteristics. Worse, contracts are often written in such a way that the first version is the final product, and additional money is rarely available for performance tuning.
- Several large government procurements have specified the use of security technology that was thought to be practical at the time but was in fact based on research still in the laboratory. When the research

failed to progress fast enough to satisfy the needs of the program, security requirements were waived and the program lost its credibility.

Industry has understood for a long time that developing a new operating system involves far more than a one-time expense to build it; rather, a high level of continuous support is required over the life of the system. The federal government seems to have realized this, as well. Not able to commit to open-ended support, the government has largely ceased direct funding for secure operating system development, concentrating instead on specific applications and various seed efforts. A few commercial vendors are now undertaking to fill the void.

REFERENCES

Ashland, R. E. 1985. "B1 Security for Sperry 1100 Operating System." In *Proceedings of the 8th National Computer Security Conference*, pp. 105–7. Gaithersburg, Md.: National Bureau of Standards.
A description of mandatory controls proposed for Sperry (now Unisys) operating systems.

Blotcky, S.; Lynch, K.; and Lipner, S. 1986. "SE/VMS: Implementing Mandatory Security in VAX/VMS." In *Proceedings of the 9th National Computer Security Conference*, pp. 47–54. Gaithersburg, Md.: National Bureau of Standards.
A description of the security enhancements offered by Digital Equipment to upgrade security on its VMS operating system.

Fraim, L. J. 1983. "SCOMP: A Solution to the Multilevel Security Problem." *Computer* 16(7): 26–34. Reprinted in *Advances in Computer System Security*, vol. 2, ed. R. Turn, pp. 185–92. Dedham, Mass.: Artech House (1984).
A minicomputer-based security kernel with sophisticated hardware protection; this system is a Honeywell product.

Organick, E. I. 1972. *The Multics System: An Examination of Its Structure*. Cambridge, Mass.: MIT Press.
A description of Multics—at that time implemented on a processor without hardware-supported protection rings.

Schell, R. R.; Tao, T. F.; and Heckman, M. 1985. "Designing the GEMSOS Security Kernel for Security and Performance." In *Proceedings of the 8th National Computer Security Conference*, pp. 108–19. Gaithersburg, Md.: National Bureau of Standards.
A description of a security kernel for the Intel iAPX 286 microprocessor offered by Gemini Computers.

Whitmore, J.; Bensoussan, A.; Green, P.; Hunt, D.; Kobziar, A.; and Stern, J. 1973. "Design for Multics Security Enhancements." ESD-TR-74-176.

Hanscom AFB, Mass.: Air Force Electronic Systems Division. (Also available through National Technical Information Service, Springfield, Va., NTIS AD-A030801.)
A description of the enhancements incorporated into Multics to support mandatory security controls.

Chapter *3*

General Concepts

This chapter introduces, at an elementary level, some general concepts of computer security that apply to all applications; it also introduces terms that will be used repeatedly in later chapters. Many of the topics discussed here will be covered later in more detail.

3.1 INTERNAL AND EXTERNAL SECURITY

Most of this book addresses *internal security* controls that are implemented within the hardware and software of the system. For these internal controls to be effective, however, they must be accompanied by adequate *external security* controls that govern physical access to the system.

External controls cover all activities for maintaining security of the system that the system itself cannot address. External controls can be divided into three classes:

- Physical security
- Personnel security
- Procedural security

Physical security controls (locked rooms, guards, and the like) are an integral part of the security solution for a central computing facility, but they alone cannot address the security problems of multiuser distributed systems. As networking becomes a more and more pervasive part of computing, the role of physical security will continue to diminish. In a large heterogeneous network, it is probably impossible to guarantee (and risky to assume) that any system other than your own is physically protected.

Personnel security covers techniques that an employer uses in deciding whom to trust with the organization's system and with its information. Most governments have procedures whereby a level of security clearance is assigned to individuals based on a personal background investigation and (possibly) additional measures such as polygraph examinations. These procedures allow the government to assign different degrees of trust to different people, depending on the needs of their particular job and the depth of their investigation. Personnel screening in industry is far less formal than in government, and people are usually given "all or none" access. Where selective access to information is required, it is determined on a case-by-case basis.

Procedural security covers the processes of granting people access to machines, handling physical input and output (such as printouts and tapes), installing system software, attaching user terminals, and performing countless other details of daily system administration.

Internal and external controls go hand in hand, and it is possible to trade off a control in one area for a control in the other. For example, even the most primitive multiuser systems today have password protection. The password mechanism is an internal control that obviates the need for external controls such as locked terminal rooms. In designing a secure system, we generally strive to minimize the need for external controls, because external controls are usually far more expensive to implement. Procedural controls are also notoriously error-prone, since they rely on people each time they are invoked.

3.2 THE SYSTEM BOUNDARY AND THE SECURITY PERIMETER

A *system* is a vague entity that comprises the totality of the computing and communications environment over which the developers have some control. Everything inside the system is protected by the system, and everything outside it is unprotected (fig. 3-1). What is important is not the generic definition of the term *system* but the definition as it applies in each particular case. In any effort to plan for security features, it is crucial to establish a clear understanding of the *system boundary* and to define the threats (originating outside the boundary) against which the system must defend itself. You cannot construct a coherent security environment without understanding the threats.

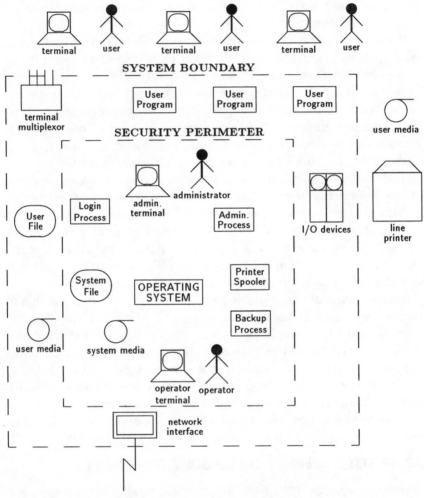

Figure 3-1. System Boundary and Security Perimeter. *The entities collected inside the system are protected by the security-relevant portions within the security perimeter, as long as rules about access to the system from the outside are enforced by means of external security controls. Rules for access to the security perimeter interface are enforced by the internal controls implemented in the security perimeter.*

Identifying the system boundary hinges on precisely specifying the interface between the system and the outside world. External security controls enforce this interface; and as long as those controls are in place, the internal controls protect information within the system against the specified threats. All bets are off, however, if something that should not be there bypasses the external controls and enters the system or if the system is threatened from the outside in an unanticipated way.

For example, a user might walk into the machine room and enter commands on the system console, or the system administrator might divulge a password to an outsider. These are failures of external controls that the system cannot defend against. It may, however, be able to defeat attempted incursions by unauthorized terminals, modems, or users who access the system remotely, as long as they are constrained to enter the system according to the rules of the system interface.

The components inside the system are of two types: those responsible for maintaining the security of the system (those, in other words, that are security-relevant), and all others. The security-relevant components implement the internal controls. Separating the two types of components is an imaginary boundary called the *security perimeter*. The operating system and computer hardware usually lie within the security perimeter; outside the perimeter are user programs, data, terminals, modems, printers, and the items that the system controls and protects. The nature of all components within the security perimeter must be precisely defined, because a malfunction in any one can lead to a security violation; in contrast, the nature of the components outside the perimeter is rather arbitrary, subject only to constraints enforced at the time they enter through the system boundary. A malfunction within the security perimeter has the effect of expanding the security perimeter to the system boundary, causing components previously outside the perimeter to become security-relevant.

Just as a precise interface must be identified across the system boundary, a well-defined interface across the security perimeter is crucial, as well. This interface is enforced by the security-relevant components. For example, the list of system calls in an operating system or the electrical specifications of a communications line are interfaces into the security perimeter. As long as the system boundary is enforced externally, the security perimeter will be maintained by the security-relevant components. In order to implement the components within the security perimeter, great care must go into defining a complete, consistent, and enforceable set of perimeter interface rules.

3.3 USERS AND TRUST

The *user* is the person whose information the system protects and whose access to information the system controls. A person who does not use the system, but who indirectly accesses the system through another user, is not a user as far as the system is concerned. For example, if your secretary is responsible for reading your electronic mail on your behalf, as well as the mail of others in your department, your secretary is the user and, as far as the system is concerned, this same user has access to all the mail in the department. You must trust your secretary, in addition to the system, to keep your mail separate from that of others.

3.3.1 Protecting the User from Self-betrayal

The system must assume that the user who owns a given piece of data or who has created that piece of data, is trusted not to disclose it willfully to another user who should not see it, nor to modify it in an inappropriate way. Of course, the user might be tricked into mishandling his data, but that's a different threat.

Though it may seem obvious, people often lose sight of the fact that computers cannot possibly protect information if the owner of the information wants to give it away.[1] It is in fact possible to design a system that does not allow users to give others access to their data, intentionally or otherwise; but such a design would be silly, because a person determined to disclose information doesn't need a computer to do so. The ability to read a file is tantamount to the ability to give that file to someone else.

While it does not make sense to go to great lengths to prevent a user from giving away information, it does make sense to ensure that the user knows when he or she is doing so. The access controls on the system must have a well-engineered user interface to minimize accidental disclosures.

3.3.2 Identification and Authentication

In order for a system to make meaningful decisions about whether a user should be allowed to access a file, the system (and other users) must have a means of identifying each user. A *unique identifier* is a name for each user (such as a last name, initials, or account number)

---

1. Various "copy protection" schemes attempt to prevent the user from copying a file (usually on a medium such as a floppy disk) in order to protect copyrighted software, but these schemes address an entirely different threat from the data protection threats that this book is about. (They also don't work very well.)

that everyone knows, that nobody can forge or change, and that all access requests can be checked against. The identifier must be unique because that is the only way the system can tell users apart. The identifier must be unforgeable so that one user cannot impersonate another.

The act of associating a user (or more accurately, a program running on behalf of a user) with a unique identifier is called *authentication*. The authentication process almost always requires the user to enter a password, but some more advanced techniques, such as fingerprint readers, may soon be available. The process of identification (associating a user ID with a program) is easy to confuse with authentication (associating the real user with the user ID), but it is important to maintain the distinction. The system must separate authentication information (passwords) from identification information (unique IDs) to the maximum extent possible, because passwords are secret and user IDs are public. The password need only be presented when the user first accesses the system. Once the unique ID is determined, the system need not refer to the password again. The unique ID, on the other hand, is used many times to make access decisions. Since the entire security of the system may be based on the secrecy of the passwords, the fewer times and fewer places they are used, the less the risk of exposure will be.

Authentication and identification are general concerns that pertain to systems and programs as well as to users. Users may need to know which system or which programs on the system they are interacting with and they need to obtain this information in a way that cannot be forged by the system or the programs. Moreover, systems on a network may need to authenticate each other, as if each were a user of the other. In many cases, the ability of a program to impersonate another program—or of a system to impersonate another system—is a serious security concern. The authentication techniques for systems and programs are quite different from those for users. In particular, passwords make very poor authenticators for systems and programs because each use of a password results in disclosure to the recipient and (therefore) the potential for abuse. Section 10.4 describes ways that systems and programs identify themselves to users. Section 13.2.2 discusses system-to-system authentication within a network.

3.4 TRUSTED SYSTEMS

Although users must be trusted to protect data to which they have access, the same is not true for the computer programs that they run. Everybody knows that computer programs are not completely trustworthy. And no matter how much we trust certain users, we cannot let the programs they use have total freedom with the data. The best programmers would agree that even their own programs can make mistakes. It would be nice (but it is usually impractical) to give programs limited access rights on a case-by-case basis, depending on what the programs need.

We can group software into three broad categories of trust:

1. *Trusted* – The software is responsible for enforcing security, and consequently the security of the system depends on its flawless operation.
2. *Benign* – The software is not responsible for enforcing security but uses special privileges or has access to sensitive information, so it must be trusted not to violate the rules intentionally. Flaws in benign software are presumed to be accidental, and such flaws are not likely to affect the security of the system.
3. *Malicious* – The software is of unknown origin. From a security standpoint, it must be treated as malicious and likely to attempt actively to subvert the system.

The quality of software that falls into each of these groups varies greatly from system to system. Most software we use daily is benign, whether the software was written by a good programmer or by an incompetent programmer, and whether that software is a system program or an application. The software is not trusted because it is not responsible for enforcing security of the system, and it is not malicious because the programmer did not intend to deceive the user. Some systems trust software that has received minimal scrutiny, while others consider anything not written by a trusted system programmer to be malicious. Hence, one system's trusted software may be as unreliable as another system's malicious software.

Within a system, a fine line separates a malicious program from a benign program with many bugs: there is no guarantee that a buggy benign program will not give away or destroy data, unintentionally having the same effect as a malicious program. Lacking an objective way to measure the difference, we often (but not always) consider both benign and malicious software to be in a single category that we call *untrusted*. This interpretation is especially common in environments where extremely sensitive information is handled, and it constitutes a fundamental tenet of the security kernel approach to building a secure system.

In most cases, the operating system is trusted and the user programs and applications are not; therefore, the system is designed so that the untrusted software cannot cause harm to the operating system, even if it turns out to be malicious. A few systems are secure even if significant portions of the operating system are not trusted, while others are secure only if all of the operating system and a great deal of software outside the operating system are trusted.

When we speak of trusted software in a secure operating system, we are usually talking about software that first has been developed by trusted individuals according to strict standards and second has been demonstrated to be correct by means of advanced engineering techniques such as formal modeling and verification. Our standards for trust in a secure operating system far exceed the standards applied to most existing operating systems, and they are considerably more costly to implement. Trusting all the software in a large system to this extent is hopeless; hence, the system must be structured in a way that minimizes the amount of software needing trust. The trusted software is only the portion that is security-relevant and lies within the security perimeter, where a malfunction could have an adverse effect on the security of the system. The untrusted software is not security-relevant and lies outside the security perimeter: it may be needed to keep the system running, but it cannot violate system security.

Within a single system, it is normally not useful to distinguish between different degrees of trusted software. Software either is responsible for security or is not. It does no good to assign more trust to some security-relevant programs than to others, because any one of them can do your system in. Similarly, we usually try to avoid establishing degrees of untrustworthiness. In most conventional systems where the security perimeter is not precisely defined, however, it is useful to distinguish between benign and malicious programs. In some instances, certain programs need not work correctly to maintain security of the system, but they nonetheless have the potential to cause damage if they are malicious. Such benign programs fall into a gray area straddling the security perimeter.

3.4.1 Trojan Horses

Most people's model of how malicious programs do their damage involves a user—the penetrator—writing and executing such programs from a remote terminal. Certainly systems do have to protect against this direct threat. But another type of malicious program, called the *Trojan horse*, requires no active user at a terminal.

A Trojan horse is a program or subroutine that masquerades as a friendly program and is used by trusted people to do what they believe is legitimate work. A Trojan horse may be embedded in a word-processing program, a compiler, or a game. An effective Trojan horse has no obvious effect on the program's expected output, and its damage may never be detected. A simple Trojan horse in a text editor might discreetly make a copy of all files that the user asks to edit, and store the copies in a location where the penetrator—the person who wrote the program—can later access them. As long as the unsuspecting user can voluntarily and legitimately give away the file, there is no way the system can prevent a Trojan horse from doing so, because the system is unable to tell the difference between a Trojan horse and a legitimate program. A more clever Trojan horse in a text editor need not limit itself to the file the user is trying to edit; any file potentially accessible to the user via the editor is accessible to the Trojan horse.

The reason Trojan horses work is because a program run by a user usually inherits the same unique ID, privileges, and access rights as the user. The Trojan horse therefore does its dirty work without violating any of the security rules of the system—making it one of the most difficult threats to counter. Most systems not specifically designed to counter Trojan horses are able to do so only for limited environments. Chapter 7 presents a detailed discussion of the problem, along with some implications that may seem surprising.

3.5 SUBJECTS, OBJECTS, AND ACCESS CONTROL

All activities within a system can be viewed as sequences of operations on objects. You can usually think of an object as a file, but in general anything that holds data may be an object, including memory, directories, queues, interprocess messages, network packets, input/output (I/O) devices, and physical media.

Active entities that can access or manipulate objects are called *subjects*. At a high level of abstraction, users are subjects; but within the system, a subject is usually considered to be a process, job, or task, operating on behalf of (and as a surrogate for) the user. I/O devices can be treated as either subjects or objects, depending on the observer's point of view, as we will discuss in section 8.5. The concepts of authentication and identification, discussed in section 3.3.2, apply to all types of subjects, although authenticating subjects internal to the computer may be implicit. It is particularly important that all subjects have an unforgeable unique identifier. Subjects operating as surrogates for users inherit the unique ID of the user, but in some cases users may invoke subjects possessing another user's unique ID.

A computer program residing in memory or stored on disk is treated as an object, like any other type of data. But when the program is run, it becomes part of a subject or process. Distinguishing between the program and the process is important because the same program may be run simultaneously by different processes on behalf of different users, where each process possesses a different unique ID. Often we loosely identify a subject as a program rather than as the process in which the program executes, but it should usually be clear when we are talking about a running program as a subject versus a program as data.

Like subjects, objects should have unique IDs. Not all systems implement explicit unique IDs for objects, but doing so is important for a secure system. Section 11.4.2 discusses this topic further.

3.5.1 Access Control

The primary purpose for security mechanisms in a computer system is *access control*, which consists of three tasks:

- *Authorization:* determining which subjects are entitled to have access to which objects
- Determining the *access rights* (a combination of access modes such as read, write, execute, delete, and append)
- Enforcing the access rights

In a computer system, the term *access control* applies only to subjects and objects within the system, not to access to the system by outsiders. Techniques for controlling access to the system from outside fall under the topics of user authentication and identification discussed in section 3.3.2. Nonetheless, the access controls in a network of systems must deal with outsiders and remote systems, as well as with subjects inside the system. Network access control is covered in section 13.3.1.

While systems may implement many types of access modes, security concerns usually center on the difference between read and write. In addition, it is occasionally useful to define access modes that distinguish between the ability to delete a file and the ability to write zeros into it (for example) or between the ability to write random data anywhere into a file and the ability to append information to the end of it only.

Subjects grant or rescind access rights to objects. Usually, a subject that possesses the ability to modify the access rights of an object is considered the object's *owner*, although there may be multiple owners.

Not all systems explicitly identify an owner; and often subjects other than the owner (such as system administrators) have the ability to grant access.

Associated with each object is a set of security attributes used to help determine authorization and access rights. A security attribute of an object may be something as simple as two bits of information—one for read and one for write—indicating the modes of access that all subjects have to the object. On the other hand, a security attribute may be complex, containing a lengthy access control list of individual subjects and their access rights to the object. Other examples of security attributes of objects are passwords, access bits, and security levels.

Some systems assign security attributes to subjects as well as to objects. These may consist of identifiers or security levels that are used, in addition to the subject's unique ID, as the basis for authorization.

Instead of using subject and object attributes as a basis for access control, some systems use capability lists. A *capability* is a key to a specific object: if a subject possesses the capability, it may access the object. Subjects may possess very long lists of capabilities. A more detailed discussion of capability lists is offered in section 6.2.2.

In talking about how access controls are implemented, we need to distinguish between the granting of access rights (which happens in advance) and the exercising of rights (which happens at the time of access), because security violations do not occur until an improper access takes place. For example, placing confidential information into a public file does not cause any harm until an unauthorized user reads the file. This distinction may seem rather subtle, but the design of some systems forces us to apply certain controls at the time access is granted and certain different controls when the access occurs.

3.5.2 Security Policy

In the real world, a security policy describes how people may access documents or other information. In order for the policy to be reflected in a computer environment, we must rewrite it using terms such as *subjects* and *objects* that are meaningful to the computer. Strictly speaking, the computer obeys security properties, while people obey a security policy. We will, however, loosely talk about the computer's security properties as if they were a policy of the computer system. In cases where the distinction between security policy and security properties is especially important (as when we discuss formal models), we will use more precise terminology.

The computer's version of the policy consists of a precise set of rules for determining authorization as a basis for making access control decisions. Authorization depends on the security attributes of users and information, unique IDs, and perhaps other information about the current state of the system. While all systems have security properties, the properties are not always explicit, and the policy on which they are based may be difficult to deduce. Often the policy is a hodgepodge of ad hoc rules that have evolved over the years and are inconsistently enforced. Lack of a clear policy—and not programming errors—is a major reason why the security controls of many systems are flawed. Section 9.5.1 shows how a security policy is converted into security properties for a system.

Chapter *4*

Design Techniques

This chapter provides an overview of the aspects of computer system design that are important to security. It discusses both the architectures of computer systems and the methods by which systems are designed and built, and it introduces terms that will be used and more thoroughly covered in subsequent chapters.

4.1 SYSTEM STRUCTURES

In the last chapter we introduced two important interfaces: the system boundary and the security perimeter. To understand better the design implications of these interfaces, it is necessary to look closely at how systems are built. We shall group systems into two types: a computer system consisting of a single machine or closely coupled multiprocessors; and a distributed system that resembles a single computer system from the outside but actually consists of multiple computer systems.

The difference between a computer system and a distributed system is reflected in the internal system structure and may not be apparent to users on the outside. Indeed, some people insist that a good distributed system be indistinguishable from a computer system. It is sometimes difficult to decide whether a networked collection of computer systems should or should not be called a distributed system: the decision depends on the observer's point of view, which differs for each application on the network.

Our concern in identifying a distributed system is not so much with terminology as with the internal security architecture of its networking mechanisms. We view a *computer system* as a self-contained entity whose system boundary does not include other systems with which it might be communicating. Such a system must protect itself and does not rely on assistance from other systems; information that leaves the system is no longer protected. We view a *distributed system* as one whose system boundary includes physically separate and relatively autonomous processors that are cooperating in some way to present an integrated environment for at least some applications. Information passing from one processor to another remains within the system and is protected.

The remainder of this section discusses the structure of computer systems, introducing concepts that are fundamental to an understanding of computer security. Chapter 13 covers concepts that pertain specifically to distributed systems and networks.

4.1.1 Structure of a Computer System

The traditional decomposition of a computer system shows hardware, an operating system, and applications programs, as in figure 4-1.[1] There may be multiple applications running simultaneously and independently, one or more for each active user of the system. The applications may be the same or entirely different. The users of the system generally interact only with the applications and not directly with the operating system, though there are important exceptions. Each application running on behalf of a user can loosely be thought of as a *process*.

Years ago, the distinction between the hardware and the operating system was obvious: the operating system was implemented with bits in memory that could be easily changed, and the hardware was implemented with circuits that stayed fixed. With many machines containing microcode or firmware, however, the distinction is now blurred. While many agonize over spelling out the differences, the differences matter only when we talk about hardware or software verification— not when we discuss security mechanisms. For the most part, we will treat *hardware* in the conventional sense, as the term is applied to contemporary machines, regardless of whether that hardware is, in fact, partially implemented in firmware or software.

1. Computer security enthusiasts seem to have a preference for drawing pictures that place the operating system underneath the applications, while much of the mainframe data-processing world puts the operating system above the applications. This book will adhere to the former, "top–down" tradition.

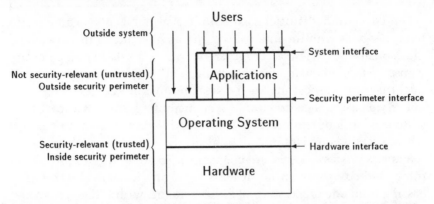

Figure 4-1. Generic Computer System Structure. Each layer uses the facilities of—and is subject to rules and restrictions enforced by—the layer below it. The interface between a pair of layers specifies the functions in the lower layer that are available to the higher layer. The operating system and hardware are security-relevant, lying within the security perimeter. The applications access the operating system through the perimeter by means of a well-defined set of system calls. The users are outside the system. They access the system through the applications or, on occasion, communicate directly with the operating system.

The division between the applications and the operating system software is usually more obvious (and more important, from our point of view) than the division between hardware and the operating system, although the nature of the software division may vary from system to system. Most people think of an operating system as being distinct from the system applications or processes that are needed to support it. The latter include processes for handling login, backup, and network interfaces. For security purposes, whether or not such processes are implemented outside the operating system is unimportant: the processes still lie within the security perimeter and must be treated as logical parts of the operating system.

A good test to use in deciding whether or not a piece of software should be viewed as part of the operating system is to ask whether it requires any special privileges to do its job—hardware privileges necessary to execute certain instructions or software privileges needed to gain access to certain data. Although utilities such as compilers, assemblers, and text editors are commonly provided by the vendor of the system (and written by system programmers), such applications do not require any privileges, because unprivileged users with programming skills can write and use their own versions.[2] Another common test is to check whether the software can have an adverse effect on the system if it misbehaves.

The horizontal lines in figure 4-1 separating the users, applications, operating system, and hardware represent precisely defined interfaces. Usually the security perimeter or operating system interface is described as a set of functions, or *system calls*, offered by the operating system; the hardware interface is described in the machine-language instruction manual. The operating system, together with the hardware, ensures that the security perimeter interface is accessed only in accordance with the rules of that interface. The system interface, on the other hand, is enforced through physical controls external to the system. There are few (if any) controls on the information that passes across that interface. For example, users are allowed to communicate freely with the applications in the system, but they can do so only through permitted physical connections such as terminal ports.

Database management systems, teleprocessing monitors, and other large applications often constitute minioperating systems of their own, running on top of the basic operating system and controlling the execution of several user applications (fig. 4-2). From the perspective of the operating system, the DBMS is just another application or process without special privileges.[3] The DBMS may be responsible for enforcing its own security policy, or the operating system may do it all. In such a design, the designers must have a very precise definition of the security requirements in order to tell whether the DBMS is security-relevant. Section 11.3 discusses the security role of such subsystems.

While most of the security features we will be discussing are intended for systems that support multiple users simultaneously, the features are usually applicable to single-user systems such as personal computers that allow serial access by multiple users. Sometimes, however, it is important to distinguish between a PC whose user has physical control over all of the hardware and software and a PC whose user does not have direct access to the operating system or hardware. This is because,

---

2. This is not universally true, however—especially for machines whose native language is a higher-order language, necessitating use of interpreters to execute the source code.

3. Again, this is an idealized view and is not universally true, since some operating systems do not provide the facilities to support multiuser applications without special privileges.

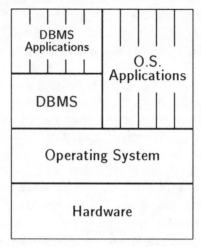

Figure 4-2. DBMS Process Structure. *To the operating system, the DBMS appears as just another user application process, while the DBMS controls its own set of applications running as individual processes within the DBMS process.*

without some physical security, no PC (or other computer) can protect itself and its data.

4.1.2 System States

A system with the structure shown in figure 4-1 or 4-2 requires some built-in support to enforce the layering and proper use of the interfaces. While it may be possible to build a system in which all the layering is enforced by software, the enforcement is tenuous, depending on correct implementation of the software on both sides of each interface. In order for the operating system to enforce constraints on the applications successfully, the operating system must have some help from the hardware.

Most machines have at least two states, domains, or modes of operation: *privileged*, and *unprivileged*. The privileged mode may also be called *executive, master, system, kernel,* or *supervisor* mode; and the unprivileged mode may be called *user, application,* or *problem* mode. When the machine is running in privileged mode, software can execute any machine instruction and can access any location in memory. In unprivileged mode, software is prevented from executing certain instructions or accessing memory in a way that could cause damage to the privileged software or other processes. Once the operating system (running in privileged mode) loads certain registers, the machine runs applications software in unprivileged mode until that software makes a call into the operating system, at which time privileged mode is restored. Privileged mode is also entered when interrupts are serviced by the operating system. Without hardware-enforced modes of privilege, the only way the operating system can protect itself is to execute applications programs interpretively—a technique that slows the machine down by several orders of magnitude.

Many modern machines, including microprocessors, have more than two domains. Several members of DEC's PDP-11 family for example, have three protection domains: user, supervisor, and kernel. The kernel mode has the most access to memory and to privileged instructions, and the user mode has the least. Having three hardware domains allows for efficient implementation of the types of system structures shown in figure 4-2. When a machine has more than three domains the domains may be numbered, with the lowest numbered domain having the most privilege. Because the domains are usually hierarchical—in the sense that each domain has more privileges than the domain above it—it is convenient to think of the domains as a series of concentric rings, a concept introduced in Honeywell's Multics (Organick 1972). Multics once proposed as many as sixty-four rings, although in practice systems commonly do not use more than a handful.

4.2 THE REFERENCE MONITOR AND SECURITY KERNELS

The security of a system can be improved in many ways without fundamentally altering its architecture. There are also a number of ways to build a fairly secure system from scratch. But for maximum protection of extremely sensitive information, a rigorous development strategy and specialized system architecture are required. The security kernel approach is a method of building an operating system that avoids the security problems inherent in conventional designs (Ames, Gasser, and Schell 1983). Based on a set of strict principles that guide the design and development process, the security kernel approach can significantly increase the user's level of confidence in the correctness of the system's security controls. Though by no means universally accepted as the ideal solution, the security kernel approach has been used more times than any other single approach for systems requiring the highest levels of security. Following is a very brief overview of the security kernel approach; chapter 10 covers the topic much more thoroughly.

The security kernel approach to building a system is based on the concept of a reference monitor—a combination of hardware and software responsible for enforcing the security policy of the system. Access decisions specified by the policy are based on information in an abstract access control database. The access control database embodies the security state of the system and contains information such as security attributes and access rights. The database is dynamic, changing as subjects and objects are created or deleted, and as their rights are modified. A key requirement of the reference monitor is the control of each and every access from subject to object.

Fundamental to the security kernel approach is the theory that, in a large operating system, a relatively small fraction of the software is responsible for security. By restructuring the operating system so that all of the security-relevant software is segregated into a trusted kernel of an operating system, most of the operating system need not be responsible for enforcing security. The kernel must be suitably protected (tamperproof), and it must not be possible to bypass the kernel's access control checks. The kernel must be as small as possible so that its correctness is easy to verify.

Compare figure 4-1 (showing hardware, software, and an operating system) to figure 4-3. The security kernel in the latter figure consists of hardware and a new layer of software inserted between the hardware and the operating system. The kernel's software and the hardware are trusted and lie inside the security perimeter; in contrast, the operating system lies outside the security perimeter, along with the applications.

In most respects, the security kernel is a primitive operating system. The security kernel performs services on behalf of the operating system

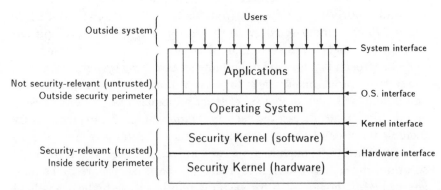

Figure 4-3. Security Kernel in a Computer System. *The kernel maintains security by controlling the actions of the operating system, while the operating system maintains a level of service by controlling the actions of the applications.*

much as the operating system performs services on behalf of the applications. And just as the operating system places constraints on the applications, the security kernel imposes constraints on the operating system. While the operating system plays no role in enforcing the security policy implemented by the kernel, the operating system is needed to keep the system running and to prevent denial of service due to errant or malicious applications. No error in either the applications or the operating system will lead to a violation of the kernel's security policy.

Building a security kernel does not require building an operating system above it: the security kernel could just as well implement all the functions of an operating system. But the more operating-system features a designer puts in a kernel, the larger the kernel becomes and the more it begins to look like a conventional operating system. In order for us to have any confidence that the kernel is more secure than an operating system, the kernel must be as small as possible. The smallness requirement must be ruthlessly enforced during design: the kernel should not contain any function not necessary to prevent a violation of the security policy. Issues such as performance, features, and convenience lie below smallness on the list of kernel design priorities.

4.3 SYSTEM DEVELOPMENT PROCESS

The development of any system involves several steps:

- *Requirements:* establishing generic needs
- *Specification:* defining precisely what the system is supposed to do, including *specification verification,* which involves demonstrating that the specification meets the requirements
- *Implementation:* designing and building the sys˙ ˌˑ, including *implementation verification,* which involves demonstrating that the implementation meets the specification

We also use the word *correspondence* as another name for the verification substeps at which two descriptions of a system are shown to be in agreement. Usually the more detailed description (for example, the specification) at a low level is said to correspond to the less detailed description (for example, the requirements) at a higher level.

The overall development of a system is guided by a *system architecture.* While most of us think of a system architecture as a description of the system as built, rather than thinking of it as a description of the process by which the system is built, a relationship exists between the result you want to achieve and the way you get there. Many of the desired characteristics of the system that help dictate the architecture (such as reliability, maintainability, and performance) have a profound impact on the development strategy. The system architecture makes itself felt either directly (through explicit development guidelines) or indirectly (through system goals).

A *security architecture* describes how the system is put together to satisfy the security requirements. If the security requirements specify that the system must attain a given level of *assurance* as to the correctness of its security controls, the security architecture must dictate many details of the development process.

Security concerns do not add steps to the development process that are not part of conventional developments. Rather, the guidelines in the security architecture are a pervasive influence on all development steps. The left-hand ("informal") side of figure 4-4 illustrates the conventional development process with one change: we have replaced *sys-*

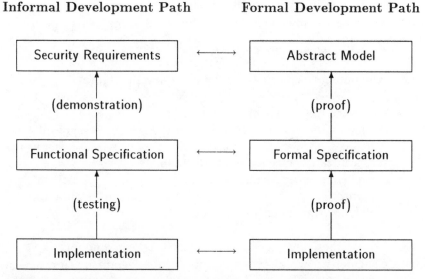

Figure 4-4. System Development Process for a Secure System. *The security-relevant aspects of the system development process are shown in two parallel paths. The informal path is conventional; the functional specifications and implementation are shown to meet the security requirements through correspondence steps involving demonstration and testing. The formal path, using mathematical techniques, is employed for systems where an extremely high level of assurance regarding the security controls is desired.*

tem requirements at the top with the *security requirements*. The security requirements, a small extract of the total system requirements, are derived from the system's security policy (not shown in the figure). The functional specification and the implementation shown in the figure are complete, not security-specific extracts. Verification of the functional specification against the security requirements—a process we call *demonstration* because it is based on informal arguments—is a far simpler task than verification of the specification against all functional requirements, since many functions described in the specification have little effect on security. Clearly verification is made easier if the functional specification is structured to locate security-relevant functions in as few (and as isolated) places as possible.

The bottom two phases in the informal path of figure 4-4, the implementation and its verification (testing), are conventional; there are no shortcuts to fully verifying the implementation against its specification, even if security is the only concern, because all functions must be examined or tested to be sure that they do not violate the security constraints.

The development process we have just discussed is called *informal* because there is no proof, in the mathematical sense, that the steps are correctly carried out. Because requirements and specification are written in a natural language (English, French, Latin) that is prone to ambiguities and omissions, formal mathematics cannot be applied to any of the correspondence steps.

The right-hand side of figure 4-4 shows a parallel formal development° path that might be used to develop a highly secure system such as a security kernel. Each phase in the informal path has a formal equivalent. The implementation, consisting of computer programs and hardware, is unchanged because the programs and hardware are already formal.

The natural-language security requirements are expressed as an abstract model, written in a mathematical notation, that is derived from exactly the same security policy as are the security requirements. The natural-language specification is expressed in a formal specification language amenable to computer processing. The correspondence steps of demonstration and testing are replaced by mathematical proofs. The horizontal arrows between parallel phases in the figure indicate equivalence, although no objective proof of that equivalence can be made.

The arrows between layers in the figure are upward, indicating that, in each case, the lower-layer description of the system corresponds to, satisfies, or is an example of a system described in the higher layer. In the formal path, especially, all of the rules in the abstract model need not be expanded in the formal specification, and all of the functions in the formal specification need not exist in the implementation; it is only necessary that the lower layer avoid violating rules or requirements of its adjacent higher layer.

The formal path for development is intended as a supplement to, not a replacement for, the informal path. It augments the informal process enough to provide the appropriate level of assurance dictated in the security requirements. Which phases of the formal path you carry out and how thoroughly you do so vary with that degree of assurance.

When you are choosing a development strategy, it is most important that you avoid gaps in the correspondence process: the boxes in the figure must be connected. Although you can choose not to write a formal specification, it is a waste of time to develop either an abstract model or a formal specification without devoting proper effort to the correspondence process. For example, you may choose to use an abstract model as an adjunct to the security requirements, without a formal specification; but in that case, you must demonstrate informally that the functional specification corresponds to the model. Alternatively, you may want to develop both a model and a formal specification but omit the formal proofs; if so, you must then use informal arguments to demonstrate correspondence among the implementation, the formal specification, and the model.

Be warned that figure 4-4 is a bit deceiving: in practice, you cannot hope to prove fully that the implementation meets the formal specification. Such a proof is a theoretical possibility, but it is not yet feasible. In other words, today's technology does not permit the right-hand path to be entirely formal. Nonetheless, the existence of a formal specification allows you to make a much more convincing, semiformal argument for implementation correspondence than you could get by testing alone.

REFERENCES

Ames, S. R., Jr.; Gasser, M.; and Schell, R. R. 1983. "Security Kernel Design and Implementation: An Introduction." *Computer* 16(7):14–22. Reprinted in *Advances in Computer System Security*, vol. 2, ed. R. Turn, pp. 170–77. Dedham, Mass.: Artech House (1984).
An overview of the reference monitor concept, the security model, and kernel implementation issues.

Organick, E. I. 1972. *The Multics System: An Examination of Its Structure.* Cambridge, Mass.: MIT Press.
A description of Multics—at that time implemented on a processor without hardware-supported protection rings.

PART II

DETAILED CONCEPTS

Chapter *5*

Principles of a Security Architecture

Building a computer system requires striking a balance among a number of requirements such as capability, flexibility, performance, ease of use, and cost. While there is nothing inherently conflicting about these requirements, features intended to satisfy them often work against each other and require you to make tradeoffs in the system design. Security is simply another requirement; and where they conflict, security features must likewise be traded off against other features, based on the importance of security to the system.

As a purist whose primary goal is to make your system secure, you might not be willing to give up a single security feature in favor of any other. But with such an outlook you are likely to fail: others will treat you as a security fanatic who is ignorant of what it means to build a practical system. By being adamant about security to the detriment of other features, you will lose most arguments over system design alternatives, and the system you are trying to influence will probably end up with few meaningful security capabilities. You are more likely to succeed in your goal of establishing a secure system if you remain pragmatic, keeping the primary goals of the system in mind and compromising on nonessential points at appropriate times. Even if you are building a security kernel for which everyone agrees that security is the most important goal, performance is almost always very close behind.

If you approach the design of a system with the attitude that you are willing to give in when necessary, your strategy should be to steer the design of the system in a direction that will avoid conflicts where possible. Many security features need not adversely affect other features. You can achieve most of your security goals without conflicts if you establish ground rules or principles to guide the system design. Once everyone on the design team agrees to these principles, the design will naturally follow a secure path.

The key to the control of the design process is the *security architecture*—a detailed description of all aspects of the system that relate to security, along with a set of principles to guide the design. The security architecture is not a description of the functions of the system; such detail belongs in a functional specification. A good security architecture is more like a design overview, describing at an abstract level the relationships between key elements of the system architecture in a way that satisfies the security requirements. The security architecture should also describe the aspects of the system development process (see section 4.3) through which adherence to the security requirements is assured. The architecture should not constrain the design in ways that do not affect security.

In the early conceptual stage of system development—even before requirements have been completely defined—a security architecture can be written that deals with high-level security issues: the system security policy, the degree of assurance desired, the impact of security on the development process, and overall guiding principles. A security architecture written at this early stage is generic, with few details about the specific system to be designed.

When the system architecture is later solidified, the security architecture should be enhanced to reflect the structure of the system. As the design progresses through stages of more and more detail, the security architecture becomes increasingly specific. While the security architecture must evolve in parallel to the system development effort, the architecture must keep ahead of that effort so that it can help guide the work to be done.

Of course, writing down a security architecture does no good unless people stick to it. The security architecture must play a dominant role in the development process, and all the developers must subscribe to it. Even during the implementation phase of a project, individual programmers will be affected by guidelines distilled from the architecture, through programming standards, code reviews, and testing.

5.1 CONSIDER SECURITY FROM THE START

Except in research projects, few systems are designed with security as the primary goal from the start. All too often the approach of the developers is "build it first, secure it later." From such a beginning, security is unlikely to be well-integrated into the system. Most designers fail to appreciate the great cost of retrofitting security.

You do not have to make security your number one goal in order to develop a secure system, but you do have to think about security from the beginning. Usually several ways are available to structure a system to satisfy a given set of requirements—some good for security, and some not. Without a security architecture to guide the early decisions, it is easy to choose a fundamentally flawed option, after which the cost of adding security controls is many times greater than would have been necessary had an equally sound alternative been selected.

This book contains many examples of situations where adding security to an existing system is made difficult by unfortunate design decisions. Practical experience in developing large systems has shown that, unless security considerations have influenced the early stages of design, little meaningful security is achieved in the final system. It cannot be stressed too strongly that, if you have any intention to incorporate security into a system, regardless of the priority of that security requirement, you must begin to think about it on the first day.

5.2 ANTICIPATE FUTURE SECURITY REQUIREMENTS

The security architecture should attempt to be far-sighted, addressing potential security features even if there is no immediate plan to use them. Usually it costs little to allow for future security enhancements, and therefore little is lost if the anticipated security is never needed.

But you must not be overly specific about anticipating security enhancements. For example, you might allow for an additional field in a protocol header to handle a security label; but when the time comes to implement the security feature, you may find it necessary to implement a third-party connection authorization scheme in order to validate the label—a feature that requires a different protocol design and can affect all existing implementations of that protocol. Another example involves error handling: while you may have made it easy to add security checks in many places in the system, such checks may introduce the possibility of new combinations of failures that existing software does not expect and cannot gracefully handle. A classic example of a new kind of failure is the inability of software to read a file even though it recognizes that the file exists.

The keys to incorporating the appropriate hooks for future security enhancements are to understand computer security requirements in general and to include those requirements explicitly as possible future needs in a security architecture. Sufficient detail in the handling of future security needs must be worked out, and such detail must be part of the design.

Anticipating security requirements not only affects the level of effort needed to make the system more secure in the future, it may also determine whether security in the system can ever be improved. Experience has shown that the security of many systems cannot be improved because the functions of the system have been defined in such a way as to depend on fundamentally insecure characteristics of the system. If the characteristics are changed, the system will no longer work as expected. In many cases, plugging security holes fixes the operating system but breaks the applications.

Consider a system that provides a scratchpad directory for use by applications programs that need to create temporary files, as is done by some versions of Unix. The directory will contain files belonging to many users on whose behalf the applications are running. But placing many users' files in a single directory readable by all users might not be secure. Even the most rudimentary security enhancements require a separate directory per user, and yet making such a separation in a clean way could be a vast undertaking if it involves modifying all applications that use temporary files.[1]

An area that demands particularly careful design planning is the definition of the security policy. A change in the security policy can have a catastrophic effect on previously good applications that violate the new policy, even when the change made in the operating system to implement the policy is simple. Had the applications been built with the new policy in mind (even if it were not enforced by the system at the time), the change would have been transparent. Of course, a documented but unenforced policy can easily be violated; you must exercise strong discipline over the applications developers. Among the applications that tend to be affected by a change in security policy are those that manage distributed information, those that maintain databases accessible to more than one user, and those that implement com-

---

1. Solutions to this particular problem in Unix have been proposed that do not require modifying all applications, but the solutions are not clean.

munications between users. Classic examples include electronic mail and database management systems. The most serious problems for such applications are caused by mandatory access control policies (see section 6.3).

5.3 MINIMIZE AND ISOLATE SECURITY CONTROLS

To achieve a high degree of confidence in the security of a system, the designer should minimize the size and complexity of the security-relevant parts of the internal design. A major reason why operating systems are not secure is that their large size leads to overall incomprehensibility. Of course, size is also the reason why operating systems are never totally free of bugs, and so will always be liable to behave unpredictably. But given that complex functional needs outside your control require you to have a big system, you still have the freedom to structure the system so that at least some parts (those that have to do with security) are small and well-defined.

If you are enhancing a system to add new security features, you may still follow this minimization principle, but constraints imposed by the existing architecture will certainly limit your flexibility. Needless to say, if improving the security of a system requires as much new mechanism as the system had in the first place, reliability of the new mechanism will be no higher than that of the original system (unless there are also significant improvements in the software engineering techniques used in those enhancements). You can always add new and useful security features, but the level of assurance may not change.

The key to minimizing the security-relevant parts of an operating system is to design the system to use only a small number of different types of security enforcement mechanisms, thereby forcing security-relevant actions to be taken in a few isolated sections. This goal, sometimes called *economy of mechanism* (Saltzer and Schroeder 1975), is simply a matter of good software engineering, but it is hard to attain for security in an operating system. The reason for this difficulty is that security permeates many different functional areas of a system—file system handling, memory management, process control, input/output, and a large number of administrative functions—so that you do not have a security module in a system as you do a device driver or scheduler.

An example illustrating the proliferation of redundant security mechanisms typical in older systems that have evolved over the years is the control of file access. One set of applications may manage its files by requesting a password before opening a file, another may use an access control list for each file, and another may use a set of access rights assigned in advance to each user (see section 6.2). Granularity of access control may also differ between applications: a DBMS worries about access on the record level; a message-handling system worries about access at the message level; and a document-processing system worries about whole files. Access control software will therefore be sprinkled throughout these applications. Not only will the security-relevant software be difficult to find and isolate, each application will have its own definition of security. Even if all the security software can be isolated in some way, the variety of mechanisms makes it difficult to design a common security solution. There is little hope for substantially improving the security in such an environment without thoroughly reexamining large parts of the system.

All operating systems—even old and complex ones—have some security mechanisms that control access to basic objects such as files, but often the common mechanism is too inflexible to be useful for many applications. The message-handling system designed to control access to individual messages within a file must bypass the operating system's access controls at the file level (by giving default read/write access to files for its users) and will provide its own security controls. If two such applications exist on the same system—for example, a database management system and a message-handling system—there will probably be two different approaches. Even systems such as Honeywell's Multics, whose design is based on the economy-of-mechanism principle, are forced to implement duplicative security controls to handle messages (Whitmore et al. 1973).

There are other reasons why we find multiple security mechanisms that do almost the same thing. When new and more flexible mechanisms are introduced in an older system, they are often incompatible with existing mechanisms; nonetheless, the older mechanism must be retained for compatibility. Some newer sophisticated mechanisms needed for certain applications are too inefficient for general use, so they are implemented as optional features. (An optional feature is not going to receive widespread use: when users are allowed to choose among several mechanisms, the decision is more likely to be based on the sophistication of the user than on the dictates of security.)

If the security-relevant mechanisms in the system are simple, easily identified, and isolated, it is usually possible to implement additional controls to protect them from damage by bugs in other portions of the system. Certainly the code that makes security decisions should be write-protected so that it cannot be modified. The databases used to make the decisions should be isolated and, if possible, protected against modification by other parts of the system.

Isolation of data should not be carried to an extreme, however. Security attributes of files, for example, are best stored along with other attributes of files, rather than in a separate database, because the synchronization mechanism needed to maintain the separate database may be complex and prone to error. In the ultimate effort to isolate security controls that is made in the security kernel approach, extreme care is devoted to separating the security-relevant mechanisms into a hardware-protected kernel of an operating system. Security kernel designers go to great lengths to minimize the size of the kernel, even if it vitiates performance or requires a significantly more complicated operating system outside the kernel.

5.4 ENFORCE LEAST PRIVILEGE

Closely related to the concept of isolating the security mechanisms is the principle of *least privilege:* subjects should be given no more privilege than is necessary to enable them to do their jobs. In that way, the damage caused by erroneous or malicious software is limited. A strictly enforced least-privilege mechanism is necessary if any reasonable degree of assurance in the security of a system is to be attained.

The philosophy of least privilege has several dimensions. The usual meaning of *privilege* in a computer system relates to the hardware mechanism that restricts use of special instructions (such as input/output instructions) and access to certain areas of memory when the processor is not operating in a privileged mode or domain. A system with only two domains (privileged and unprivileged) has a difficult time enforcing least privilege except at the coarsest level: the privileges accorded are either all or none. An architecture with three or more states provides finer degrees of control, where each state has access to less memory than the previous state as you "move out" from the most privileged state. But the hierarchical nature of the domains does not always match the requirements of applications. A capability architecture with nonhierarchical domains allows the finest degree of control but requires complex hardware support. Section 8.4 covers hardware protection features that support least privilege.

Similar to the hardware privileges are the software privileges assigned to certain programs by the operating system. These privileges permit programs to bypass the normal access controls enforced on user programs, or to invoke selected system functions. There may be a number of such privileges, providing a fine granularity of control over what a program can and cannot do. For example, the system backup program may be allowed to bypass read restrictions on files, but it need not have the ability to modify files. The restore program might be allowed to write files but not to read them.

While a system with many types of software privileges allows a fine degree of control over least privilege, privileges should not be used as a catch-all to make up for deficient and inflexible access controls. It is usually possible to design the normal access controls to accommodate most system functions without privileges. For example, Multics does not require the backup process to bypass any controls; the backup process is treated just as any other process is that is explicitly given read access to files to be backed up. Users can revoke the backup's read access to a file if they choose, and thereafter the file will not be backed up. A system that relies on a bewildering variety of privileges to carry out routine system functions securely probably has poorly designed access controls.

Another dimension of least privilege is enforced by the way in which the system is built through techniques such as modular programming and structured design. By establishing programming standards that restrict access by procedures to global data, for example, a system designer can minimize the possibility that an error in one area will affect another area. Such conventions amount to no more than good programming practice; but where security is concerned, the motivation for strict adherence to these standards must be greater. In particular, use of a layered architecture (discussed in section 11.1) can go a long way toward increasing the reliability of a secure operating system.

A final dimension for least privilege involves actions of users and system administrators. Users and system managers should not be given more access than they need in order to do their jobs. Ensuring least privilege for a user means deciding exactly what the user's job is and configuring the system to constrain the user to his or her duties. The system must provide the necessary support through flexible, fine-grained access controls and through its overall architecture.

The area of administrative functions is a particularly good place to enforce least privilege. Many systems (Unix being the most notorious) have a single "superuser" privilege that controls all system administrative functions, whether they are security-relevant or not.

Examples of administrative functions that are not security-relevant include mounting tapes, taking dumps, starting and stopping printer queues, bringing up and bringing down various background system processes, reconfiguring hardware, and entering certain user attributes. The functions are privileged because a malicious user of them could wreak havoc on the system, but misuse is unlikely to compromise security.

Administrative security functions include assigning and resetting passwords, registering new users, specifying security attributes of users and files, and breaking into someone's account in emergency situations. Misuse of these functions (or even slight slips at the keyboard) could cause lasting security problems.

By isolating day-to-day administrative functions from security administrative functions, and by using separate privileges for the different types of functions, a system would provide the capability for a site to give more people access to the administrative functions without risk of compromising security. Only a very determined malicious user of administrator privilege would be able to affect the security functions. In a system based on a security kernel, we often go so far as to make it impossible for a person with administrator privilege to affect security.

5.5 STRUCTURE THE SECURITY-RELEVANT FUNCTIONS

In discussing the system development process in section 4.3, we observed the need to demonstrate that the functional specification of the system satisfies its security requirements. If such a demonstration entails careful scrutiny of hundreds of functions in a large system, the demonstration is not only difficult but of dubious value. It is essential that the architecture of the system permit the security-relevant aspects of the system to be easily identified so that large sections of the system can be examined quickly. With a good security architecture, this simply requires good documentation: the security controls will be isolated and minimized, and there should be a clean and easily specifiable interface to the security-relevant functions.

If we look at a description of system calls in an operating system, we usually find that many, if not most, functions have to make some security-relevant decisions. It is not possible to isolate all security-relevant activities in one place. Any function used to access an object has to determine access rights, and many functions must check their arguments for validity. Consequently, it is necessary to identify clearly which checks are security-relevant and which are courtesy checks for the programmer. In particular, many important checks to prevent denial of service are not relevant if the security requirements do not address denial of service.

5.6 MAKE SECURITY FRIENDLY

The following three principles should be kept in mind in any effort to design security mechanisms:

- Security should not affect users who obey the rules.
- It should be easy for users to give access.
- It should be easy for users to restrict access.

The first principle means that, in the average case of a user doing an assigned job, security should be transparent. When security repeatedly gets in the way, users lose productivity and may seek a way to bypass the controls. The security controls must be flexible enough to accommodate a wide range of user activities while fully enforcing the principle of least privilege.

No system can anticipate all possible user activities, so a user will occasionally need to understand and use the security mechanisms. In some systems the seemingly simple act of giving or restricting access to a file requires a system administrator action. Such systems view security as a concern only to system managers. Under such burdensome procedures, system administrators are likely to give out more access than is needed, and only the most highly motivated users are likely to take the action needed to protect their information.

The second principle ensures that the user will provide access to information only when required and will not set up excessively permissive defaults to avoid complex procedures. The third principle increases the likelihood that the user will protect information when necessary.

A fourth design principle can be identified to help satisfy the preceding three principles:

- Establish reasonable defaults.

This includes both system-defined defaults and a mechanism for user-definable defaults.

A security administrator could argue that users of highly secure systems should constantly be made aware of their security responsibilities; otherwise, they might forget to take action to protect especially sensitive information when necessary. An obvious way to keep users on their toes is to configure the system so that the default action taken by the system is very restrictive (for example, arranging that nobody but the creator of a file can get access), while building in the option for a user to overrule the default when necessary. But if users are burdened with the need to override the default repeatedly in order to do their job, they will find a way to do so automatically; and an automatic override operates whether it is needed or not.

Some people insist that overriding the default controls should be difficult, requiring extraordinary effort. The government, in handling classified information, wants to make it extremely difficult for a user with access to the information to expose that information voluntarily within the computer, despite the fact that the user is fully trusted not to expose the information outside the computer. The rationale is that information in a computer is more subject to careless exposure than information on a sheet of paper. But as has been noted, making disclosure of one's own information extremely difficult only deters those who are not determined to make such a disclosure.

An improperly implemented user-defined default can be dangerous. In some versions of Unix, for example, the user can specify a default set of access modes to be assigned to all newly created files during a session. But the mechanism does not model the way people work: sometimes users operate on private files and sometimes they operate on public files, alternating between one and the other in the same session. A user who specifies a session default to make files publicly accessible is probably going to forget to turn off the default when creating private files.

A better design, used in Multics and eventually added to DEC's VMS, allows the user to specify default access modes for files based on the directory in which the file is located. Users are inclined to use different directories, rather than different sessions, for different aspects of their job. People can easily adapt their work habits to such a mechanism and are more likely to give access only where necessary.

These arguments demonstrate that making security friendly requires a thorough understanding of the applications for which the system will be used. This is much easier to do in some systems than in others. Designers of general-purpose systems have a difficult time deciding what the users will do, and in an attempt to please everyone they are likely to offer multiple redundant mechanisms, thereby violating the economy-of-mechanism principle.

5.7 DO NOT DEPEND ON SECRECY FOR SECURITY

Except in the handling of passwords and encryption keys, a primary goal for the security architecture of a system is to avoid depending on the secrecy of any part of the system's security mechanisms. In other words, it is unsafe to assume that users will not be able to break into a system because they do not have the manuals or source listings of the software. Of course, a penetration is certainly harder without the information, but you never know what information the penetrator has obtained, and the safest assumption is that the penetrator knows everything.

Fortunately secrecy of design is not a requirement for even the most highly secure systems. If you are building a system from the ground up, you have the opportunity to incorporate the necessary mechanisms so that even a person who helped develop the system cannot break into it. But if you are enhancing an existing system, you do not have that freedom, and you may have to make a guess as to how clever the penetrator will be. In such a case, you might well avoid publicly describing exactly what security enhancements you have made.

Revealing the internals of a system does not mean revealing ways to penetrate the system. Even the most secure systems have flaws, detected either as part of a penetration analysis or as a result of an actual penetration. No system will ever be free of all covert channels (see section 7.2).

Disclosing the design of a system's security mechanisms can actually improve security because it subjects the system to scrutiny by a much larger audience. Vendors often find that their customers report security problems in their systems as bugs before any serious penetration takes place. Of course, proprietary designs must be appropriately protected, but such protection should not be a requirement for system security.

REFERENCES

Saltzer, J. H., and Schroeder, M. D. 1975. "The Protection of Information in Computer Systems." *Proceedings of the IEEE* 63(9):1278–1308. Reprinted in *Advances in Computer System Security*, vol. 1, ed. R. Turn, pp. 105–35. Dedham, Mass.: Artech House (1981).
A set of principles for the design of protection features in computers— particularly those used in Multics.
Whitmore, J.; Bensoussan, A.; Green, P.; Hunt, D.; Kobziar, A.; and Stern, J. 1973. "Design for Multics Security Enhancements." ESD-TR-74-176. Hanscom AFB, Mass.: Air Force Electronic Systems Division. (Also available through National Technical Information Service, Springfield, Va., NTIS AD-A030801.)
A description of the enhancements incorporated into Multics to support mandatory security controls.

Chapter *6*

Access Control and Multilevel Security

The primary purpose of security mechanisms in a system is to control access to information. Until the early 1970s, it was not generally realized that two fundamentally different types of access controls exist. *Discretionary access control* is the most common: users, at their discretion, can specify to the system who can access their files. Under discretionary access controls, a user (or any of the user's programs or processes) can choose to share files with other users.

Under *nondiscretionary* or *mandatory access control,* users and files have fixed security attributes that are used by the system to determine whether a user can access a file. The mandatory security attributes are assigned administratively (such as by a person called the *security administrator*) or automatically by the operating system, according to strict rules. The attributes cannot be modified by users or their programs. If the system determines that a user's mandatory security attributes are inappropriate for access to a certain file, then nobody—not even the owner of the file—will be able to make the file accessible to that user.

6.1 ACCESS TO THE SYSTEM

Before we worry about access to information within the system, we should pause to consider control of access to the system itself. For some systems, physical controls are entirely adequate, but most systems need to be accessible from locations that are not under the physical control of the site administration.

A system can protect itself in two ways:

1. It can limit who can access the system.
2. It can limit what people can do once they access the system.

The first way requires the system to implement a two-step process of *identification* (asking you who you are) and *authentication* (asking you to prove it), as we discussed in section 3.3.2.

Until technology provides something better, the much-maligned *password* will continue to be the most common authentication technique. Despite their drawbacks, passwords, if properly used, are very effective for user authentication. Following are some time-honored principles for password management:

- Use passwords only for user authentication (see section 6.2.1), not for access control or system identification.
- Encrypt passwords stored in the system database in such a way that someone reading system dumps or the database cannot read the passwords. Using a *one-way cipher* (National Bureau of Standards 1985) where, for example, the password is the key to its own encryption— makes it impossible to decipher the database.
- Assign a given password to no more than one person.
- Minimize the number of times a password must be entered by the user (to limit its exposure).
- Do not store passwords in programs or files that could be revealed by someone reading the program.
- Minimize the number of different passwords a person has to remember.
- Discourage users from using the same password on different machines.
- Educate users who choose their own passwords about easy-to-guess passwords. Instead of allowing users to choose passwords, some systems (such as Honeywell's Multics and DEC's vms) provide an automated password generator that assigns random pronounceable words (Gasser 1975).
- Have users change passwords occasionally, but not so frequently that they need to write them down.
- Change a user's password the day that person leaves the organization. In a large organization with scores of machines of various sizes, this means keeping good enough records to be able to find all the systems on which the user has an account.

The National Bureau of Standards and the National Computer Security Center have published comprehensive guidelines for the creation and management of passwords (Department of Defense 1985; National Bureau of Standards 1985).

The second way for a system to protect itself is to make available a very limited and controlled set of functions for users whom it cannot identify. A transaction processing system, for example, might limit users to a specific set of menu options, with no opportunity for running arbitrary commands. While such *limited service systems* have their place, they should never be used in lieu of proper authentication. This cannot be stressed too strongly: the only appropriate use for a limited service system as a substitute for user authentication is where it is impractical to register users in advance, such as on a public terminal in an airport providing flight information and reservation services.

If you think you can avoid a lot of implementation effort and password management headaches by implementing a limited service interface for a given application, you are thinking dangerously. Limiting what a user can do on a general-purpose operating system is extraordinarily difficult. Try as you might to close the loopholes, there always seems to be a way for a clever user to break out of the limited system and obtain access to the operating system's underlying facilities. Even if you do succeed in containing the user, it may be nearly impossible to prevent malicious misuse of the limited system, except in the case of extremely limited systems that provide read-only access to a small amount of data. If a security breach occurs and you have not taken steps to require proper identification, there is no way to track down the perpetrator.

As dangerous as they are when used as a substitute for authentication, limited service systems make sense in cases where you need to limit what certain users (who have been properly identified and authenticated) can do.

6.2 DISCRETIONARY ACCESS CONTROL

Early systems had no internal access controls; any user could access any file simply by knowing its name. Access control consisted of an operator's deciding whether to mount a tape or card deck for reading or writing. This decision was rarely reliable. For example, the operator might look at the user name punched on a special ID card at the head of a batch card deck to ensure that the job requesting a tape to be mounted belonged to the owner of the tape. These ID cards might contain colored stripes to make them more difficult to forge. Such systems worked despite their flaws because the value of the information that could be gained by a penetration was rarely worth the risk or effort.

Access control became a more serious issue with the emergence of disk storage, on which files of many users could be stored online—well before the days of networks or interactive computing. Indeed, controlling access to disk files was probably the first widespread computer security concern, because for the first time the system, rather than the operator, was required to enforce access control.

6.2.1 Passwords for File Access

Very simple password-based access control mechanisms were used to protect files at first; and even as technology changed from batch computing to online interactive computing, these password schemes remained the primary protection mechanism.

In a password-based access scheme, each file is given a password. A user can access a file by providing to the system the password for that file. This password has nothing to do with any password the user might need to log into the system. Each new user who needs to access the file must be notified of the file's password. In some systems that use passwords on files, only system managers can assign the passwords; in others, the owner of a file can change the password at will. There usually must be at least two passwords per file: one to control reading, and one to control writing.

While passwords are excellent for user authentication, they are unsuitable for file access control. The following problems (some of which were discussed in section 2.4) render such use highly dangerous:

- There is no way to revoke one user's access to the file (by changing the password) without revoking everyone's access. This problem is only partially corrected by using multiple passwords per file.
- There is no way for the system to keep track of who has access to the file, since passwords are distributed manually without the system's knowledge.
- Passwords for file access tend to be embedded as character strings within programs that need to use the files; so one user's program can be run by another person who does not necessarily know the passwords for all of the files the program needs in order to operate properly. Accidental and undetected exposure of passwords is greatly increased whenever passwords are written down in any form.
- Requiring a user to remember a separate password for each file is an

unreasonable burden. Most likely the user will end up writing down a list of the passwords on a sheet of paper and taping it to the terminal.

In a large organization where users come and go daily, a password-based protection scheme for all files becomes impossible to manage.

6.2.2 Capability List

Another type of access control is the *capability list* or *access list*. A *capability* is a key to a specific object, along with a mode of access (read, write, or execute). A subject possessing a capability may access the object in the specified mode. At the highest levels in the system, where we are concerned with users and files, the system maintains a list of capabilities for each user. Users cannot add capabilities to this list except to cover new files they create. Users might, however, be allowed to give access to files by passing copies of their own capabilities to other users, and they might be able to revoke access to their own files by taking away capabilities from others (although revocation can be difficult to implement).

This type of access control, while much better than passwords, suffers from a software management problem. The system must maintain a list for each user that may contain hundreds or thousands of entries. When a file is deleted, the system must purge capabilities for the file from every user's list. Answering a simple question such as "who has access to this file?" requires the system to undergo a long search through every user's capability list.

The most successful use of capabilities is at lower levels in the system, where capabilities provide the underlying protection mechanism and not the user-visible access control scheme. We will discuss this lower-level use of capabilities by hardware in section 8.4.2 and by software in section 11.6.

6.2.3 Owner/Group/Other

A more effective, but simple and very common discretionary access control scheme (implemented in Unix, DEC's RSX and VMS, and many other systems) uses only a few bits of access control information attached to each file:

Owner			Group			Other		
R	W	E	R	W	E	R	W	E

These bits specify the access modes for different classes of users. There usually are no more than four classes: the owner of the file, users belonging to the owner's group or project, special system users, and the rest of the world. In a large system where users are grouped by project or department, most access control needs are satisfied by this technique. The scheme falls apart when access across specific groups is required. A major drawback of the scheme is its inability to specify access rights for an individual user: there is no way for Smith to specify that only Jones, and nobody else, should have access to a file, unless there is a group defined in the system to which only Smith and Jones belong. This drawback usually results in users giving world access to their files, even though they only want to make the file accessible to specific users.

6.2.4 Access Control Lists

One of the most effective access control schemes, from a user's perspective, is the *access control list*, or *ACL* (usually pronounced "ackle"), placed on each file (fig. 6-1). The access control list identifies the individual users or groups of users who may access the file. Because all the access control information for a file is stored in one place and is clearly associated with the file, identifying who has access to a file, and adding or deleting names to the list can be done very efficiently.

One alleged disadvantage of an access control list scheme is performance: the access control list has to be scanned each time any user accesses (or opens) a file. But with suitable defaults and grouping of users, access control lists rarely require more than a handful of entries. The only performance penalty might be due to there being an extra disk I/O required to fetch the ACL each time a file is opened. This could have a noticeable impact on systems where large numbers of files are opened in a relatively short time. Another disadvantage is storage management: maintaining a variable-length list for each file results in either a complex directory structure or wasted space for unused entries. This tends to be a problem only for systems having huge numbers of very small files (typical of the way in which Unix systems are used).

Largely because of the complex management required, only a few systems—such as Honeywell's Multics, DEC's VMS, and Data General's AOS—provide the most general form of access control list. If performance is a problem, one approach is to employ a combination of owner/group/other and access control lists. The access control list is only used for files where the granularity of owner/group/other is insufficient to specify the desired set of users. (VMS uses this dual approach—but for compatibility with older programs, not for performance.) This approach

FILE ALPHA   FILE BETA

Jones.CRYPTO	rew
*.CRYPTO	re
Green.*	n
.	r

Smith.DRUID	r
.	n

*Figure 6-1. Access Control List. The scheme above, similar to that used in Multics and VMS, employs a list of identifiers of the form USER.GROUP, where a * is a wildcard symbol matching any user or group name. When a user opens a file, the list is scanned and the allowed access corresponds to the first match. In this example, user Jones in group CRYPTO has rew access to file ALPHA, while all others in group CRYPTO have re access. Green has no access (n) unless he is in the CRYPTO group. All other users have r access.*

is an example of a performance and compatibility tradeoff that violates the principle of economy of mechanism discussed in section 5.3.

6.2.5 Trojan Horse Threats

Discretionary access controls have one major drawback, regardless of the specific implementation scheme used: they are, by their very nature, subject to Trojan horse attacks. With discretionary controls, programs acting on the user's behalf are free to modify access control information for files that the user owns. The operating system cannot tell the difference between a legitimate request to modify access control information desired by the user and a request made by a Trojan horse that the user did not intend. By eliminating some flexibility, a system can limit the ability to modify access control information to special programs that have privileges. But there is still no general way, under discretionary controls, to prevent a Trojan horse in one process from transmitting information to another process via shared objects: files, messages, shared memory, and so on. See chapter 7 for a more complete discussion of the Trojan horse problem.

6.3 MANDATORY ACCESS CONTROL

Mandatory access controls prevent some types of Trojan horse attacks by imposing access restrictions that cannot be bypassed, even indirectly. Under mandatory controls, the system assigns both subjects and objects special security attributes that cannot be changed on request as can discretionary access control attributes such as access control lists. The system decides whether a subject can access an object by comparing their security attributes. A program operating on behalf of a user cannot change the security attributes of itself or of any object—including objects that the user owns. A program may therefore be unable to give away a file simply by giving other users access to it. Mandatory controls can also prevent one process from creating a shared file and passing information to another process through that file.

Many different mandatory access control schemes can be defined, but nearly all that have been proposed are variants of the U.S. Department of Defense's multilevel security policy (section 6.4). Consequently, it is difficult to discuss mandatory controls apart from multilevel security. A few general concepts, however, apply to all mandatory policies.

Mandatory controls are used in conjunction with discretionary controls and serve as an additional (and stronger) restriction on access. A subject may have access to an object only if the subject passes both discretionary and mandatory checks. Since users cannot directly manipulate mandatory access control attributes, users employ discretionary controls for their own protection from other users. Mandatory controls come into play automatically as a stronger level of protection that cannot be bypassed by users through accidental or intentional misuse of discretionary controls.

As we will see in later examples, mandatory access controls unavoidably impose some severe constraints on users with respect to their own data. Because these constraints are so visible, it is easy to forget that the underlying purpose of mandatory controls is not to restrict the user. If we simply wanted to prevent users from accessing other users' files, discretionary controls would be sufficient. On the other hand, if we wanted to prevent a user from giving away a file, nothing the computer can do would be sufficient, as it is always possible for a user who can read a file to pass the contents of the file to another user manually. But if our intention is to prevent a program (in the form of a Trojan horse) from giving away a user's file, mandatory controls are needed. Exactly how a Trojan horse is foiled by mandatory controls is discussed in chapter 7.

In practice, mandatory controls do provide a benefit over discretionary controls, even if Trojan horses are not a threat, in cases of accident or irresponsibility. Mandatory controls make it more difficult for a user unintentionally (via an errant program or manual mistake) to give away information in an unauthorized manner. In fact, a mandatory policy can be set up so that the only ways users can pass information to other users is by means of pencil and paper or by giving away their passwords. Using mandatory controls for these purposes is quite reasonable, as long as you remember that mandatory controls can do little to prevent malicious users from revealing their own data.

Mandatory security controls have been implemented in all security kernel-based systems (see chapter 10) and in a handful of conventional (nonkernelized) operating systems. The latter include Honeywell's Multics (Whitmore et al. 1973), DEC's SES/VMS (Blotcky, Lynch, and Lipner 1986), and Sperry (now Unisys Corp.)'s 1100 Operating System (Ashland 1985).

6.4 MULTILEVEL SECURITY

The idea of *multilevel security* originated in the late 1960s when the U.S. Department of Defense decided it needed to develop some way of protecting classified information stored in computers (Ware 1970). Until that time it was against regulations to process classified information on a system to which uncleared people had access, because no machine was trusted to protect the classified data. Today the situation is not much different, but it should change as systems supporting mandatory controls become more widely available.

6.4.1 Military Security Policy

The Department of Defense has a strict policy for manually handling and storing classified information, which we will call the *military security policy*. All information (usually in the form of a document) possesses a *classification*, and every person possesses a *clearance*. In order to determine whether a person should be allowed to read a document, the person's clearance is compared to the document's classification.

A classification or clearance is made up of two components:

- A *security level* (also called *sensitivity level* or just *level*), consisting of one of a handful of names such as UNCLASSIFIED, CONFIDENTIAL, SECRET, and TOP SECRET
- A set of one or more *categories* (also called *compartments*), consisting of names such as NATO and NUCLEAR from among a very large number of possible choices used within the Department of Defense

A classification contains a single security level, while its category set may contain an arbitrary number of categories. We will write a classification as a security level name followed by a list of category names:

{SECRET;NATO,NUCLEAR,CRYPTO}. In practice the category set is often empty, and it is rarely larger than a handful of names.

The purpose of the multilevel security policy is to prevent compromise, whereby a user is able to read information classified at a level for which he or she is not cleared. In particular, the policy says nothing about the modification or destruction of information.[1]

The military classification scheme has many parallels in industry, even though the terms used in industry are different (Clark and Wilson 1987; Lipner 1982). Although industry does not usually employ the concept of hierarchical security levels, most of the theory and practice for handling classified information in a computer are directly applicable to techniques for handling commercially sensitive or "privacy" information. Because a great deal of research has gone into automating the military security policy, and because the concepts are well-defined, we will continue to use terms such as SECRET and TOP SECRET. You can directly map these onto terms used in industry such as PRIVILEGED and COMPANY CONFIDENTIAL. An industry parallel to categories might be the division of a company into departments (ACCOUNTING, PAYROLL, PERSONNEL, and so on), subsidiaries, and various product development groups.

6.4.2 A Note on Terminology

To avoid confusion when reading other literature (or perhaps to confuse you more), you should notice a few things about terminology. In the context of computer security, there is no difference between a *classification* and a *clearance:* one term simply applies to an object, and the other applies to a subject. This book uses the term *access class* for both. Elsewhere you will run into very loose usage of all these terms. Often the terms *security level* and *level* are used as synonyms for *classification*, which is fine as long as the level and category breakdown of the classification is not important (it rarely is). In some documents you may see the meanings of *classification* and *level* interchanged from those given here. Again, the distinction rarely matters: *access class, security level, clearance,* and *classification* can all be safely taken to mean the same thing. In the remainder of this chapter, we will continue to speak about the components of an access class individually. In the

---

1. Of course, the Department of Defense does care about information destruction, but preventing destruction is the not the main reason for classifying information.

rest of the book, we will note the rare cases where the distinction between the level and the categories matters.

6.4.3 Mathematical Relationships

The security levels in an access class are *linearly ordered*; for example:

UNCLASSIFIED < CONFIDENTIAL < SECRET < TOP SECRET

One requirement of the military security policy is that, in order to obtain information legally, a person must possess an access class whose level is greater than or equal to the level of the access class of the information.

Categories are independent of each other and not ordered. To obtain access to information, a person must possess an access class whose category set includes all the categories of the access class of the information.

When categories and levels are combined, several relationships are possible between two access classes (mathematically called a *partial ordering*—see section 9.5.3).

1. The first access class *dominates* the second; that is, the level of the first is greater than or equal to the level of the second, and the category set of the first contains all the categories of the second.
2. The second access class dominates the first.
3. The access classes are equal, which is a special case where both 1 and 2 above are true.
4. None of the above is true: the access classes are disjoint and cannot be compared. The first contains a category not in the second, and the second contains a category not in the first.

The word *dominates*, when used to express a partial ordering relationship, has a meaning similar to "greater than or equal to." While they are not mathematically correct, we will continue to use the words *greater than* or *less than* with respect to access classes and will only use the word *dominates* in contexts where a more precise meaning is required.

As an example, consider a document with access class {SE-CRET;NATO,NUCLEAR}. A user with access class {TOP SE-CRET;NATO,NUCLEAR,CRYPTO} can read the document, because the user possesses a higher level and all the categories of the document. A user with access class {TOP SECRET;NATO,CRYPTO} cannot read the document, because the user is missing the NUCLEAR category.

6.4.4 Multilevel Security Rules

Multilevel security, also known as *MLS*, is a mathematical description of the military security policy, defined in a form that can be implemented in a computer. The first mathematical model of a multilevel-secure computer system, known as the *Bell and La Padula model* (Bell and La Padula 1973), defined a number of terms and concepts that have since been adopted by most other models of multilevel security. The Bell and La Padula model is often equated with multilevel security or MLS, but researchers have developed other models of multilevel security. In fact, many of the concepts of the Bell and La Padula model originated in work done at Case Western Reserve University (Walter et al. 1974). Section 9.5.3 discusses the Bell and La Padula model in detail.

Multilevel security has a number of subtleties that make it a not-so-obvious transformation of the military security policy. Access classes are easy to represent in the computer, and appropriate checks can readily be made when a user tries to access a file. Enforcing multilevel security in a mandatory way, so that neither users nor their programs can change users' clearances or files' classifications, is also easy to do. This straightforward enforcement of multilevel security is commonly called *simple security* in the Bell and La Padula model.

Consider a system with two files and two processes (fig. 6-2). One file and one process are UNCLASSIFIED, and the other file and other process are SECRET. The simple security rule prevents the UNCLASSIFIED process from reading the SECRET file. Both processes can read and write the UNCLASSIFIED file. Despite enforcement of the simple security condition, however, a violation of the intent of the military security policy

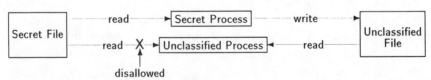

disallowed

Figure 6-2. Security Violation with Simple Security Controls. *In this example, despite the presence of the simple security restriction of multilevel security controls, a Trojan horse in the SECRET process is able to use the UNCLAS-SIFIED file as a medium for passing SECRET information to the UNCLAS-SIFIED process.*

can easily occur if the SECRET process reads information out of the SE-CRET file and writes it into the UNCLASSIFIED file. This is equivalent to an unauthorized *downgrade* (lowering of the access class) of information, except that no access class of any file has been changed. Thus, while the letter of the policy has been enforced, the intent of the policy to avoid compromise has been violated. Though the actual compromise does not take place until the downgraded information is read by the unclassified process, the specific act that permits the eventual compromise is the writing of information. When a process writes information into a file whose access class is less than its own, we call the act a *write-down*. The write-down problem is a continual source of frustration, because even the best technical solutions to the problem adversely affect the usability of systems.

In general, multilevel security requires the complete prohibition of write-downs by untrusted software. Such a restriction is clearly not present in the world of people and paper: a person with a SECRET clearance is rarely prohibited from writing an UNCLASSIFIED document, despite having a desk cluttered with SECRET documents, because the person is trusted to exercise appropriate judgment in deciding what to disclose.[2] The restriction on write-downs in a computer is necessary because a bug or Trojan horse in the user's program cannot be trusted to exercise the same judgment. This restriction has been given the rather uninformative name *-property* (pronounced "star-property") in the Bell and La Padula model—a term that has become accepted in the computer security community. We will instead use the more descriptive name *confinement property*.

To summarize, the multilevel security model has two basic properties (fig. 6-3):

- **Simple security:** A subject can only read an object if the access class of the subject dominates the access class of the object. In other words, a subject can read down but cannot read up.
- **Confinement property:** A subject can only write an object if the access class of the subject is dominated by the access class of the object. The subject can write up but cannot write down.

It follows that, in order for a subject to both read and write an object, the access classes of the subject and object must be equal. Although

2. As a half-serious proviso, it might be noted that UNCLASSIFIED reports written by cleared individuals working on a classified project are often subject to a manual review before publication, which is a kind of write-down restriction.

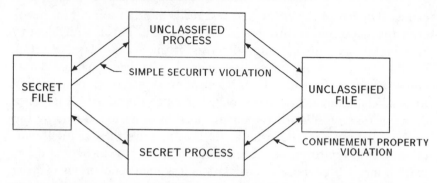

Figure 6-3. Multilevel Security Rules. A process cannot read an object at a higher access class (simple security) nor write an object at a lower access class (*-property or confinement property).

these properties allow a subject to write into an object at a higher access class, the write-up capability is often not too useful, and most systems implementing multilevel security restrict write access to objects that are of an equal access class. But from the standpoint of information compromise, there is no reason why a write-up need be disallowed. The Bell and La Padula model of multilevel security also makes use of an append access mode that allows a subject to attach information to the end of a file it cannot read. Although conceptually this seems a nice idea, implementing practical one-way writes in reality is very difficult.

6.5 INTEGRITY

Even though the confinement property of the multilevel security policy controls the writing of information, its goal is to prevent unauthorized disclosure. The multilevel security policy deals only with secrecy and does nothing to control unauthorized modification of information.

Soon after the Bell and La Padula model of multilevel security was defined, people began to wonder how to model the unauthorized modification of information. One crude way is simply to eliminate the ability to write up. But just as eliminating read-up does not alone prevent the unauthorized disclosure of information (the confinement property is also needed), eliminating write-up does not fully prevent unauthorized modification. Something akin to the confinement property is needed to prevent a process at a higher access class from reading down and being adversely influenced by information at a lower access class.

The *Biba integrity model* (Biba 1977) addresses the modification problem by mathematically describing read and write restrictions based on integrity access classes of subjects and objects (Biba uses the terms *integrity level* and *integrity compartment*). The integrity model looks exactly the same as the multilevel security model, except that read and write restrictions are reversed:

1. A subject can write an object only if the integrity access class of the subject dominates the integrity class of the object (simple integrity),
2. A subject can read an object only if the integrity access class of the subject is dominated by the integrity class of the object (integrity confinement).

Rule 1 is the logical integrity write-up restriction that prevents contamination of high-integrity data. Figure 6-4 illustrates the reason for rule 2, the equivalent of an integrity confinement property.

It is easiest to think about integrity if you completely ignore multilevel security for a moment. A high-integrity file is one whose contents are created by high-integrity processes. The two rules just identified guarantee that the high-integrity file cannot be contaminated by information from low-integrity processes. Furthermore, the high-integrity process that writes the file cannot be subverted by low-integrity processes or data. The integrity class label on a file therefore guarantees that the contents came only from sources of at least that degree of integrity.

When you consider secrecy (that is, multilevel security) and integrity together, you must be careful not to confuse the secrecy access class with the integrity access class, as they have nothing to do with one another: secrecy and integrity are independent qualities.[3] You may, for example, use a spreadsheet program obtained from a public bulletin board to display TOP SECRET data. The process in which the program runs will have low integrity but high secrecy; the output may be erroneous, but the program cannot compromise the top secret data.

Conversely, an UNCLASSIFIED process may never have access to any classified information, but if the process's job is to perform a system management function that must work correctly to keep the system running, the process should be of high integrity. You would like to feel

---

3. Biba originated the confusion by using the same names for both secrecy access classes and integrity access classes.

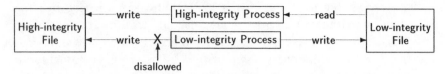

Figure 6-4. Contamination with Simple Integrity Controls. A low-integrity process is not allowed to write into and contaminate a high-integrity file; but through some error, the high-integrity process may receive low-integrity data and may write that data into the high-integrity file.

sure that the process cannot be influenced by low-integrity programs or be tricked by running with low-integrity data.

Although implementing integrity is straightforward, using hierarchical integrity as an adjunct to multilevel security has not fully caught on. Its application is seen as too complicated for many purposes. Whereas there are good reasons for having four or five different secrecy levels and ten or twenty categories, nobody has thought of a reason to use more than a couple of integrity levels; and on top of that, integrity categories are difficult to apply. Some people have warned that, with both secrecy and integrity fully in place, it will be all too easy to set up situations in which processes will be unable to access anything at all.

It has been proposed that eliminating the integrity confinement property restriction (rule 2) might simplify things. After all, a program of high integrity should be trusted to protect itself from low-integrity data. Although it is still possible for an "integrity Trojan horse" in that program to read the low-integrity data and write the data into a high-integrity file, one may wonder how a Trojan horse has gotten into a high-integrity program. The integrity confinement property is probably more suited to containing errors than Trojan horses.

Probably one of the most important reasons why the idea of integrity as an exact dual of multilevel security has problems in practice is that the notion of integrity is somehow related to the notion of trustedness. Secrecy, on the other hand, says nothing about trust, while requiring trusted software for its enforcement. We can construct any number of simple scenarios that would result in malicious software running at a high secrecy access class, but it is hard to think of a reason why malicious software would be running at a very high integrity level. As long as we already have to worry about the distinction between trusted and untrusted software for security purposes, many of the aspects of the integrity model seem superfluous.

Nonetheless, the integrity model is so clean and appealing that aspects of it have been implemented in several systems, leaving its use up to the system managers. In fact, it is possible to combine the integrity and secrecy access classes into a single access class that is rarely separated into the two components; files, processes, and users are then assigned security attributes that combine both secrecy and integrity. In such a system, the rule for reading a file would be as follows: the integrity access class of the file must dominate the integrity access class of the process, and the secrecy access class of the process must dominate the secrecy access class of the file. This rule combined with the appropriate rule for writing result in a rather complex series of checks, especially given that both integrity and secrecy access classes are composed of level and category components.

It may seem at first that integrity addresses the denial-of-service problem by preventing random destruction of data (which other security techniques do not address). But, there are many ways to cause denial of service other than by destroying data: executing illegal instructions or making illegal system calls that halt the system; crashing or slowing down the system by using up too many resources; and so on. Integrity is strictly a technique to prevent unauthorized modification.

In the systems where integrity has been implemented, the primary application has been to avoid modification of certain system programs and system databases that are important to the operation of the system and yet do not involve information with any secrecy content. For example, the list of users allowed to access the system might not be secret, but it must be protected from modification by untrusted software. This protection must be stronger than the discretionary protection provided for user files, and a mandatory integrity mechanism provides that type of protection. It has been proposed that integrity categories might be quite useful in a commercial environment (Lipner 1982)—perhaps more so than mandatory secrecy controls.

REFERENCES

Ashland, R. E. 1985. "B1 Security for Sperry 1100 Operating System." In *Proceedings of the 8th National Computer Security Conference*, pp. 105–7. Gaithersburg, Md.: National Bureau of Standards.
A description of mandatory controls proposed for Sperry (now Unisys) operating systems.

Bell, D. E., and La Padula, L. J. 1973. "Secure Computer Systems: Mathematical Foundations and Model." M74-244. Bedford, Mass.: Mitre Corp. (Also available through National Technical Information Service, Springfield, Va., NTIS AD-771543.)
Highly mathematical description of the original Bell and La Padula model.

Biba, K. J. 1977. "Integrity Considerations for Secure Computer Systems." ESD-TR-76-372. Hanscom AFB, Mass.: Air Force Electronic Systems Division. (Also available through National Technical Information Service, Springfield, Va., NTIS AD-A039324.)
The Biba integrity model.

Blotcky, S.; Lynch, K.; and Lipner, S. 1986. "SE/VMS: Implementing Mandatory Security in VAX/VMS." In *Proceedings of the 9th National Computer Security Conference,* pp. 47–54. Gaithersburg, Md.: National Bureau of Standards.
A description of the security enhancements offered by Digital Equipment to upgrade security of its vms operating system.

Clark, D. D., and Wilson, D. R. 1987. "A Comparison of Commercial and Military Computer Security Policies." In *Proceedings of the 1987 Symposium on Security and Privacy,* pp. 184–95. Washington, D.C.: IEEE Computer Society.
Argues that a commercial security policy has some characteristics that differ from the lattice nature of the military security policy.

Department of Defense. 1985. "Password Management Guideline." CSC-STD-002-85. Ft. Meade, Md.: National Computer Security Center.
A thorough discussion of password management guidelines.

Gasser, M. 1975. "A Random Word Generator for Pronounceable Passwords." ESD-TR-75-97. Hanscom AFB, Mass.: Air Force Electronic Systems Division. (Also available through National Technical Information Service, Springfield, Va., NTIS AD-A017676.)
Versions of this password generator are used in Multics and vax/vms.

Lipner, S. B. 1982. "Non-Discretionary Controls for Commercial Applications." In *Proceedings of the 1982 Symposium on Security and Privacy,* pp. 2–10. Silver Spring, Md.: IEEE Computer Society.
Proposes a way to use military-style mandatory security controls in a commercial environment.

National Bureau of Standards. 1985. "Password Usage Standard." FIPS PUB 112. Gaithersburg, Md.: National Bureau of Standards.
Another password management guideline, with recommendations suitable for government and industry.

Walter, K. G.; Ogden, W. F.; Rounds, W. C.; Bradshaw, F. T.; Ames, S. R.; and Shumway, D. G. 1974. "Primitive Models for Computer Security."

ESD-TR-4-117. Hanscom AFB, Mass.: Air Force Electronic Systems Division. (Also available through National Technical Information Service, Springfield, Va., NTIS AD-778467.)
An early discussion of a multilevel security model, interesting for historical reasons.

Ware, W. H. 1970. "Security Controls for Computer Systems: Report of Defense Science Board Task Force on Computer Security." R-609-1. Santa Monica, Cal.: Rand Corp. (Reissued October 1979.)
A comprehensive discussion of computer security threats and policy recommendations, providing the foundation for much of the subsequent government work in this field; now largely of historical interest only, although many of the concepts are still valid.

Whitmore, J.; Bensoussan, A.; Green, P.; Hunt, D.; Kobziar, A.; and Stern J. 1973. "Design for Multics Security Enhancements." ESD-TR-74-176. Hanscom AFB, Mass.: Air Force Electronic Systems Division. (Also available through National Technical Information Service, Springfield, Va., NTIS AD-A030801.)
A description of the enhancements incorporated into Multics to support mandatory security controls.

Chapter *7*

Trojan Horses and Covert Channels

When people began thinking about making systems more secure, they naturally speculated about specific penetration techniques. At first, the approach to securing operating systems was directed toward closing the holes inadvertently left by designers. These holes typically allowed a penetrator to gain control of the operating system, or at least to bypass some particular access control mechanism. Some penetration techniques identified by "tiger teams" searching for holes were incredibly complex, as were the countermeasures.

The Trojan horse route to penetration, however, was not formally identified until surprisingly late in the history of computing.[1] This route was far easier to exploit than many of the highly sophisticated penetrations people were trying to thwart. Worse, this simple type of penetration was fundamentally impossible to prevent on nearly all systems. Only a complete change in the philosophy of protection and a complete restructuring of the system could come close to addressing the problem. The most insidious aspect of the Trojan horse attack is that it requires no discovery and exploitation of loopholes in the operating system. A successful Trojan horse attack can be mounted through the use of only the most well-documented and obviously desirable features of a flawless, bug-free system.

1. The term *Trojan horse* was first used by Dan Edwards (Anderson 1972).

Do not assume that the Trojan horse problem is so esoteric that it only applies to computers entrusted with military secrets. Once you understand how easy it is to carry out a Trojan horse attack, you may wonder why anyone should have any confidence in the safety of any information in their system, why more systems are not constantly being penetrated, and why you should bother to close every small hole in your system while leaving gaping Trojan horse holes that are so easy to exploit.

One sentence can explain what a Trojan horse is, but chapters are needed to cover all the implications. Many who initially think they understand the Trojan horse are surprised when confronted with its ramifications. If you explain the Trojan horse problem to the management of a large computer installation, the likely response you will receive is "we don't have that problem here, because. . . ." But if you ask about that installation's existing security controls, you will usually find multiple redundant measures strengthening "conventional" aspects of the system while leaving wide-open paths for a Trojan horse attack. After such a discussion, you might be able to convince the management that many of the controls in these conventional areas serve only to reinforce the iron links in a paper chain.

7.1 TROJAN HORSES AND VIRUSES

Most references define the Trojan horse in one or two sentences. A *Trojan horse* is a computer program that appears to the user to perform a legitimate function but in fact carries out some illicit function that the user of the program did not intend. The victim is the user of the program; the perpetrator is the program's developer.

We can identify several key requirements for launching a successful Trojan horse attack:

- You (the perpetrator) must write a program (or modify an existing program) to perform the illicit act in a way that does not arouse the suspicion of any future user of the program. The program should perform some interesting or useful function that will entice others to use it.
- You must have some way of making the program accessible to your victim—by allowing the victim access to the program, by installing it in a system library (which could require help from an honest but gullible system administrator), or by physically handing the victim a tape or disk.
- You must get the victim to run your program. This might happen incidentally (if your program replaces an existing program that the

victim normally uses) or intentionally (if your program is directly invoked by the victim).

- You must have some way to reap the benefits of the illicit act. If the act is to copy private information (our primary concern), then you have to provide a repository for it that you can later access. This is normally quite easy if you have an account on the victim's system.

A special type of Trojan horse that propagates itself through a system or network of systems is the *virus* (Cohen 1984). "Infecting" a system with a virus usually requires a high level of skill on the part of the perpetrator, but once installed it can cause a great deal of harm and may be particularly difficult to eliminate.

7.1.1 Trojan Horse Examples

In section 3.4.1 we discussed some simple examples of the Trojan horse threat. Following are a few more sophisticated examples of both Trojan horses and viruses:

- A program that plays the game *Adventure* uses idle time when the user is thinking to scan the user's directory and give "world" read access to all the victim's files. You (the perpetrator) later log in normally and read the files. The victim might eventually find out that the access rights were changed, but may still have a hard time figuring out which program did it and whether anyone read the files.
- A new improved list_directory program that everyone wants to use functions as advertised but never exits upon completion. Instead, it pretends to exit, mimicking the response of the system command processor. The program reads and processes the victim's further commands normally (possibly by invoking the real command processor for each command) and never reveals the fact that it is still there. When the user finally types logout, the program simulates a genuine logout, but does not really log out. The next time any user walks up to the terminal and types login, the program reads the user's name and password and discreetly sends you (the perpetrator) a message containing the user's password. Then the program mimics a normal login procedure and finally does exit, returning the user to the command processor. The user never knows that all the prior input has been monitored, and you now have the user's password.
- An *Adventure* game, copied by the user from a public bulletin board where you have placed it for free distribution, modifies the user's command search list to cause a search of one of your own directories before searching the system libraries. In all subsequent sessions, every

time the user types a system command, any one of a number of Trojan horse programs in your directory may be invoked instead of, or in addition to, the desired system command. Once the search list is modified, you can get the victim to run any of your programs practically at will. One of these Trojan horse programs might be an altered version of show_search_list that hides from the user the fact that your directory is on the user's list. You would probably also want to include a doctored version of modify_search_list to prevent your own directory from being deleted from the list. This example shows that, with a little planning on your part, a single mistake by a user can result in permanent compromise of the user's security.

- You quietly place your Trojan horse in a public user directory, and give it an interesting name like *Superspreadsheet*, hoping some user will find it and try it. Besides operating as a spreadsheet, the program scans the user's directories, looking for executable binary files (other programs) that the user owns and appending a section of Trojan horse code to each such file. It modifies the calling sequence in those files to transfer temporary control to the Trojan horse each time one of those programs is called. When one of those programs is later used— possibly by a different user—the Trojan horse scans that user's directories, looking for more files to append itself to. Of course, the operation of the programs modified by this Trojan horse is not visibly affected. On a system where many users share each other's programs, this virus will quickly infect most of the user software in the system. If system programmers or administrators ever use someone else's programs, the virus can infect system programs as well. Since nobody ever looks at object code to see if it matches compiled code, this virus is unlikely to be detected as long as it does no visible harm.

    Your hope is that someone on a compiler development team will use a program infected with your virus; your virus is designed to recognize when it is appended to the compiler, and it will thereafter cause the compiler to append the virus to all compiled programs automatically. In this way, recompiling a program will not eliminate the virus.

    This virus causes no functional harm to the operating system other than using up a little memory along with each executable program. You can use your imagination to decide what additional features an interesting virus might have.

    A primitive type of virus was installed as a penetration exercise on an early version of Honeywell's Multics (Karger and Schell 1974).

As you can see, the illicit activity of the Trojan horse or virus need not hamper or frustrate the legitimate function of the command in which it is embedded, although the simplest Trojan horses might just go after the information the particular command already uses. The best Trojan horses do their dirty work and leave no traces. Modifying the access rights to all the user's files can be very damaging, but it is also easily detected and potentially traceable to the program that caused it. Trojan horses that persist indefinitely (like the virus) can cause a great deal of harm while they exist, but a program that causes trouble has a chance of being detected eventually. A clever Trojan horse might even be programmed to delete itself if the user tries to do something that might reveal its presence. Because most systems keep track of logins, stealing and using a password is unlikely to work more than a few times before the penetration is detected (although password theft is probably the easiest route to computer crime and can certainly cause a great deal of damage).

The common goal in these examples is to allow you (the perpetrator) to read a user's information to which you have no access. The Trojan horse either copies the information into one of your files, or sets up access modes so that you can later read the information directly from the user's files. The success of the Trojan horse depends on the extent to which you can retrieve the information.

So far we have not directly talked about Trojan horses that delete, modify, or damage information. A Trojan horse or virus whose goal is to modify files can do its job without your having to log in. In fact, you do not need to have any access to the user's system at all (provided that you had some way of giving the program to the user in the first place). A write-only Trojan horse used unknowingly by a system administrator and acting to modify a system file can be particularly insidious. In keeping with the general philosophy of this book that computer security is primarily concerned with information disclosure, we will continue to think of the Trojan horse as a means of illicitly obtaining read access to information. Although the write-only Trojan horse attack is somewhat simpler to carry out, solutions to the Trojan horse information disclosure problem (to the extent that they are solutions) generally address the information modification problem, as well.

7.1.2 Limiting the Trojan Horse

Preventing a Trojan horse from doing its damage is fundamentally impossible without some mandatory controls, and keeping a Trojan horse out of your system is extremely difficult. While simple or special-purpose systems might be protected to a degree, no general-purpose system can be protected adequately. A few of the techniques discussed here can reduce the possibility of a successful Trojan horse attack; but these techniques are somewhat dangerous, in that they can give you a false sense of security. Before adopting any of them, therefore, be sure you understand their limitations.

Restricting Access Control Flexibility

As was discussed in section 6.2.5, a Trojan horse can defeat any type of discretionary access control mechanism. As long as it is possible for the legitimate user to write a program that alters access control information for his or her own files, it is possible for a Trojan horse invoked by that user to do the same. Since the ability to write programs that alter access control information is a feature of most modern systems, it is difficult to imagine anyone being willing to eliminate this ability for the sake of security.

But suppose we do build a system that provides no unprivileged subroutine interface to the access control mechanism. In such a system, the only way for a user to specify access control information is by invoking a privileged system utility that sets the information based on input from the user's terminal—not on input from another program. (This utility program would have to make sure it was really reading input from the terminal, and not from a command file, for example.) Since we trust users not to give their own files away, it might seem that the Trojan horse threat to discretionary access control could thus be eliminated.

Notice, however, that several of the examples in section 7.1.1 do not require the Trojan horse to alter any access control information. For a Trojan horse to copy a user's files into the perpetrator's directory, the system need only allow the perpetrator to create a file manually that is writeable by the unsuspecting user. To avoid suspicion, the perpetrator might create a file that is writable by anyone, rather than solely by the specific user being targeted.

Let us then go further and mandate that the system not allow anyone to create a world-writable file (which is not a particularly useful feature anyway). In that case the Trojan horse might use a mail utility or an interprocess message to communicate information. If these facilities do not exist either, the Trojan horse might find a world-readable file belonging to the user and store the information in it. No one could reasonably suggest that a system not allow a user to create world-readable files.

These examples should convince you that, except in very limited systems, it is usually not fruitful to try to prevent a Trojan horse attack by limiting the ways in which users can exchange information.

Procedural Controls

Within a general-purpose operating system, nobody has come up with a practical scheme for detecting a Trojan horse. If the system allows any user programming at all, there is no way to prevent a user from implementing a Trojan horse and convincing another person to use it. As used here, the term *programming* includes the ability to write command files, macros, and any other instructions that enable a user to cause things to happen outside the user's direct control.

Procedurally, however, users can be warned not to run any programs other than those in the system libraries, and they can be cautioned not to carry out any action that might accidentally invoke a "foreign" file in their directory as a command or program. Users need not be prevented from writing their own programs for their own use (because it would be pointless for a user to plant a Trojan horse in his or her own program), but users should be suspicious about any program that someone else has written. The effectiveness of such voluntary restrictions depends, of course, on the dedication of the users. The interesting aspect of such restrictions is that users are only protecting themselves (and information entrusted to them): one user's violating a voluntary restriction against using an outside program will not compromise any other user's private information.

Unfortunately, voluntary restrictions are highly unreliable. Even sophisticated users may inadvertently violate the rules or be misled into doing so. In our earlier example where the search list was modified, a one-time, possibly accidental use of a Trojan horse renders the user permanently vulnerable thereafter. The difficulties of the voluntary approach are exacerbated by the fact that those who would build a Trojan horse are not restricted. One can imagine an open system in which scores of users litter the system with Trojan horses in the hope that one of a handful of honest and careful users might one day make a mistake and type the wrong command name. In a multiuser system that allows data-sharing, there is no practical way to prevent program-sharing.

In contrast to voluntary restrictions, enforced restrictions can be more nearly foolproof. In one approach (Karger 1987), a trusted mechanism in the system prevents programs called by a user from accessing files other than those intended by the user based on predefined usage patterns of each program that the user calls. The Trojan horse can still damage the files it is legitimately given, but it cannot access additional files without the user's knowledge. While such techniques are an interesting possibility, none has yet been implemented in practice.

System Controls: No Programming

Clearly the best restrictions are ones that the system automatically enforces. Limiting sharing is not practical, so the only restriction left involves programming.

Eliminating user programming might at first seem fairly easy: just get rid of all the compilers, assemblers, interpreters, and similar applications. In fact, many systems on which users do not need to write programs are operated this way. But if the system has a text editor and a command language, the ability to write command procedures (both batch and interactive) must also be eliminated, either by changing the command processor or by getting rid of all text editors. A DBMS that allows users to store complex queries as procedures for later access must be eliminated or restricted. Even without a command processor or DBMS, many text-processing tools such as editors and formatters are practically programming languages in their own right; these would have to be eliminated, too. (Remember that a successful Trojan horse might be as simple as a 1-line copy command embedded in an editor macro.) Even spreadsheet programs have features for user programmability.

By the time you eliminate all possibility of writing any type of program on a system, you have probably limited the use of the system to a few very specialized applications. Certainly no general-purpose system can be operated that way. But many large systems are in fact special-purpose and need no kind of programmability. Large organizations such as airlines and banks use their operational computers solely for transaction processing, with separate computers for development. But even when the operational system has no need for programming, it is rare for designers to make more than half-hearted efforts to eliminate the ability to write programs. Usually such efforts are aimed at saving memory and storage rather than at increasing security.

It is frequently argued that even the best efforts at eliminating programming are doomed. After all, any system on a network is a potential recipient of a Trojan horse from another system that does allow programming. Moreover, Trojan horses need not always resemble a program. A list of financial transactions could contain a Trojan horse in the form of illicit transactions. But, while it is indeed very difficult (or perhaps impossible) to guarantee that no Trojan horse has entered the system, the guarantee need not be absolute. Through a systematic analysis of all possible paths into the system, it is possible to weigh the effort a penetrator must make to install a Trojan horse against the value of the information gained or damage done. A partial closing of such paths (which, to be of practical benefit, must still be relatively complete) is adequate in many cases.

Scrutinizing Vendor Software

One route to installing a Trojan horse that we have not considered is via the vendor of the software. Most organizations certainly trust their vendors not to plant Trojan horses (although rumors are not lacking about features such as time bombs that inactivate the software when the rental period expires). Indeed, prior to initial purchase of a software package, there is little reason for an organization to fear that there might be a Trojan horse in the software specifically targeted at that organization. Once the software is installed, however, a site with very sensitive data has good reason to fear updates to that software supplied by the vendor—not because the vendor is likely to be malicious, but because the vendor probably has no more control over the actions of its employees than the organization has over its. Imagining a scenario where a disgruntled employee quits an organization to work as a programmer for a vendor that supplies the organization with software is not difficult. Unless appropriate control is maintained over the acquisition of new or updated vendor software, the value of closing all other Trojan horse channels is limited.

Probably the only practical technique for screening vendor software— a method used by the government at certain highly secure installations—is to accept software updates from a vendor only in the form of source code, to be scrutinized manually for malicious code by site personnel and to be compiled locally. Programs that highlight only the differences between earlier and later versions of the source code are used as an aid. This technique, though laborious, is considered useful because of the assumption that a Trojan horse in source code is easy to spot. Nonetheless, a clever programmer might be able to hide a Trojan horse, especially within a complex program. Rather than providing 100 percent assurance, the technique of scrutinizing the source code probably only serves as a deterrent to penetrators by increasing the work required to hide a Trojan horse.

Mandatory Controls

As was stated in section 6.3, the only effective way to handle the Trojan horse threat is to use mandatory access controls. Under mandatory access controls, a Trojan horse is prevented from giving away information in a way that would violate the mandatory access restrictions. Consider, for example, the multilevel security model discussed in section 6.4.4 and illustrated in figure 6.3. The confinement property prevents a Trojan horse in a process running at the SECRET access class from writing SECRET information into an UNCLASSIFIED file. Everything writable by a SECRET process must have at least a SECRET access class.

It is important to remember that mandatory controls only thwart Trojan horse attacks that attempt to cross mandatory access class boundaries. The Trojan horse in our example can still bypass discretionary rules by copying information from the victim's SECRET file into another user's SECRET file. Since it is impractical to assign a different mandatory access class to each user, mandatory controls are only used to protect information that is more sensitive than information that is simply private to a single user.

For example, suppose that a corporation allows its competitors to buy time on its computer system. Corporate proprietary information in that system is assigned a mandatory access category, and only employees of the corporation are given access to that category. A Trojan horse used by one of those employees will not be able to pass information to competitors outside the category, but it will be free to transfer information among users within the category.

7.2 COVERT CHANNELS

A key notion behind the Trojan horse attack is illicit communication through a legitimate information channel intended for interprocess communication: a file, an interprocess message, or shared memory. Mandatory access controls can prevent such communication across access classes. But a system usually allows processes to communicate in numerous other ways that are not normally used for communication and are not normally protected by mandatory controls. We call these other paths *covert information channels*, or simply *covert channels* (Lampson 1973; Lipner 1975).

Covert channels have also been called *leakage paths* because information can escape unintentionally. People worry about leakage paths because it is impossible to predict how much information an errant program might leak through such a channel. The practical impact of unintentional leakage, however, is usually minor and not a primary concern to us; much more serious is the intentional leakage caused by a Trojan horse.

Systems abound with covert channels. Every bit of information in the system (that is, every object) that can be modified by one process and read by another—directly or indirectly—is potentially a covert channel. Where mandatory controls prevent a Trojan horse from communicating information through files and other conventional objects, any bit of information not protected by mandatory controls is potentially an alternate path.

A covert channel's most important parameter is its *bandwidth*—the rate, in bits per second, at which information can be communicated between processes. This bandwidth is a function of the number of bits in the object and of performance characteristics of the system that determine the rate at which the object can be changed or modulated.

There are two types of covert channels: a *storage channel* is any communication path that results when one process causes an object to be written and another process observes the effect; a *timing channel* is any communication path that results when a process produces some effect on system performance that is observable by another process and is measurable with a timing base such as a real-time clock.

7.2.1 Covert Storage Channels

Covert storage channels use three types of information:

- Object attributes
- Object existence
- Shared resources

Object Attributes

The easiest-to-use and most common storage channels in systems are usually file names. A 32-character file name can be changed by one process and read by another process, resulting in a 32-character message transfer between the processes even if the file itself is not readable or writable by the processes. This channel can usually be eliminated by designing the access controls so that file names are objects protected by mandatory access controls in the same manner as the files are.

The use of file names is one example of the use of file attributes as storage channels. File attributes are items of information about a file that the operating system maintains in addition to the data in the file. Examples of other file attributes include length, format, date modified, and discretionary access control lists. The file attributes may be directly readable (as are file names), or their values may be indirectly inferred. Unlike file names, however, the values of most attributes are not directly modifiable by a process, and communicating via the attributes requires encoding the message to be sent in a form that uses the legal range of values of those attributes. For a process to change the file length, for example, the process may have to rewrite part of the file. This file length channel is limited to communicating a relatively small number of bits at a time, depending on the range of possible lengths. Changing the file format might be easy and direct, but the formats possible might be very few, leading to a rather narrow channel. Surprisingly, the access control list often provides one of the largest covert storage channels, since the list may be quite long and there might be few restrictions on the format of the user names on the list (see section 6.2 and figure 6.1). The values of the date and time when a file was last modified are usually difficult to control with any precision. The operating system usually updates the date and time at relatively long intervals, and the value may be no more accurate than to the nearest second. The bandwidth of such a channel can be no greater than one bit every 2 seconds; nonetheless, over a long period of time, an undetected Trojan horse can patiently transmit a significant amount of information by modifying a file at specific intervals.

Object Existence

File attributes are storage objects that are indirectly writable. Storage channels also include any items of information about the file that can be deduced by a process. For example, the fact that a given file exists is a bit of information; and even if you have no access to any of a file's attributes, you may still be able to infer whether a particular file exists. A simple way to do so would be to try to access the file and check the returned status condition. Some systems obligingly tell you whether your problem is `file does not exist` or `you have no access to the file`. If the system can support ten file creations or deletions per second, the Trojan horse can communicate ten bits of information per second.

If the system does not tell you directly whether a file inaccessible to you exists, you might try to create a new file with the same name as that file. If the system gives you a `name duplication` or other error, you will have confirmed that the file already exists. If the system allows you to create and use the new file, you will have established that the file did not previously exist.

The single bit of information about existence of a file may not seem like much information, but some systems strive to provide high-speed file creation and deletion. Thus, though the information channel is narrow, its bandwidth can be high, especially if multiple files are used.

Shared Resources

The use of file existence as a one-bit covert storage channel is an example of a more general single-bit channel involving shared or global resources. Almost every system contains certain resources that are pooled among a number of active processes or users. Such resources include disk blocks, physical memory, I/O buffers, allocated I/O devices, and various queues for shared devices such as printers and plotters. Without per-process quotas, these types of shared resources can be consumed by a single process. For example, one process could submit so many print jobs that the printer queue fills up. When that happens, other processes on the system simply receive some kind of error condition when they try to submit a job. A one-bit channel exists between the sending process that fills the queue and the receiving process that gets the error message. The sending process can transmit multiple bits in a serial fashion by alternately submitting and then canceling the last job on the queue. Some systems tell a process how many total jobs there are on a printer queue; communication via the queue is then easy and does not require filling the whole queue, and the information about the total number of jobs provides a channel that is wider than a single bit.

One way to minimize the queue overflow channel (or any shared resource exhaustion channel) is to use a per-process quota. In our printer queue example, a limit could be imposed on the number of jobs that any one process might place on the queue. If the system guarantees that a process will always be able to submit jobs up to its quota, then for all practical purposes the queue appears to each process as a private queue, revealing no information about other processes' jobs on the queue. But a queue structured in this way is not actually a shared queue, and all of the benefits of resource sharing are eliminated when resources are statically allocated to each process. Nonetheless, static allocation is often necessary to ensure complete closure of certain high-bandwidth shared-resource covert channels.

A way to reduce the bandwidth of resource exhaustion channels is to limit the rate at which a process can discover that the resource is exhausted. Usually a process cannot directly ask how much of a shared resource is available. The only way it can determine how much space is on a printer queue is to see how many jobs it can submit to the queue. When the process reaches the end of the queue, the system can delay the process for a certain amount of time before allowing it to attempt to put additional jobs on the queue. Since it is highly abnormal for a process to constantly bang away at the end of a queue, delaying a process trying to do so—even for several seconds—is unlikely to affect the performance of any legitimate operation.

One problem with such a bandwidth-limiting scheme is that the process may have access to many different shared resources. Therefore the limit must be based on the total number of resource exhaustion conditions that a process may be able to detect, not just on each resource individually. We also have to worry about the possibility that several processes can work in collusion, thereby multiplying the bandwidth by the number of processes.

Probably the simplest way to address the shared resource channel is to audit each case of resource exhaustion, in order to detect an excessive number of such cases within a given time interval. The threat of audit and detection might well suffice to deter a penetrator from using this technique. While auditing is usually not a reliable method of distinguishing between legitimate and illegitimate actions, resource exhaustion happens rarely enough that establishing a relatively low audit threshold (minimum number of incidents to trigger an audit) could be a valuable security measure.

7.2.2 Covert Timing Channels

Because the usefulness of covert storage channels is measured as a bandwidth, in bits per second, people often mistake certain types of storage channels for timing channels. In order for a covert channel to be classified as a timing channel, a real-time clock, interval timer, or the equivalent must be involved. The clock allows the receiving process to calculate relative amounts of real time between successive events. A channel that does not require a clock or timer is a storage channel. The distinction is important because, without any way for a process to determine the passage of time, a timing channel disappears. Storage channels, on the other hand, are not affected when access to a clock is eliminated.

A simple example of a timing channel is the percentage of CPU time available to a process. A Trojan horse in one process transmits 1's and 0's by using up varying fractions of CPU time at 1-second intervals in a busy loop. The receiving process reads the bits by counting the number of its own loops that it is able to perform in each interval. If these two processes are the only ones running on the machine, the receiving process's loop count in each second is a direct function of the sending process's CPU utilization. The bandwidth of this channel depends on the range of values for the loop count that can be predictably communicated.

Timing channels tend to be noisy because they are affected by processes on the system other than the ones actually communicating. The noisier a channel is, the lower the effective bandwidth becomes; however, it is usually possible to minimize the noise caused by other processes by running late at night, when few other processes are running. An effective Trojan horse can choose the times it runs.

It is often suggested that timing channels be eliminated by removing the ability for a process to read a clock. Our example above does not work if the receiving process has no time reference. But even if the receiving process has no direct access to a clock, there are ways for it to determine passage of time. For example, the process can measure 0.1-second intervals by counting characters received from a terminal while the user (who is the penetrator on the receiving end) holds down a repeat key that enters characters at the fixed rate of 10 per second. The process may even be able to manufacture its own clock by counting the number of disk accesses it can make or the number of characters it can write to a terminal between specific events to be timed. On multiprocessor systems, one process can use program loops to determine time intervals on behalf of another process. Even if none of these techniques works, the user can always operate a stopwatch at his or her terminal and count the seconds between events.

Timing channels are insidious for two reasons: there are no formal techniques for finding them in a system; and there is usually no way to detect their use and hence to audit them. Whereas storage channels can often be countered by controlling the rate at which specific, identifiable objects in the system are modified, timing channels do not involve observation of any identifiable objects.

Computer security technology has little to offer those who wish to find and block timing channels. Computer security projects to date have failed, by and large, to address the problem in a systematic way. The best advice for planners designing a new system would be to understand the timing channel problem from the start of the system design and to be constantly aware of the threat. Most obvious channels are uncovered during the design and development process. You cannot completely close many of the channels you find, but at least you will have a good idea of where they are and can deal with them on an individual basis.

At the current state of the art in secure operating systems, the timing channel is far more difficult for a penetrator to exploit than many other avenues. Perhaps someday, when these other routes are closed, we will have better solutions to the timing channel problem.

7.3 TRAP DOORS

The *trap door* (Karger and Schell 1974) is an illicit piece of software in an operating system that provides a way for a penetrator to break into the operating system reliably and without detection. The trap door is activated by a special command or unlikely sequence of events that the penetrator can cause at will and that no one else is likely to discover by accident. A trap door is only useful in software that runs with privileges that the penetrator does not otherwise have; otherwise, the trap door does not give the penetrator anything not already obtainable. For this reason, we usually think of trap doors in operating systems and not in applications.

A trap door is much like a bug in an operating system that permits a penetration. Indeed, a penetration might be necessary to install the trap door in the first place. A trap door may also be installed by a dishonest employee of the vendor of the operating system. The techniques for inserting trap doors are much like those for inserting Trojan horses, but they are more difficult to carry out in an operating system.

Unlike Trojan horses and covert channels, trap doors can only be installed by exploiting flaws in the operating system or by infiltrating the system's development team. Hence, trap doors can be avoided by employing the usual techniques for developing reliable trusted software: no special techniques are required.

REFERENCES

Anderson, J. P. 1972. "Computer Security Technology Planning Study." ESD-TR-73-51, vols. 1 and 2. Hanscom AFB, Mass.: Air Force Electronic Systems Division. (Also available through Defense Technical Information Center, Alexandria, Va., DTIC AD-758206.)
The first study to document the government's computer security problem and the proposed solutions in the form of the reference monitor and the security kernel; now no longer useful as a primary technical reference, but historically significant.
Cohen, F. 1984. "Computer Viruses: Theory and Experiments." In *Pro-*

ceedings of the 7th National Computer Security Conference, pp. 240–63. Gaithersburg, Md.: National Bureau of Standards.

The term virus *was first introduced in this paper.*

Karger, P. A. 1987. "Limiting the Potential Damage of Discretionary Trojan Horses." In *Proceedings of the 1987 Symposium on Security and Privacy*, pp. 32–37. Washington, D.C.: IEEE Computer Society.

Discusses a technique to limit discretionary Trojan horses on the basis of built-in knowledge of usage patterns, and provides a good overview of the problem and helpful references to related techniques.

Karger, P. A., and Schell, R. R. 1974. "Multics Security Evaluation: Vulnerability Analysis." ESD-TR-74-193, vol. 2. Hanscom AFB, Mass.: Air Force Electronic Systems Division. (Also available through National Technical Information Service, Springfield, Va., NTIS AD-A001120.)

A discussion of penetrations of Multics, pointing out several classic types of flaws in various areas; useful as a guide to detecting flaws in other operating systems.

Lampson, B. W. 1973. "A Note on the Confinement Problem." *Communications of the ACM* 16(10):613–15.

One of the first papers to discuss covert channels (called confinement *or* leakage paths*) and techniques for closing them.*

Lipner, S. B. 1975. "A Comment on the Confinement Problem." *ACM Operating Systems Review* 9(5):192–96.

In response to Lampson's paper, this paper discusses some fundamental problems involved in attempting to close covert channels in a system with shared resources.

PART *III*

IMPLEMENTATION

Chapter *8*

Hardware Security Mechanisms

It is fortunate that most of the hardware mechanisms needed to implement a secure system are also required by conventional operating systems; otherwise, there would be little hope of seeing these features on today's machines. This is not a coincidence: good protection features are essential to an efficient and reliable operating system. Even if security is not a major concern, systems must provide reasonable protection against errant user software. Many of today's sophisticated features that protect against malicious software are logical extensions of early features designed simply to contain bugs in benign user programs.

Some hardware security features are useful only for highly secure systems (such as the security kernel), but most are commonly found in machines from mainframes through microprocessors. Some features, though eminently practical, have never been implemented in exactly the form discussed here, although approximations exist. Numerous theoretical features—particularly features pertaining to so-called "capability machines"—are little-used or highly experimental (despite being academically interesting and being studied by all computer science students). Such features are given only token consideration in this chapter.

This chapter is not written for machine designers, although anyone responsible for the hardware architecture of a new machine should understand the mechanisms discussed here. Instead, it is for software designers who have the option of choosing one of several machines for an application or who want to understand how to use specific security mechanisms. You will be most likely to use these features if you are developing an operating system or application that runs on a bare machine, since most of the features are intended to be used by the lowest levels of the system. Many of the security features in some recent microprocessors (for example, the Intel 80286 and Motorola 68000 families) are not used by most of the popular personal computer operating systems (Unix and MS-DOS), because the operating systems evolved on earlier hardware architectures that had few security features.

If you have been exposed to Honeywell's Multics operating system, you will notice a strong Multics slant to much of this chapter. Multics is one of the first large commercial operating systems to have included security as a major goal from its inception. The protection features of the Multics processor were tailored to the needs of a general-purpose operating system, and many of the security features offered by other machines have been influenced by the Multics architecture. Multics is an excellent example to use when discussing protection features because the protection features of most other machines are a subset of the Multics features. Furthermore, much of the terminology and philosophy developed in conjunction with the Multics project is useful for discussing hardware security features. The features discussed here should not, however, be taken as a description of Multics. Some features are not in Multics, and those that resemble Multics have been simplified for the purposes of this chapter. Some concepts described here are also borrowed from Honeywell's SCOMP, a minicomputer that employs many of the Multics features but on a far smaller scale (Fraim 1983). The SCOMP hardware also addresses some areas, such as mapped I/O, that Multics does not.

For a complete description of Multics and its protection features, as implemented on the GE-645 processor, see the book by Organick (1972). That processor was redesigned as the Honeywell 6180, whose major new feature was hardware protection rings (Schroeder and Saltzer 1972).

8.1 HARDWARE/FIRMWARE/SOFTWARE TRADE-OFFS

Many security mechanisms that were once implemented in software are now implemented in hardware. Some features remain in software, either because of their complexity or because the hardware designers do not want to lock in a particular implementation. For the most part, the distinction between firmware and hardware is not important to the understanding or use of security features, and we shall largely ignore the difference. If you should choose to do any verification of the hardware or firmware, however, the verification techniques are apt to be quite different. See chapter 12 for a discussion of verification.

You do not need sophisticated hardware to build a secure operating system. Indeed, theoretically, a secure operating system can be built on a very primitive processor. Hardware security features are favored over software features for three reasons:

1. The features are alleged to be more reliable and to be correctly implemented.
2. Putting the feature in hardware yields a much cleaner architecture.
3. Hardware permits higher performance (speed of execution) than does software.

Reason 1 is largely a misconception: hardware is fundamentally no more correct than software; it seems more reliable because it performs simpler functions. If an entire operating system were to be implemented with transistors and wires, it would have at least as many bugs as the equivalent software (and it would be much harder to fix). Furthermore, unlike software, hardware is subject to random failure of parts, making it less reliable as it ages. The only way in which hardware might be considered more reliable is that it cannot be damaged by errant software, but it is no more reliable in this sense than is software in read-only memory.

Reason 2 is a valid reason that directly affects security. A well-structured architecture increases the reliability of the overall system.

Reason 3 is also valid. While performance is only indirectly related to security, nobody is likely to use a security mechanism that unacceptably degrades performance. Performance is one of the primary reasons for putting security features in hardware.

8.2 PROCESS SUPPORT

A fundamental requirement for a secure operating system is that the system isolate users from one another while permitting exchange of information through controlled paths. All modern operating systems support some notion of a *process* as a surrogate for a user. In a timesharing or multiprogramming system, each user may have several processes operating on his or her behalf.

Because multiprogramming is central to the construction of a secure multiuser operating system, it is important that a process switch be very fast. In a system supporting many users at once, the process switching overhead can have a significant effect on performance. If this impact is great enough, software developers may be tempted to avoid process switching where possible.

One common way to minimize process switching is to use a single process for several simultaneous users, rather than giving each user a separate process. An example is a database management system that interacts directly with a number of users who submit queries to a common database (see figure 4-2). The danger of multiplexing a number of users onto a single process is a greatly reduced level of security, because the hardware's process isolation mechanism is no longer used for user isolation.

The minimum hardware support required for multiprogramming is the ability to capture the internal state of a process so that a suspended process can later be restarted ("dispatched"). This internal state includes at least the program counter and the processor registers visible to programs. Early processors required software to store and reload these registers one at a time. Most processors today perform a bulk load and restore with a single instruction.

There must also be some way of saving the addressable memory (address space) of the process. On simple machines this may involve keeping a copy of the base and the bounds of each process's address space and loading these values into the appropriate registers when the process is dispatched. The memory itself may stay put, or can be transferred ("swapped out") to disk by the operating system when the process is not running.

On machines with more complex memory management, involving segmentation or demand paging when a process's address space consists of noncontiguous pages in physical memory, much more information must be restored when a process is dispatched. Originally machines required software to load a series of memory descriptor registers, individually or in bulk. More advanced machines use a single descriptor base register that points to a table of memory descriptors. Under this arrangement, a process restart only requires software to load the single descriptor base register; however, the process may still be slow to start up if hardware must fetch many descriptors from memory as the process references different portions of its address space. A mechanism to retain active memory descriptors in a cache across process switches is therefore useful. The various technical terms in this and the previous paragraph are discussed more completely in the subsections of section 8.3.

8.3 MEMORY PROTECTION

Probably the most fundamental hardware requirement for a secure system is memory protection. On systems that run a single process in memory at a time, on behalf of a single user, memory protection is needed to prevent the user's programs from affecting the operating system. On systems with multiprogramming, memory protection also isolates the process's memory areas from each other. The mechanisms behind memory protection go hand-in-hand with memory management mechanisms designed for efficient use of memory. We shall first cover some of the important aspects of memory management hardware, and then consider how the features support memory protection.

8.3.1 Virtual Address Space

A process in execution has a *private address* space that contains its programs and data. This address space does not include secondary storage (disk) that the process may access using I/O instructions. Each word in the process's address space has a fixed *virtual address* that the programs in the process use to access the word. Most systems support some type of *virtual memory* that enables the physical location of a word with a given virtual address to vary, possibly changing each time the process is dispatched.

In executing a memory reference instruction, the hardware computes the virtual address that identifies the target location of the reference, using a value or offset contained in a field of the instruction plus some index registers and address registers. The virtual address is then translated, or *mapped*, by hardware into a *physical address*. This translation is transparent to the program. Early machines did not use the terms *virtual address* and *virtual memory*, but we shall apply the terms liberally to any system that maps memory addresses.

Machines that support indirect addressing determine the target virtual address by following a chain of one or more *pointers* (virtual addresses stored in memory), as specified by the instruction. The *effective address* is the virtual address of the target location.

8.3.2 Virtual Memory Mapping

The earliest systems that employed any kind of memory management required a process's address space to lie in contiguous physical memory locations. A base register pointed to the beginning of the physical memory area, and a bounds register pointed to the end or indicated the size of the area. A user program running in the process could not reference outside these limits and could not modify the registers. By automatically adding the value of the base register to all memory addresses, hardware obviated the need for programs to be concerned about the absolute location of the address space.

In a large system where many processes with address spaces of different sizes are swapped in and out of memory, the requirement that a process's memory be contiguous would result in fragmentation of physical memory. More efficient use of physical memory is achieved by dividing physical memory into a number of *pages* of fixed size, and allowing a process's address space to be scattered among these pages. Under this arrangement, swapping in a large process only requires finding enough total unused pages, not a single large contiguous space.

Scattering a process's virtual memory among many physical pages requires a set of hardware *mapping registers,* each of which points to the start of a page in physical memory that is accessible to the process (fig. 8-1). The total number of pages available to the process may be limited by the number of mapping registers, or it may be specified in a single bounds register.

When an instruction references memory, it must indicate which mapping register or which page is to be used. If we view the virtual memory of a process as a linear address space with locations numbered beginning at zero, the page selection is done automatically by hardware and remains transparent to software: a machine instruction specifies a virtual address of a location in virtual memory and hardware determines the page number or mapping register number by examining the

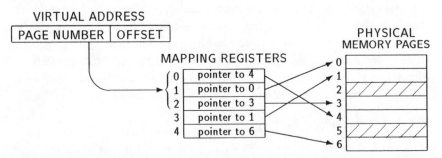

Figure 8-1. Mapping Pages in Virtual Memory. The page number portion of the virtual address identifies the mapping register to be used in finding the location of the page in physical memory. Pages 2 and 5 in physical memory are unused by the current process.

high-order bits of the virtual address. To the hardware, the virtual address has a two-dimensional structure:

VIRTUAL ADDRESS: | PAGE NUMBER | OFFSET |

In a paged system, when a process is ready to be dispatched, the operating system determines the correspondence between virtual and physical page numbers and sets up a table of page descriptors in memory. A *page descriptor* is a pointer to a physical page that contains some additional control information. As the process is dispatched, software or hardware loads the descriptors into mapping registers (or into a cache) for high-speed access by hardware on each memory reference. The loading of registers from the descriptor table may be dynamic—done transparently by hardware the first time each page is referenced by a program.

8.3.3 Demand Paging

Some modern machines permit a process to have a virtual memory that is many times the size of the physical memory of the machine; to accomplish this, a demand paging mechanism is used to move pages between secondary storage and physical memory, as required. The process must be able to be run without keeping track of which pages are memory-resident. The operating system constructs a table of page descriptors for the entire virtual memory of the process, setting an "on-disk" flag in the descriptors whose pages are not in physical memory (fig. 8-2). When the process references a page, the address translation mechanism sees the "on disk" flag and traps to the operating system, signaling a page fault. The operating system finds a free page in physical memory, reads in the page from disk, resets the descriptor to point to the page, and resumes execution of the process at the point of fault.

In order to minimize disk access time, pages in a demand-paged system tend to be small—equal to the size of a disk block, such as 512 or 1,024 words. Small pages also allow a process to run with a small amount of reserved physical memory. In a non-demand-paged system, where a process's entire address space must reside in physical memory, page size is less critical. The small size of pages limits their usefulness as a basis for memory protection, as we shall discuss more completely in section 8.3.5. With declining memory costs and faster disks, these trade-offs are changing.

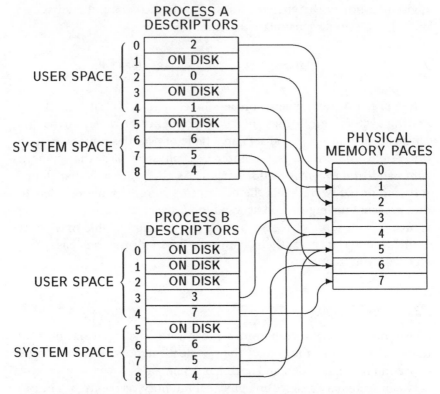

Figure 8-2. Demand Paging. *In a demand-paged system, some of the pages may not be in memory. The operating system takes care of reading the contents of the appropriate page from disk, as needed. Shown are two processes that share some of the same physical pages.*

8.3.4 Segmentation

In most systems, the virtual address space of a process is divided into at least two distinct portions, or *segments,* one for user programs and data (called *user space*) and the other for the operating system (*system space*). The partitioning is usually simple and static. In figure 8-2, for example, all virtual addresses for pages 0–4 are in user space, and all virtual addresses for pages 5–8 are in system space. Typically, one copy of the operating system (code and data) lies in memory, shared by all processes. The figure shows the system space for both processes occupying the same physical pages. The user space pages are separate, although some systems allow processes to share selected user pages.

The two-segment scheme is common but limited. The most flexible architecture, the *segmented virtual memory,* allows many segments to be included in each process, any of which can be shared. The virtual address is a two-dimensional value containing a segment number and a segment offset:

VIRTUAL ADDRESS: | SEGMENT NUMBER | SEGMENT OFFSET

Each segment contains an independent identifiable object—a procedure, a large program, the process stack, a shared data area, or the like—and segments need not all be the same size (though there is a maximum, based on the size of the segment offset field). When a process is stepping through consecutive locations in a segment (during program execution, for example), there is no notion of overflowing into the "next" segment when the end of the segment is reached: the segment number of an object bears no relationship to neighboring segment numbers. If the two-dimensional virtual address is treated as a single large number, the virtual address space can be described as being full of holes, each corresponding to the addresses that lie beyond the end of one segment and before the beginning of the next. Though a large number of unused virtual memory locations lie at the end of each segment, no physical memory is wasted by the existence of these holes.

Some machines have memory segments but cannot conveniently map segments to distinct objects, either because the hardware supports too few segments or because the operating system architecture does not permit it. The segmentation is simply a memory-partitioning convenience, and memory addresses flow continuously from one segment into the next.

A translation mechanism for virtual memory addresses that accommodates variable-size segments in conjunction with demand paging requires an extra level of memory descriptor, as shown in figure 8-3. Notice that the segment offset in the virtual address is composed of a page number and a word number. Instead of there being one page table for the whole process, as was the case in figure 8-2, there is a variable-length page descriptor table for each segment, and each process has a variable number of segments. The fixed-size pages permit efficient use of physical memory, and the variable-size segments permit efficient sharing of segments among processes. Figure 8-4 illustrates the use of a shared segment. Notice that the segment number of the shared segment can be different for each process. This permits each process to lay out its virtual address space as it chooses, without having to es-

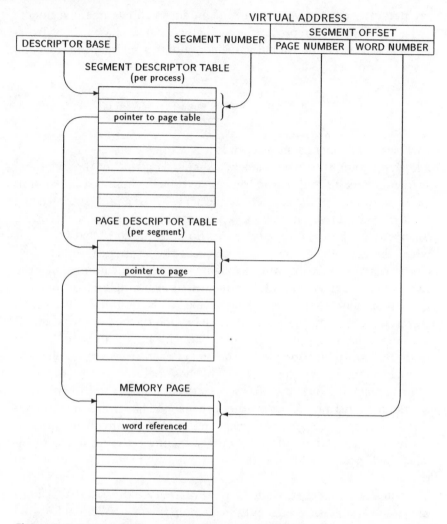

Figure 8-3. Virtual Address Translation with Segments. *A process has a descriptor base register that points to the segment descriptor table for the process. In a virtual address, the segment number selects a segment descriptor that points to the page table for the segment. The high-order bits in the segment offset constitute the page number, which points to a page descriptor that identifies the location of the page in physical memory. The low-order bits in the segment offset constitute the word number, which identifies the location of the word within the page.*

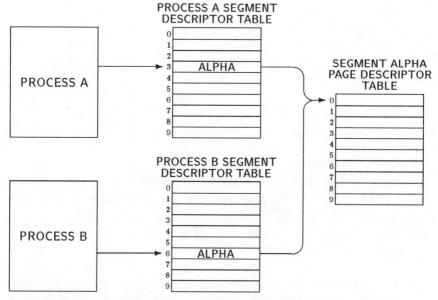

Figure 8-4. Sharing Segments in a Virtual Memory. Each process has its own segment descriptor table that specifies page tables for the segments and access modes to the segments. The shared segment ALPHA has one page table, used by both processes. ALPHA is referenced as segment number 3 by process A and as segment number 6 by process B.

tablish any "agreements" ahead of time with other processes that share the same segments.

8.3.5 Access Control with Memory Management

Where the address space is divided into two segments—*system* and *user,* as in figure 8-2—the process must not be allowed to write into system space when running unprivileged programs in user mode. When running in system mode, the process is permitted to read and write all of virtual memory. A context switch from user mode to system mode is accomplished by using a special instruction that transfers control to one of a set of restricted locations in system space. Since the partition between system space and user space is static, hardware can easily enforce these access restrictions based on the privilege mode (context) of the process. For greater flexibility, however, it is desirable to allow the system software to specify exactly which pages of the process's address space are readable and/or writable in each context.

Before machines provided transparent memory management, access decisions were based on the identity of the physical page. Each physical page was labeled with information such as a key and some access bits indicating whether the page was readable or writable. Each process was assigned a key that had been loaded by the operating system into a process status word. The hardware checked the key on each memory reference, prohibiting access unless the process status word key matched the memory key and unless the access bits matched the desired read or write access mode. A design similar to this was used on IBM 360 machines.

The approach of associating access information (keys and access bits) with physical pages becomes unmanageable when pages are not fixed in memory for the life of a process. Each time ownership of a physical page changes (as when a page is swapped), the access information has to be modified. And, if two processes share a page—one for reading and one for writing—the access information has to be changed on each process switch.

With a descriptor-based address translation mechanism, where each process has a private set of descriptors, a process's access modes to a page or segment of memory are specified in the descriptors. There may be two sets of access modes, one for use while the process is running in user context and the other for use while the process is running in system context:

System   User

MEMORY DESCRIPTOR: | W | R | E | W | R | E | PHYSICAL ADDRESS |

where the fields W, R, and E are single bits that indicate whether the process has write, read, or execute access to the specified segment or page of memory. Because the descriptors are already fetched during address translation, descriptor-based access control imposes little or no additional overhead in process switching, in context switching within a process, or in swapping processes into or out of memory.

In figure 8-3, where there are two levels of descriptors, the access information should be contained in the segment descriptors, not in the page descriptors. Otherwise, it would not be possible to specify different modes of access for two processes sharing the same segment.

Use of Virtual Memory to Map Objects

When a user program reads a file, it asks the operating system to carry out an I/O operation that reads the contents of a block of the file into a buffer somewhere in the user space of the process's virtual memory. Another way for a program to access a file is for the operating system to map the file directly onto the virtual address space of the process. The file (or a portion of it) is paged into memory and the words in the file become accessible through memory reference instructions, just as if they were words in the process's virtual memory. The process must keep track of the starting virtual address of the file; it then computes the virtual addresses of words in the file as offsets from that starting address. In such an architecture, the entire file system is potentially part of each process's virtual memory, although a single process will only have a small number of files mapped at any one time.

The idea of translating a virtual address into a location in a file is not unlike the concept of demand paging, by which portions of a process's virtual memory are kept on a paging disk and copied into physical memory when referenced. The difference is that the process specifically requests that a particular file be mapped into a particular range of virtual memory locations. The major benefit of mapping files directly into virtual memory is that no privileged I/O is required to access a file once it is mapped: the normal demand paging and memory management mechanisms are used. Random access to any location in the file is also made easier, and performance improves somewhat because a system call is not required on each access; these benefits, however, are not security concerns.

The technique of mapping files into virtual memory, although routine in Multics, is rare elsewhere. (The feature is available in vMS and probably in other systems, but it is not routinely used for all file accesses.) Programmers traditionally use read and write system I/O calls for accessing files; giving programmers a way to access a file as a long string of characters or as an array of words requires rethinking how applications are designed. To be practical, this technique must be well-integrated into the programming language.

The simplest way to implement file-to-virtual-memory mapping is to associate a single segment with an object. Thereafter, the process need simply keep track of the segment number of each file it has mapped and need not reserve virtual memory space for objects prior to mapping. Associating hardware segments with system storage objects has advantages from a security standpoint, because the hardware's access control mechanisms are used without additional software control.

In order to represent objects as segments efficiently, however, the range of possible segment sizes must span several orders of magnitude. If a typical object exceeds the size of a maximum-length segment, a mechanism must be available for building large objects out of several segments, and this means that direct access to a word in an object cannot consist of a simple offset from the beginning of a segment. Mapping multisegment objects onto consecutive segment numbers in virtual memory leads to an awkward software structure, although it is done in the SCOMP (with considerable difficulty) because of the small segments. The small segments in the Intel 80286 cause similar programming difficulties. Even Multics, which supports segments of up to 2^{18} 36-bit words (over 1 million characters), has a multisegment file facility for the occasional very large file that will not fit into a segment. These multisegment files are not mapped into contiguous segments, so all applications that might potentially use them must use a special application package that provides an I/O-style interface for file access rather than direct memory reference—thereby defeating some of the performance advantages of direct memory reference to files.

Another performance problem that occurs with multisegment files managed by applications is the need for a process to *initiate* (map for the first time) a number of segments each time the file is opened. Segment initiation is a relatively slow process, comparable in overhead to the opening of a file in conventional file systems. Moreover, the operating system (which treats each segment independently and knows nothing about the relationship between segments in a multisegment file) must maintain separate access control information for each segment in the file, even though all segments are accessed identically. These performance and overhead problems have no adverse effect on security per se, except that the poor performance of such features might drive people to find shortcuts that bypass the security controls.

The preceding discussion indicates that, if you are to represent files as segments efficiently, a reasonably large file should fit into one segment. It is also necessary that the system support enough segments for each process to free most processes from concern about *terminating* (unmapping) segments no longer in use. If a process runs out of segment numbers as it brings new objects into its address space, the process must find a segment to terminate that it knows is not needed by any programs in the process. Determining which segments are no longer in use and avoiding inappropriate reuse of segment numbers for deleted objects pose a difficult problem and an undesirable complication—complete cooperation by user applications is required. For example, when a program is finished with a file or segment, that program cannot simply unmap the segment because other programs in the process might still retain pointers to virtual memory locations in the original segment. If a new file is later mapped into the same virtual memory locations, thereby inheriting the same segment number, those other programs, using their stored pointers, will access the wrong file. As in the case of small segments, these problems are security issues only to the extent that they may so complicate the applications that people will seek shortcuts that bypass the controls.

In addition to mapping files into virtual memory as segments, executable programs can also be mapped. On most systems, executable programs are in fact stored in files. Usually, however, all separately compiled programs that will run in a process must be linked in advance into one large executable image that is stored in a single file or series of segments. At execution time, the image is mapped into virtual memory as one or more memory segments. From an access control standpoint, the image is one object to which the process has execute access permission, and no finer-grained control on the programs within the image is enforced.

Dynamic linking is a sophisticated capability used in Multics that allows separately compiled programs to remain in individual segments without prior linking. The first time a program is called by a process, the segment containing the program is mapped into the virtual address space, and all linking between the process and the program takes place at execution time.[1] An advantage of dynamic linking (and the ability to retain each program in its own segment) is that the protection attributes of the program (obtained from its segment) remain enforced by hardware, thereby permitting different programs in the same process to have different attributes. The importance of this will become more apparent as we discuss execution domains in the next section.

8.4 EXECUTION DOMAINS

Hardware features that support execution domains are as pervasive as memory management features. Even systems that lack memory management or multiprogramming usually support execution domains. Our use of the term *execution domains* includes commonly used terms such as *execution mode, state,* and *context.*

When there are two domains, *system* and *user,* the domains are hierarchical. The more privileged domain has access to all of memory and all instructions, and the less privileged domain has access to a portion of memory and a subset of the instructions. A three-domain machine

1. Because of the performance overhead of dynamic linking, even Multics provides a prelinking or binding facility for collections of programs that are routinely used together.

is likewise hierarchical. Both two- and three-domain machines are special cases of a general hierarchical domain architecture based on *protection rings*, so called because a picture of the hierarchy is shown as concentric rings (fig. 8-5). The lowest-numbered, innermost ring has the most privilege; and the highest-numbered, outermost ring has the least. Each ring has access to at least the same memory as the next-less-privileged ring (fig. 8-6). Though Multics has proposed instituting as many as sixty-four rings, rarely are more than three or four rings

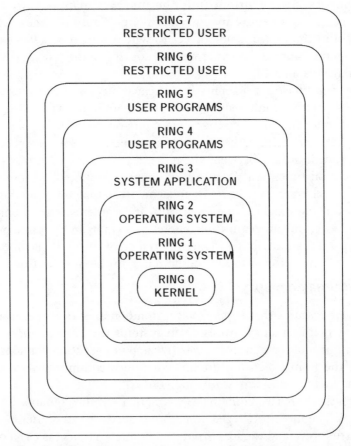

Figure 8-5. Hierarchical Domains. *The rings of privilege show the most privileged ring in the center, with less privileged rings as we move outward. The operating system occupies the innermost rings, users do their programming in intermediate rings, and certain restricted users might be given access to the outermost rings only.*

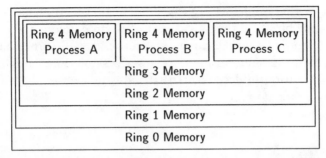

Figure 8-6. Hierarchical Domain Memory Access. *The most privileged domain (ring 0) can access all of memory, while the least privileged domain (ring 4) has the most restricted access. Memory accessible to the less privileged domains is segregated by process, whereas the more privileged domains tend to share the same memory across all processes.*

used. The International Computers Limited (ICL) 2900 mainframe supports sixteen rings, and most of them are used on the VME/B operating system (Parker 1981).

It is easy to understand the purpose of having two rings: to separate the operating system programs from user programs, but it is less easy to see the purpose of having three or more. One way of viewing rings is in terms of scope of control. The innermost ring contains the operating system that controls the whole computer system. Outside it might be a ring in which large applications—such as database management systems and transaction processing monitors—are run. These large applications control various user applications in an outermost ring.

The important security concept here is that the domain mechanism protects each ring from those outside it and allows each ring to control applications efficiently in the less privileged rings. The process isolation mechanism is orthogonal to the domain mechanism: a given process may run in any one of several rings at any one time, moving from ring to ring during execution. When a process is running in a given ring, that process is protected from damage by other processes running in the same ring because the system normally isolates processes from one another. On the other hand, the innermost rings are the ones most likely to choose to share system-wide data or data belonging to multiple users; and in a given ring, the processes are only isolated to the extent that the software in that ring chooses to keep its data separate from the data of other processes.

Hardware that implements a two-domain architecture needs a single process state bit: *on* if the process is in system domain, and *off* if it is in user domain. As was discussed in section 8.3, the processor determines which segments in memory are accessible in each domain by using information in descriptors that indicate access modes for each segment in each domain:

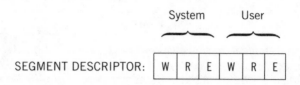

If hardware supports many hierarchical domains, maintaining a separate set of W, R, E bits in each segment descriptor for the access modes for each ring is unwieldy. Fortunately, there are shortcuts. We know that, if ring n has a given mode of access to a segment, all rings 0 through $n - 1$ also have that mode of access. Therefore, for each type of access mode, it is necessary to specify in the descriptor only the greatest ring having that mode of access. Instead of maintaining three access mode bits per ring, we have three fields, each containing a ring number (one for each of the access modes):

SEGMENT DESCRIPTOR: | R1 | R2 | R3 |

We call these three ring numbers (R1, R2, and R3) *ring brackets,* where

0–R1 is the write bracket.
0–R2 is the read bracket.
0–R3 is the execute bracket.

For example, the set of ring brackets (4, 5, 7) within a segment descriptor would tell us that the segment was writable from rings 0 through 4, readable from rings 0 through 5, and executable from rings 0 through 7. As a simplifying assumption, we can assume that the ring brackets always satisfy the relation

$$R1 \leq R2 \leq R3$$

since there is little reason to prevent a domain from reading a segment that it is allowed to write, or to prevent it from executing a segment that it is allowed to read. It is dangerous (and pointless) for a process to execute a segment from an inner ring that is writable from a less privileged ring, so it is reasonable to restrict the execute bracket to the range R1–R3; however, such a restriction only serves to limit the damage caused by errors in an inner-ring program and is not, strictly speaking, a security requirement.

A segment with brackets (0, 0, 0) is only accessible from within the innermost ring, while a segment with brackets (7, 7, 7) is readable and writable from all rings. Since ring 0 is the most privileged, there is little security reason to prohibit access to a segment from a user in ring 0 (though, for reliability, Multics does allow ring 0 to write-protect its segments from itself).

As we saw in figure 8-4, each process that uses a shared segment has its own segment descriptors and (possibly different) set of access modes to the segment. It might at first seem useful to allow each process to have a different set of ring brackets for a given segment, so that two processes that share a segment would have different access to the segment in different rings. But the set of ring brackets is better treated as a system-wide attribute of the segment—one that defines the domains in which the segment may be used, regardless of which process uses the segment. Instead of giving each process a different set of ring brackets for a segment, we can use the same set of ring brackets for all processes and alter the three access mode bits W, R, and E in situations where access differs per process. The access mode bits restrict access to a segment in a way that is more restrictive than that implied by the ring brackets. The segment with ring brackets (4, 5, 7), for example, is writable from rings 0 through 4 only if the write access mode bit is also on. The access control information in the segment descriptor thus includes one set of ring numbers and three access mode bits:

SEGMENT DESCRIPTOR: | R1 | R2 | R3 | W | R | E |

Each process's segment descriptor table contains this information for each segment; and only the W, R, E bits may differ among processes sharing the same segment.

8.4.1 Transfer of Control Across Domains

In executing a program, the processor fetches instructions from the sequential virtual memory locations indicated by a program counter. This sequential flow is altered when the processor encounters one of three types of *transfer instructions* that load a new virtual address into the program counter:

- jump changes the program counter to a specified virtual address.
- call saves the program counter on the process stack and changes the program counter to a new value.
- return restores the program counter to a value previously saved on the stack.

In general, these instructions may specify arbitrary locations in virtual memory. Whether instruction execution at that new location takes place or not depends on whether the segment or page of virtual memory is marked *executable* and possesses the proper ring brackets.

In a system with two domains and two segments—system space and user space—a process running in the user domain that performs a simple jump to a random location in system space does not change domains. While the locations in system space may be addressable and executable by a process running in the user domain, the process will have no system privileges, and the system code will eventually fail when it attempts an access that is not permissible from user domain. A domain change is only permitted through a call to prescribed legitimate entry points in system space. Most machines implement such a call as a trap to a predetermined location or to a transfer vector in system space. Return to user domain is accomplished with the return instruction. Hardware does not need to restrict the target location of return, but of course you cannot use a return instruction to switch from user domain to system domain.

In a ring architecture, the processor maintains a current ring of execution in place of a single user/system mode bit. A domain change can only be accomplished by transferring control through a call instruction to prescribed locations in special *gate segments* that are designated as entry points into an inner ring. The reason for designating some segments as gates is to prevent a program from calling into an inner ring and executing at an arbitrary location. The single-bit gate indicator, along with the new ring of the segment, is specified in the segment descriptor along with the other access control information:

SEGMENT DESCRIPTOR:	R1	R2	R3	W	R	E	RING	GATE

The permissible locations in the gate segment where entry is allowed may be specified in additional fields in the segment descriptor (Multics has a call limiter field that is the maximum address to which control can be transferred), but simply restricting entry to location zero of the gate segment is adequate because multiple entry points can be designated by values passed in registers.

Even though the ring brackets and mode bits of a segment may specify that the segment is executable (using any type of transfer instruction) from any ring, the current ring number will only change if the segment is a gate and a `call` instruction is used.

Once a process has entered an inner ring through a gate, that gate segment may transfer control to other segments executable within the new current ring. Some nongate segments, such as language utilities, are useful in many rings and therefore have an execute bracket that spans all rings; the current ring of execution remains unchanged when those segments are called. Other segments are useful only in inner rings and may not be executable or callable from outer rings. From a security standpoint, an outer ring can only damage itself by calling or transferring illegally to an inner-ring segment, because the current ring number will not change and the code will fail. Still, there may be reasons to hide the contents of programs in inner-ring segments by preventing their execution as well as the reading of their contents (as when a program contains secret algorithms).

Multics has the additional concept of a *call bracket* that specifies the maximum ring from which a segment may be called. Such a feature is more of a convenience than a requirement for security, since in any case the gate procedure can check whether it has been called from a ring within a given range.

8.4.2 Argument Passing Across Domains

Figure 8-7 illustrates a tree of procedure calls that occur within a process as the process traverses several rings. For simplicity we will assume that each procedure is in its own segment, but nothing prevents us from prelinking several procedures in the same ring into a single segment.

When procedure *A* calls procedure *B*, the current ring remains unchanged because both procedures are part of ring 4 (the user ring). Procedure *B* has the same access to information as procedure *A*. When procedure *B* calls procedure *C* or *D*, however, there is a ring change, and therefore procedure *C* or *D* can access additional information belonging to ring 2. Procedures *C*, *D*, *E*, and *I* are gate procedures into their respective rings. Also shown in the figure is a `call` from procedure *H* to procedure *I* that drops directly from ring 4 into ring 0. Finally,

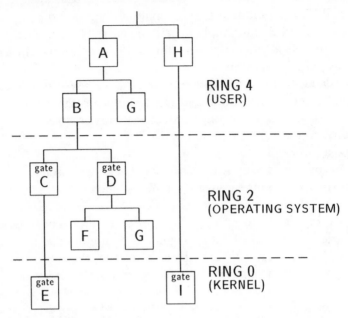

Figure 8-7. Domain Crossing. *Each box represents a procedure within a system supporting hierarchical domains (rings). The tree of procedure calls spans user, operating system, and kernel rings.*

notice that procedure *G* is accessible from and runs within either ring 4 or ring 2. Its execute bracket includes rings 2 through 4.

When *A* calls *B*, programming practices might dictate that *B* check the arguments passed to it for validity. While such checks might help find bugs in *A*, the checks do nothing for security because *A* and *B* have access to exactly the same information. Consequently, *A* can obtain access to any information used by *B*, whether or not *B* checks its arguments.

On the other hand, procedure *D*, being a gate into ring 2, is responsible for ensuring that arguments passed by *B* cannot harm ring 2. Operating systems typically go to great lengths to check arguments received from user programs. Many of the checks are simple, such as ensuring that an argument is within a prescribed range of values, and they are often used to catch errors in user programs rather than to protect the operating system. Other checks are security-relevant, designed to ensure that one user's process cannot illegally obtain access to data belonging to another user, or to ensure that part of the operating system is not damaged. In order to prevent asynchronous modifications to arguments (by other processes or processors) between the time they are checked and the time they are used, arguments passed across a gate must usually be copied into a safe place within the ring of the gate. Argument copying and most general-validity and access checks are implemented by software in the gate procedure of the inner ring; the ad hoc nature of these checks means that hardware can do little to help. The software impact of argument validation is discussed in section 11.2.

Hardware can help significantly in one particular type of argument validation, however: address validation. In figure 8-7, one way that ring 4 can use procedure B to obtain ring 2 information is to fool D into copying that information into a place accessible to ring 4. As an example, assume that D is an I/O procedure that writes data from a buffer specified by the caller into a file also specified by the caller. The calling sequence from B to D might be

```
call write_file (file_name, buffer_ptr)
```

where the argument buffer_ptr is a *pointer* to (a virtual address of) the buffer. The buffer is supposed to lie in an area of memory accessible to ring 4. If write_file does not check the validity of the buffer pointer, procedure B may be able to pass a pointer to an area of ring 2's memory, thereby causing write_file to write ring 2 data into the file. The normal hardware access control mechanism does not prevent a ring 4 procedure from constructing a pointer to ring 2 data, nor does it prevent the data from being accessed by the ring 2 procedure. Therefore, procedure D must carry out some type of pointer validation on the buffer_ptr.

Pointer validation done completely by software tends to be time-consuming because of the number of steps involved: finding and examining the target segment descriptor, fetching indirect references, validating intermediate addresses, and calculating index information. For better performance, some hardware support for pointer validation is desirable when the machine has several rings, segmented virtual memory, multiple levels of pointer indirection, or indexing information in pointers. Machines that have just two or three rings and simple pointers in which a one-dimensional virtual memory is statically assigned to domains probably do not need hardware help.

There are two general types of hardware pointer validation schemes: *explicit* and *implicit*. The explicit scheme is more common and requires inner-ring software to invoke the validation mechanism as required.

The implicit scheme requires software cooperation but no direct assistance.

Explicit Pointer Validation

The simplest explicit pointer validation mechanism is a machine instruction that asks some form of the question, "What mode of access does ring x have to the area of memory designated by pointer p?" This technique requires software to validate the pointer explicitly, prior to use.

A somewhat more sophisticated mechanism uses a two-instruction sequence: the first instruction asks the machine to "execute the following instruction using the access rights of ring x rather than the rights of the current ring"; and the second instruction is a normal memory reference instruction that uses indirection through the pointer. The second instruction will fail with an access violation, if access was not allowed in the outer ring x. To eliminate the possibility of asynchronous modification, the machine automatically suspends interrupts between the pair of instructions. Each time software makes a reference through a pointer that might have come from an outer ring, the reference must be preceded by the special instruction. This technique allows software to postpone validation until the time that the pointer is actually used.

With either technique for explicit pointer validation, software must decide when to check the pointer: at the point of entry into the inner ring (in the gate procedure), or in conjunction with its normal use. In figure 8-7, the buffer_ptr passed from procedure B to procedure D might not be used until procedure G is called, so the task of validating the pointer appears to lie most appropriately with G. For procedure D to validate the pointer properly, it would have to know whether the buffer was to be read or written by G, and it would have to know the length of the buffer (to ensure that the buffer could not overflow onto an area not accessible to ring 4).

Another complicating factor is that arguments may contain pointers. For example, the write_file I/O call might require as an argument a data structure containing information such as file name, location in file to be written, space for returning a status code, and buffer to be written. The data structure itself is passed by means of a single pointer as an argument. To keep the structure compact and to avoid moving a great deal of data around on each call, the data structure contains pointers to the items rather than containing the items themselves. This means that all the pointers in the structure (as well as the pointer to the structure itself) have to be validated. Requiring the gate procedure to validate these pointers forces it to be intimately familiar with the format and use of the data structure, even if the gate's only role is to pass the data structure on to another procedure for processing. This requirement violates good software layering and information-hiding principles.

On the other hand, one could argue that the task of a gate procedure such as D is to make all appropriate argument checks and to relieve inner procedures from having to make such checks. For example, procedure G might be a general-purpose I/O routine that can perform I/O on behalf of either the user or the operating system. If so, procedure G may not know whether the buffer pointers or embedded pointers passed to it should be validated with respect to the user's ring or to the operating system's ring. Such information might be passed to G by every caller; but if G happens to be embedded deep in a tree of procedure calls, this extra information must be passed down by every caller in the tree.

A problem with explicit pointer validation in advance of use is that the information on which the validation is based (like the segment descriptors) may be changed by other processes or processors by the time the pointer is used. This is possible even if the pointer itself is copied into a safe place so that it cannot change.

Ensuring that the segment descriptors have not changed between the time a pointer is validated and the time it is used may require suspending interrupts and stopping all other processors (on multiprocessor systems) during the interval. This is rarely a feasible option, although suspending interrupts on a single-processor system for a brief period by using the delayed validation approach is possible.

Despite its drawbacks, explicit pointer validation is the only type of hardware assist provided on most machines. Through various techniques (based largely on programming and calling sequence conventions), operating system software does the best it can to ensure that the validation information has not changed. From a security standpoint, perhaps our biggest concern with this technique—as with any technique that requires explicit software action—is the possibility that security holes will remain as a result of overlooked or incorrect checks.

Implicit Pointer Validation

The implicit pointer validation mechanism requires little or no software assist and avoids most of the asynchronous change problems of pointer validation. The hardware automatically validates every pointer at the time of use. In order to be efficient, the hardware validation cannot require extra machine cycles, since the vast majority of pointers need no validation. Aside from the obvious benefit of avoiding software errors, a major advantage of this mechanism is that the programmer of an inner-ring procedure need not worry about the origin of the pointer.

Automatic pointer validation requires that the pointer contain a field indicating the ring number of its origin:

POINTER: | RING | VIRTUAL ADDRESS |

This ring number is inseparable from the pointer, staying with it as the pointer is passed between procedures. When a program finally uses the pointer as an indirect reference, hardware computes access rights to the target location based on the ring number in the pointer rather than on the current ring of execution.

Refer again to figure 8-7, where procedure B in ring 4 calls procedure D in ring 2. If B passes a pointer to D, the pointer looks like this:

POINTER: | RING = 4 | VIRTUAL ADDRESS |

indicating that the pointer originated in ring 4. The pointer might get copied from place to place in ring 2 prior to use; if so, the ring number of 4 is preserved during copies. When procedure G makes an indirect reference through the pointer, hardware will validate access to the target based on the effective ring number 4, rather than on the current ring number 2. Pointers originating in ring 2 have a ring number of 2 and the effective ring for them is 2, correctly validating the pointer with respect to the current ring. In both cases, the programmer of procedure G has done nothing to assist validation.

Since ring 4 constructs the pointer, it is possible for procedure B to lie about the origin of the pointer and insert a 2 in the RING field. This deception must be prevented by checking the RING number in the pointer at the time it is first copied into ring 2. Hardware assist to prevent this form of attack is a special copy_pointer instruction that operates much as any other data copying instruction does, but performs an additional validation on the ring field to ensure that its value is no less than the ring of the segment from which the pointer is copied. By using copy_pointer for all pointer copying, software can safely pass the pointer through several rings.

The purpose of `copy_pointer` is not just to save a little software checking: an important additional benefit is that the pointer need not be copied into the inner ring by the gate procedure; it can be copied at any later time. The gate procedure need not know anything about the intended use of the arguments, and the procedure that uses the pointer and does the copy need not know where the pointer originated, thereby fostering clean software layering.

But procedures do not always have a reason to copy pointers into an inner ring prior to use, so an additional mechanism exists to allow the pointer to be validated at the time of use even while still residing in the outer ring. During address calculation, hardware sets the effective ring number to the maximum of the RING field of the pointer and the ring of the segment in which the pointer is located. In this way a pointer can remain in ring 4, and a ring 2 procedure can make an indirect reference through that pointer with assurance that access will be computed relative to ring 4.

While the pointer validation mechanism discussed here is unique to Multics, it demonstrates the possibility of freeing software from any concern about the origin of pointers and attendant access checks in most cases.

Extension to Nonhierarchical Domains (Capabilities)

Our discussions about pointer validation, though based in the context of a ring architecture, apply equally to all hierarchical domain architectures. Architectures with two domains do not need as complicated a mechanism as architectures with four or more domains, because the solutions do not have to be as general.

With nonhierarchical domains, solutions to argument validation are difficult and complex. Nonhierarchical domains provide greater flexibility for support of mutually suspicious subsystems (a topic covered more fully in section 11.3) than do ring-based systems, although proposals have been made for using rings in such systems (Schroeder 1972). The main problem is that, when domains are not hierarchical, hardware has no simple "greater than" relationship to use in comparing the relative access rights of two domains. Controlled sharing between mutually suspicious domains means preventing each domain from accessing the memory of others, while allowing domains to pass selected pointers to each other's memory.

When the domains are nonhierarchical, this in effect requires that hardware implement the concept of an *object,* where a primitive object is indicated by a special kind of pointer that identifies a range of consecutive virtual memory locations. A domain that receives a pointer to an object as an argument from another domain cannot modify that pointer and cannot reference words outside the range of the pointer. A domain cannot construct a pointer to anything outside its address space. A pointer that identifies an object is called a *capability* because the domain that possesses the pointer has the capability to access the object. Capabilities can be passed freely between domains. Designs based on such concepts are given such names as *object-oriented architectures, domain machines,* and *capability machines.*

There are two common ways for hardware to manage capabilities. One is to store all capabilities in special areas of memory that are directly accessible only to privileged programs or to the hardware. This approach is always used in systems that implement capabilities in software, but is also used in some hardware architectures. Another, more flexible approach uses *tagged memory,* whereby each word of memory contains an extra bit that indicates whether the word contains a capability or simple data. In both cases, moving a capability from place to place requires special instructions or system calls.

Several commercial hardware architectures are based on capabilities. These include the Intel iAPX 432 microprocessor and the midrange IBM System/38.

8.5 INPUT/OUTPUT ACCESS CONTROL

Among the functions of a typical large operating system, input/output tends to be the most complex. While the hardware to support processes, memory management, and domains is geared toward the convenience of the programmer, hardware support for input and output seems to work against any programmer concerned with implementing an easy-to-understand I/O system. People who search for security holes in an operating system look first at the I/O area, because hardware rarely, if ever, provides any assistance for secure I/O. The design goals for the hardware that supports I/O in most large machines are geared toward cost and performance, not security. The hardware is replete with idiosyncrasies that frustrate attempts to implement a well-structured secure interface to I/O functions.

Almost universally, I/O is a privileged operation that can be carried out only by the operating system. All operating systems provide high-level system calls to read and write files; in these procedures, the user need exercise no control over the details of the I/O operation. Some systems, to enhance flexibility and performance, enable the user to specify many details and may even allow the user to write *channel programs* (lists of instructions executed by I/O controllers). While this flexibility makes it appear as if the user has direct control over the I/O device, the operating system must carry out many complex internal checks to ensure that the requested operations in the channel program are secure. Operating systems based on IBM's 370 architecture are representative of this approach.

Operating systems could be far simpler if they did not have to mediate all I/O operations. The Multics structure, in which files are mapped into virtual memory segments, avoids the need to perform explicit I/O for file access, but it does not eliminate the need for operating system-supported I/O for terminals, tapes, printers, and foreign (non-file-system) disks. Operating systems must carry out much of the same I/O on their own behalf: they must access their own system disks and tapes to keep the system running. But in principle, the operating system need not play a part in providing or controlling access to devices that are owned by a single user or process. With the proper hardware support, complete control over these devices could be relegated to applications programs outside of the operating system.

From an access control perspective, a generic I/O instruction issued by a process involves identifying the following items:

1. The I/O device
2. The affected medium or portion of medium (which particular tape reel, disk pack, or sector of disk)
3. The locations in memory of the buffers involved in the data transfer
4. The locations where device status information will be stored and where commands to the device will be obtained

Regardless of their complexity, access requirements of I/O operations can be decomposed into some combination of these four primitive elements.

Hardware security support for memory management concentrates solely on processor-to-memory access (shown on the right side of figure 8-8). When I/O is included, several additional information paths appear: device-to-medium, device-to-memory, and processor-to-device. Access control decisions for these interfaces must be based on the identity of the subject (process) on behalf of whom the device or processor is operating, and on the object (area of memory or medium) that is affected.

I/O operations initiated by the processor include both *control operations* to the device (sending commands, reading status) and requests for data transfers to or from the medium. Some control operations, such as "rewind tape," do not require a data transfer; others, such as "write end-of-file" and "erase disk block," clearly do. Certain status

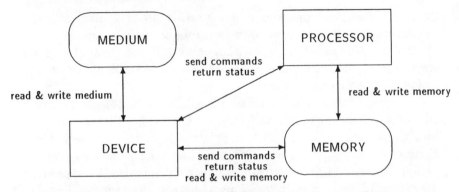

Figure 8-8. Access Paths for I/O and the CPU. *The processor and the device operate on behalf of subjects (processes) that access the objects (the memory and the medium). The device and processor may also access each other as objects. In general, information flows in both directions along all four paths. Multiple processors and devices may operate on behalf of different subjects, accessing different areas of memory and media.*

conditions may indirectly reveal information about contents of data on the medium ("parity error," "byte count"), while other status conditions either are unpredictable hardware conditions or reveal information about the state of the device controller and are not a function of the data on the medium. For security purposes, control operations that influence or are influenced by the medium must be viewed as if they were write or read data transfer operations. A pure control operation is one that involves no data transfer as a side effect.

Looking again at figure 8-8, we can view a "rewind tape" operation issued by the processor as a write from the processor to the device, possibly followed by a write from the device to the processor or to memory to return the status of "rewind done." A "read data" operation requires several steps:

1. Processor sends "read" command to device.
2. Device reads additional command information from memory (location of buffer, number of words, and so on).
3. Device reads data from medium.
4. Device writes data to memory.
5. Device sends status to processor.

Step 1 illustrates why all I/O operations must be viewed as "writes" to the device—even those that only read data from the medium or status from the device.

Figure 8-8 is the most general view of the access paths for I/O. Where the device or the medium is outside the system or security perimeter, the device may be indistinguishable from the medium, from a security standpoint: reads and writes to the device must be controlled in exactly the same manner as reads and writes to the medium are. For example, if the device is an intelligent controller managing a number of disk drives whose firmware is user-supplied and not under the control of the operating system, the operating system can only control the commands and data that are written to the controller—not what the controller writes to the individual drives. Terminals are devices that commonly fall under full user control: sending a command to a terminal is tantamount to displaying it to the user; anything the processor receives from a terminal must be treated as if the user entered it. On the other hand, if a controller and the disk drives it manages can be trusted to carry out requests of the operating system, the controller effectively becomes part of the operating system (within the security perimeter), and data transfer to the disk packs—not to the controller—is the important security concern.

The simplest view of I/O access control treats both the device and the medium as one object, as if both were outside the security perimeter. Since all I/O operations are data transfers to and from the device, a process carrying out I/O must have both read and write access to the device. In figure 8-8, this means that the device-to-medium path can be collapsed, and that the processor-to-device path is always bidirectional.

Devices in figure 8-8 can also be viewed as autonomous subjects that are trusted to read and write memory in a manner specified by the processor. (Trusted subjects are discussed in section 10.5.) Such a view mostly affects the security model of the system (a topic covered in chapter 9, where subjects and objects are enumerated), rather than the hardware architecture. Some techniques however—particularly the *fully mapped* technique, covered in section 8.5.4—permit a device to be treated as an untrusted subject.

From an access control perspective, hardware can support I/O in four ways (from simplest to most complex):

- Programmed
- Unmapped
- Premapped
- Fully mapped

Programmed I/O is synchronous, in that the processor is in direct control of every word of data transferred to or from the I/O device. The other three types of hardware support are varieties of *DMA* (*direct memory access*) I/O, whereby the processor tells the controller to begin a lengthy I/O operation (such as reading one or more blocks of disk), and the controller carries out the operation autonomously and asynchronously from the processor. Each of these four support systems has different implications for hardware access control. Much of the discussion that follows echoes aspects of the SCOMP design. Multics has no hardware support for I/O mediation.

8.5.1 Programmed I/O

Programmed I/O was the only type available before I/O controllers became intelligent enough to operate autonomously (without the help of the processor). Under programmed I/O, software loads a register with a word of data to be transferred and executes an I/O instruction with an argument naming the device. Later, when the transfer is complete, the processor receives an interrupt (or alternatively, software periodically scans a status register). Even today, programmed I/O is often used for slow-speed devices such as terminals, especially on microprocessors that perform only one function at a time and can afford to dedicate the processor to terminal I/O.

Because I/O is carried out through a processor register, no device-to-memory path is involved in the transfer. The only security concern is whether the process making the request has access to the I/O device. A straightforward way to support device access is to use a *device descriptor table,* which maps a virtual device name into a physical device name, much as a virtual address is mapped onto a physical address (fig. 8-9). The device descriptor contains information similar to the segment descriptor:

DEVICE DESCRIPTOR: | R | W | C | PHYSICAL DEVICE ADDRESS |

Instead of using the execute mode for memory access, we have a control mode that specifies whether the process can carry out a control operation.

If you intend to implement a pure control mode in order to allow a process to manipulate the device without affecting the medium, you have to be careful to define control operations in a way that cannot confuse another process sharing the device. For example, a process that has been given only control access can secretly backspace a tape and

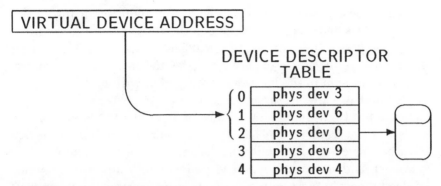

Figure 8-9. Mapping Device Names. *A virtual device name is mapped by hardware into a physical device name. If the device is in the process's device descriptor table, the process has access to the device.*

cause another process to write information onto the wrong place on the tape.

Some device characteristics can be changed quite drastically through a control operation, making it impossible to isolate the actions of one process from those of another that shares the device. Systems that support such operations might use the control access mode as a privileged mode of access rather than as a restricted mode.

8.5.2 Unmapped I/O

Unmapped I/O is by far the most common type of direct memory access I/O: software sends the device an I/O command that specifies the physical location of a buffer in memory. The device acts as a trusted subject and is allowed to read or write physical memory. It is trusted to execute the command correctly.

Since user programs do not deal with physical addresses, unmapped I/O can be initiated only by the operating system. The operating system must translate virtual buffer addresses (supplied by the user) into physical addresses. Although hardware could provide a translation for virtual device names, as described above for programmed I/O, such a translation does not relieve the operating system of having to validate and carry out the I/O request.

8.5.3 Premapped I/O

Also called *virtual I/O,* premapped I/O allows software to specify virtual buffer addresses. When the I/O instruction is issued, the processor translates these virtual addresses into physical addresses, using the descriptor tables and mapping registers of the current process; the processor then passes the resulting physical address to the device. During the translation, the processor checks whether the process has the correct access permission to the locations to be read or written. From the device's point of view, I/O is physical (the device never sees a virtual address); but from the process's point of view, the I/O is virtual and access control is enforced by hardware. As in unmapped I/O, the device must be trusted to access only the desired locations in memory.

Even if hardware does support virtual I/O, user programs may not be able to issue I/O instructions without operating system intervention. A mechanism is needed to prevent the operating system from unknowingly reassigning (for example, through swapping) the affected pages of memory while user-initiated I/O is in progress. Mechanisms designed to inform the operating system that DMA I/O is in progress are complex and are rarely seen. The virtualization frees the operating system from the chore of performing address translation and access control—but not from the task of managing and keeping track of the I/O operations. The SCOMP comes close to allowing user-initiated virtual I/O by providing (through a combination of hardware and software) primitives that specify when pages should be wired down in memory, and by ensuring that I/O can only take place in pages that have been previously wired.

8.5.4 Fully Mapped I/O

With premapped I/O, the initial translation of the virtual buffer address to the physical address, together with the associated access check, provides sufficient protection as long as the I/O controller is a trusted subject that references only the intended physical addresses and obeys the read/write restrictions that the processor has previously checked. But some I/O controllers are very complex: some are even microprogrammed with firmware downline-loaded from memory. In highly secure systems, it may be improper to assign such a high level of trust to hardware and firmware that are relatively uncontrollable. It is definitely improper to do so if the device itself is outside the security perimeter, as when the device resides remotely in a user-controlled area.

A much safer form of virtual I/O consists of hardware carrying out a virtual-to-physical translation on each memory reference made by the device. The device acts as an untrusted subject (possibly even containing a Trojan horse), presenting only virtual addresses as it reads or stores information in memory; translation hardware within the security perimeter does the mapping and access checks. The translation hardware uses the same memory descriptors that belong to the process initiating the I/O. Because the translation and the access check are made on each word transferred, there is no security problem if the operating system reallocates memory during the I/O operation (although the I/O operation is likely to abort with an error if a page fault is encountered while I/O is in progress).

Fully mapped I/O is not a simple enhancement of the premapped approach. Because I/O is asynchronous, a virtual address presented by an I/O device may not necessarily lie within the address space of the currently running process. While the I/O device is operating on behalf of one process, the processor may be operating on behalf of another. Complex address translation hardware is required to keep track of all processes for which I/O is in progress, so that the proper descriptors can be fetched from memory during address translation. In effect, each I/O device must be treated as a separate processor with its own descriptor tables. Translating every address during high-speed operations that cannot be stalled also has performance implications: unless all descriptors in the translation path are cached, a translation requiring a fetch of multiple descriptors from memory may not be able to keep up with the I/O.

Finally—though it is not a security concern here, as it is for premapped I/O—the operating system must know when I/O to a given page of memory is in progress, in order to avoid a page fault during I/O. Thus, primitives to wire pages are still needed.

8.6 MULTIPROCESSOR SUPPORT

A multiprocessor system, in which a number of processors share the same physical memory and run different processes, introduces a host of complexities. Most of these complexities revolve around the issue of consistent maintenance of shared information, such as descriptor tables that might be modified at any time during execution of a process. Software is responsible for handling most of these problems. Hardware helps only by providing a primitive locking mechanism for communication between processors, using "read-alter-rewrite" or "test-and-set" instructions that read and write locations in a single indivisible operation. (Such instructions also simplify interprocess communication on a single-processor system.) Few of these problems are unique to security, but support by hardware can improve the performance of certain security-related operations.

Memory management, already very complex, becomes even more so with multiple processors. These complexities center on descriptor cache management. Each processor usually has its own memory descriptor cache. When one processor modifies a descriptor in memory or in its own cache, the other processors must be told to invalidate their copies and to fetch a new copy from memory. A simple mechanism that accomplishes this is an interprocessor signal (initiated by software) that forces all processors to purge all descriptors whenever a descriptor is changed. While a total cache purge is often used on single-processor systems, such purges can cause serious performance problems on large systems where each user operates several processes and where descriptors get changed very frequently. (Consider that a descriptor is invalidated each time a page fault is processed.) A much better (but complex) approach is a mechanism that invalidates only the descriptor that is changed. The logically simplest approach (which, unfortunately, is usually impractical from the standpoint of hardware implementation) is to implement a single descriptor cache shared by all processors; this is also the most secure approach because it minimizes the chance for error caused by flawed coordination mechanisms.

We have already discussed the problem of argument validation, where the information on which the validation is based can change between the check and the use of the argument. This problem is far worse on a multiprocessor system because it is not feasible, without a severe performance impact, for one processor to disable interrupts or instances of process switching on other processors for extended periods of time during critical sections of code.

Vendors often build computers first as single-processor systems and enhance them later to support multiple processors. If multiple-processor support is not considered during the original hardware design, such enhancement is very painful and introduces a host of software incompatibilities. Likewise, even with the best hardware support, enhancing an operating system designed for a single processor to fit a multiprocessor operating system usually requires major software modifications. Even the best security architecture is not likely to survive such a hardware/software overhaul. Needless to say, the best time to consider multiprocessor support in a system is during the initial system design, when the hooks for multiprocessor support cost relatively little.

There has been considerable interest, but few practical results, in efforts to prove the correctness or security of multiprocessor systems. Verification and formal modeling techniques (subjects of chapters 9 and 12) typically model a system as a single "state machine" with a single thread of execution; consequently, they are not strictly suitable for multiprocessor systems. But given that the current state of the art of program verification does not permit a full formal proof of even single-processor systems, the additional uncertainty introduced by multiple processors is not significant. Multiprocessor handling is best addressed informally as part of implementation correspondence (see section 12.8).

REFERENCES

Fraim, L. J. 1983. "SCOMP: A Solution to the Multilevel Security Problem." *Computer* 16(7):26–34. Reprinted in *Advances in Computer System Security*, vol. 2, ed. R. Turn, pp. 185–92. Dedham, Mass.: Artech House (1984).
   A minicomputer-based security kernel with sophisticated hardware protection controls; this system is a Honeywell product.
Organick, E. I. 1972. *The Multics System: An Examination of Its Structure.* Cambridge, Mass.: MIT Press.
   A description of Multics—at that time implemented on a processor without hardware-supported protection rings.
Parker, T. 1981. "ICL Efforts in Computer Security." In *Proceedings of the 4th Seminar on the DoD Computer Security Initiative*, pp. L1–L22. Gaithersburg, Md.: National Bureau of Standards.
   Describes the ICL 2900 machine and the VME/B *operating system, supporting sixteen protection rings.*
Schroeder, M. D. 1972. "Cooperation of Mutually Suspicious Subsystems in a Computer Utility." Ph.D. dissertation, MIT. Project MAC Report #MAC TR-104. DARPA Order #2095. (Also available through National Technical Information Service, Springfield, Va., NTIS AD-750173.)
   Discusses mutually suspicious subsystems and proposes a way to use the Multics ring-based architecture to support them.
Schroeder, M. D., and Saltzer, J. H. 1972. "A Hardware Architecture for Implementing Protection Rings." *Communications of the ACM* 15(3):157–70.
   A thorough discussion of protection rings, domain-crossing mechanisms, and argument validation as used in Multics.
Tangney, J. D. 1978. "Minicomputer Architectures for Effective Security Kernel Implementations." ESD-TR-78-170. Hanscom AFB, Mass.: Air Force Electronic Systems Division. (Also available through National Technical Information Service, Springfield, Va., NTIS AD-A059449.)
   Discusses hardware protection features that are suitable for a secure operating system (such as a security kernel).

Chapter 9

Security Models

Success in achieving a high degree of security in a system depends on the degree of care put into designing and implementing the security controls. But even the most careful application of the best software engineering practices is inadequate unless you clearly understand the system's security requirements. The purpose of a security model is to express those requirements precisely.

A security model has several properties:

- It is precise and unambiguous.
- It is simple and abstract, and therefore easy to comprehend.
- It is generic: it deals with security properties only and does not unduly constrain the functions of the system or its implementation.
- It is an obvious representation of the security policy.

For high-security systems, especially those based on a security kernel, the requirement for precision is satisfied by writing the model in a formal mathematical notation. However, the concept of modeling a system does not require the use of mathematical techniques. Even for medium-grade security, if your goal is to modify an existing system to improve its security properties, writing a natural-language model can be well worth your while.

The property of simplicity is satisfied by modeling only the security properties of a system, and not the functions. It is important to avoid the tendency to turn the model into a formal specification (a topic of chapter 12) by including too many functional properties of the system that are irrelevant to the security policy.

9.1 ROLE OF A SECURITY MODEL

There are two reasons why a system may not be as secure as expected: there is a bug in the security controls; or the definition of what it means to be secure is flawed. The first problem is one of software reliability and is overcome by good software engineering in conjunction with the design techniques and principles specific to security that are discussed throughout this book. Chapter 12 covers formal specification techniques that, in part, address software reliability.

The second problem—defining what you want the system to do—is not a particularly hard problem for most systems, but it is relatively difficult for security because the definition must be much more precise. The security model plays a pivotal role in the formal system development path illustrated in figure 9-1. Figure 9-2 explores several ways to carry out the formal development path. The goal of each of these options is to demonstrate, to varying degrees of assurance, that the implementation corresponds to the model.

Paths (a) and (b) do not involve any formal work beyond the definition of the model. Path (a) assumes that you have developed a formal or informal model but have no additional specification of the security properties from which to implement the system. (This does not imply that you have no specification at all: it is assumed that you have a functional specification, but that the specification does not specifically elaborate on the security requirements expressed in the model.) In path (b), you have an informal specification of the security properties as an intermediate step between the model and the implementation. Both paths require informal arguments and testing to support the correspondence argument.

Because of the huge jump in level of detail between the model and the implementation, the correspondence argument in path (a) is very tenuous. Consequently, the model is of dubious value. Path (b), on the other hand, permits you to make a far more credible correspondence argument. In particular, you can use the informal specification in path (b) as a basis for designing and implementing the system, just as you would use any functional specification.

Paths (c) and (d) employ formal specifications and proofs, and both require a formal model. Path (c) uses a single formal specification in

Informal Development Path   Formal Development Path

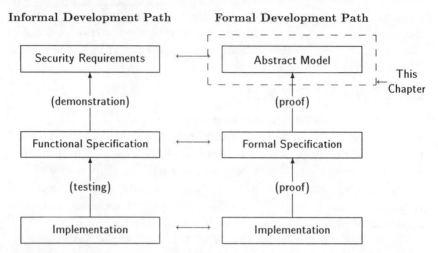

Figure 9-1. System Development Paths. *The abstract security model is the first step in the formal development path that corresponds to the informal security requirements phase.*

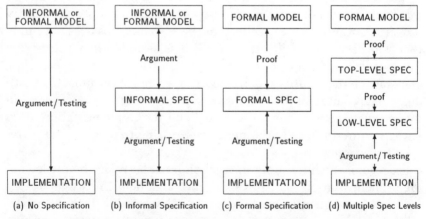

Figure 9-2. Model Correspondence Alternatives. *As we add more intermediate levels of formal specification between the model and the implementation, and as we carry out proofs between the more formal levels, the overall assurance of the system increases. The specifications referred to in this figure represent specifications of security properties, not specifications of functional properties.*

place of (or in addition to) the informal specification in path (b). The formal specification incorporates the same level of detail as the informal specification in path (b), but it is far more precise and unambiguous. The formality of the specification provides the basis for a mathematical proof that the specification corresponds to the model. While the correspondence argument between the implementation and the formal specification remains informal, as in path (b), the argument can be much more precise.

Path (c) significantly raises the level of assurance over path (b). Nonetheless, a large gap remains between the levels of abstraction of the formal specification in path (c) and of the implementation. Path (d) shows two or more levels of formal specification between the implementation and the model, thereby reducing the gaps that must be filled by informal justification. The state of the art in verification today does not permit us to eliminate the informal argument between the implementation level and the lowest level of formal specification, and this informal step remains the weakest link in the overall model-to-implementation correspondence argument.

The benefit of additional levels of specification beyond the top begins to diminish rapidly. Too many levels can even reduce the degree of confidence in the correspondence, because the large number of intermediate proofs increases the probability of error. Even the best automated verification systems cannot eliminate all sources of human error. Incorporating many levels of specification also significantly increases the maintenance costs of the specifications and intermediate proofs, as the system undergoes revisions.

The precise meaning of *levels of specification* in figure 9-2(d) is addressed more thoroughly in chapter 12, where we cover paths (c) and (d) and formal proofs. In this chapter, we are concerned primarily with the development of the model used in all paths and in the informal correspondence arguments of paths (a) and (b).

9.2 PRACTICAL APPLICATIONS OF A MODEL

People shy away from modeling because of its abstract nature, and many have a difficult time appreciating its relevance to a real system. Indeed, it is all to easy to get carried away with modeling details and mathematical formalism to the point where the model does not help you to design the system. This chapter explains how to develop a model and how to prove that it is a reasonable description of your security requirements; it also tells you how to apply the model to the system development process.

9.2.1 Security Model as a Security Specification

When you write a functional specification early in the life cycle of a system, you usually have not done enough detailed design to specify every possible aspect of the system's behavior. In fact, if you write a highly detailed functional specification at this point to cover all unusual error conditions, you will unnecessarily constrain the design. A functional specification should leave the designers free to define for themselves the course of action to be taken in the numerous "don't care" conditions that will be identified as the design progresses. The functional specification is most useful in describing the particular aspects of the system that are needed to satisfy the obvious requirements of the system. When the system is completed, chances are that the designers will have exercised reasonable judgment, and that the course of action taken for all the "don't cares" will not violate the spirit or unwritten intent of the specification.

But the specification of a secure system cannot leave certain things to chance. Despite good intentions and knowledgeable designers, subtle security flaws such as covert channels can show up at any spot where the functional specification has left a loophole. A functional specification for a secure system need not cover every function in excruciating detail, but wherever detail is omitted the specification must constrain the possible designs so that the system cannot simultaneously meet the specification and violate the intent of the security policy.

Most of us are not accustomed to writing functional specifications with the degree of precision necessary to close all security loopholes. A security model can help. Used as an adjunct to the functional specification, the model constrains the design to meet the security requirements without constraining the functions. Because the model must be proved or demonstrated to obey the security properties derived from the security policy, a system implemented in accordance with the model (subject to the vagaries of proving that accordance) will have no security flaws. The functional specification continues to serve as a guide to the functions of the system, and the security model serves as a guide to the security-relevant behavior of the functions.

9.2.2 When Is a Model Useful?

It is unfair to imply that the only good way to specify the security properties of a system is to use a mathematical model—or any modeling technique at all. Modeling requires considerable effort and is worth doing only if you have the freedom and resources to carry out one of the correspondence paths in figure 9-2 fully and properly. If your system is already built and your job is to make major add-on enhancements, an informal natural-language model is probably adequate for your needs. If you only have the chance to make a few changes here and there to an existing system ("closing the holes"), you cannot do much to improve security of the system anyway, and modeling is probably fruitless. Although this chapter focuses on mathematical models, the process of developing an informal model is conceptually the same.

Fortunately for many organizations, using a model is not synonymous with developing one. A few security models exist that are sufficiently generic to be tailored to many systems with minimal alteration. The Bell and La Padula model discussed in section 9.5.3 has been used repeatedly for security-kernel-based systems.

9.3 TYPES OF SECURITY MODELS

Security models are not easy to classify because models tend to differ markedly from one another. While people talk about modeling as a general concept, only a handful of security models have had widespread exposure (Landwehr 1981; Millen and Cerniglia 1984), and even fewer have been applied to real systems. Nonetheless, certain characteristics are common to this handful. Do not be discouraged by the relatively small number of different models: this is due not to a problem with the concept of modeling, but to the widespread applicability of the few existing models.

A *state-machine model* describes a system as an abstract mathematical state machine; in such a model, *state variables* represent the state of the machine, and *transition functions* or *rules of operation* describe how the variables change. Most of the models described in this book are of the state-machine type. The idea of modeling a system as state machine is quite old, but state-machine models have not played a leading role in software development because modeling all possible state variables of an operating system is infeasible. The security model deals only with the most prominent security-relevant state variables, and so is far simpler than a complete state-machine model of a system.

The *access matrix model* (Harrison, Ruzzo, and Ullman 1976) is a state-machine model that represents the security state of the system as a large rectangular array containing one row per subject in the system and one column per subject and object (fig. 9-3). The entry in each position of the array specifies the modes of access each subject has to each object or other subject. This access matrix is one of several state

	OBJECTS			SUBJECTS		
	Object 1	Object 2	Object 3	Subject 1	Subject 2	Subject 3
Subject 1	read write	read		—		send
Subject 2		read execute	read write		—	send
Subject 3		read write	execute			—

Figure 9-3. Access Matrix. The intersection of a row and a column specifies a subject's modes of access to an object or to another subject. Allowed modes of access are read, write, and execute to objects and send to another subject.

variables of the state-machine model. The transition functions of the model describe how changes to the access matrix and to other variables take place.

Another common way to describe the security state of the system is in terms of security attributes of subjects and objects. The access modes that a subject has to an object are determined by comparing their security attributes, rather than by looking them up in a matrix. A model may use both an access matrix and security attributes. All such models based on subject-to-object access might be termed *access models*.

A variant on the access model is the *information flow model* (Denning 1983), which—rather than checking a subject's access to an object—attempts to control the transfer of information from one object into another object, constrained according to the two objects' security attributes. The difference between flow models and access models (which we will discuss later in this chapter) may seem rather subtle, but its most practical effect is that access models do not help you find covert channels, whereas flow models do so nicely.

Another type of model that has recently been developed is the *non-interference model*, where subjects operating in different domains are prevented from affecting one another in a way that violates the system's security properties (Goguen and Meseguer 1982). This model is still undergoing development as it is being applied by Honeywell in the Secure Ada Target research project (Boebert et al. 1985; Haigh and Young 1986).

9.4 CHARACTERISTICS OF A SECURITY MODEL

People often have a hard time understanding the difference between a model of a system and a description or specification (such as a formal specification) of the system. When developing a model for a specific system, it is all too easy to get lost in detail, and the result is a model that does not serve its purpose.

The primary characteristic of a good model is that it is easy to comprehend. It should be possible to describe, in natural language, all the important aspects of the model in a very few pages, or to explain it in a few minutes. Of course, the precise mathematical version of the model might be difficult for a nonmathematician to follow, but any person trained in the notation should be able to understand it easily.

The model must be simple because it is a restatement, in mathematical terms, of the security properties you want your system to obey. If the restatement is not obvious, you will have a hard time convincing anyone that the model reflects the intended policy. There is no way to prove mathematically that a policy written in natural language corresponds to the model, so "convincing argument" is the best we can do. If you look at the most popular models for security, their correspondence to the real-world policy will be patently obvious.

On the other hand, the model will likely have a number of characteristics whose purpose is not obvious. Because a model tries to be mathematically perfect (complete and consistent) in defining the properties that represent the policy, it often calls for the inclusion of restrictions or additional properties that were not originally intended. For example, suppose you were to model multilevel security that controls disclosure of information. As we have seen in section 6.4, such a model would have to include restrictions on writing, as well as reading, information. Without the write restriction, the model might not be strong enough to prevent someone from circumventing the read restriction that is the primary goal of the policy.

9.5 STATE-MACHINE MODELS

State-machine models were originally favored because they represent a computer system in a way that mimics the execution of an operating system and hardware. A state variable is an abstraction for each of the bits and bytes in the system that change as the system is running. Thus, every word in memory, on disk, or in registers is a state variable. The state transition functions are abstractions of system calls into the operating system that describe exactly how the state can and cannot change. While other promising techniques to modeling do exist, as discussed in section 9.3, the state machine concept is so pervasive that everyone doing modeling work should understand it.

A security model does not deal with all state variables and functions of the system. It is up to you to choose the security-relevant variables and functions to be modeled.

Developing a state-machine security model involves specifying the elements of the model (variables, functions, rules, and so on), along with a secure initial state. Once you have proved that the initial state is secure and that all the functions are secure, mathematical induction tells you that if the system begins in a secure state, the system will remain in a secure state, regardless of the order in which the functions are invoked.

The following specific steps are involved in developing a state-machine model:

1. Define the security-relevant *state variables*. Typically, the state variables represent the subjects and objects of the system, their security attributes, and access rights between subjects and objects.
2. Define the conditions for a *secure state*. This definition is an *invariant* that expresses relationships between values of the state variables that must always be maintained during state transitions.
3. Define *state transition functions*. These functions describe changes to state variables that may take place. They are also called *rules of operation* because their purpose is to constrain the types of changes that the system may make, rather than to specify all possible changes. The rules may be very general and may allow functions that your system does not have; however, your system cannot modify the state variables in a way that the functions do not allow.
4. Prove that the functions maintain the secure state. To make sure that the model is consistent with the definition of the secure state, you must prove for each function that if the system is in a secure state prior to the operation, the system will remain in a secure state after the operation.
5. Define the *initial state*. Pick a value for each of the state variables that models how the system starts out in an initially secure state.
6. Prove that the initial state is secure in terms of the definition of the secure state (step 2).

The above description may seem a bit abstract for those accustomed to writing computer programs and not mathematical descriptions of programs. Section 9.5.1 describes, step by step, how a security policy is translated into a complete model, using a simple example of multilevel security that resembles (but is definitely not) the Bell and La Padula model (discussed in section 9.5.3). We shall discuss how the model is proved to satisfy the secure state invariant, after which we shall consider some additional constraints that the model may have to satisfy (and that are not listed in the above steps).

9.5.1 Example of a State-Machine Model

Consider the following real-world security policy:

Policy: *A person may read a document only if the person's clearance is greater than or equal to the classification of the document.*

This policy is a simplified statement of the military security policy discussed in section 6.4.1. Our goal is to develop a model for a computer system that enforces the intent of this policy. For now we shall assume that there are no other rules in the policy.

We must first develop some computer abstractions of the elements of the policy, restating the policy in terms of those abstractions. We shall make the following substitutions:

Real-world Item	Computer-world Abstraction
person	subject
document	object
clearance	access class
classification	access class

The resulting translation of the policy is as follows:

Property (a): *A subject may read an object only if the access class of the subject is greater than or equal to the access class of the object.*

Equating both *clearance* and *classification* with *access class* is valid only because we know that both have identical structures and interpretations (as was discussed in section 6.4). Instead of using *subject* and *object*, we could have said *process* and *file*, but these words have a fairly specific connotation in the computer world, and their use would unnecessarily restrict the ways in which *person* and *document* are represented. Some models do use more specific terms when the real-world policy has different rules for different types of objects.

Although the abstractions we have made are valid, property (a) does not guarantee the intent of the original policy. As was noted in section 6.4.4, there has to be a corresponding write-down (confinement property) restriction:

Property (b): *A subject may write an object only if the access class of the object is greater than or equal to the access class of the subject.*

This property is more constraining than the real-world policy because people can write documents at lower access classes.

STEP 1. DEFINE THE STATE VARIABLES

Our state variables correspond to the computer-world abstractions of the policy, plus some additional variables that we will use in later examples:

$$S = \text{set of current subjects}$$
$$O = \text{set of current objects}$$
$$sclass(s) = \text{access class of subject } s$$
$$oclass(o) = \text{access class of object } o$$
$$A(s,o) = \text{set of modes, equal to one of:}$$

$\{r\}$	if subject s can read object o
$\{w\}$	if subject s can write object o
$\{r,w\}$	if both read and write
$\emptyset$	if neither read nor write

$$contents(o) = \text{contents of object } o$$
$$subj = \text{active subject}$$

The symbol $\emptyset$ designates the empty set.

The subjects and objects are modeled as members of the sets S and O. The two-dimensional access array A, which resembles the access matrix in figure 9-3, is but one way to represent all subjects' current access rights to all the objects.

We have defined two variables that are not directly mentioned in property (a) or property (b): *contents(o)* which represents the *state* of (the information contents of) each object; and *subj*, which is the identity of the subject that is currently active and is invoking the transition functions. You can think of *subj* as a variable that is equal to one of the current set of subjects and that may change to an arbitrary value at any time (thereby modeling the process switching that takes place in a real system). Since these two variables are not mentioned in the properties, we might consider them not to be security-relevant; but there are reasons you might want to include them in the model, as we shall discuss in later examples.

The state of the system at any one time is expressed as a set of values of all the state variables:

$$\{S,O,sclass,oclass,A,contents,subj\}$$

STEP 2. DEFINE THE SECURE STATE

The definition of the secure state is a mathematical translation of property (a) and property (b) into an invariant:

> **Invariant:** The system is secure if and only if, for all $s \in S$, $o \in O$,
> if $\mathbf{r} \in A(s,o)$, then $sclass(s) \geq oclass(o)$,
> if $\mathbf{w} \in A(s,o)$, then $oclass(o) \geq sclass(s)$.

The notation $s \in S$ means "s is contained in set S."

Although they are straightforward, we cannot prove that our translation and our definitions of the state variables accurately portray the original policy. It is thus very important that the properties in the model be so simple and obvious that no one will question their correspondence to the real-world policy.

Neither the properties nor the invariant says whether any subject can in fact read or write any object. In other words, all values of A may be null, and the system would still be secure according to the invariant. A different policy might require certain accesses to be allowed, but in general security policies do not place any constraints on the usefulness of the system.

STEP 3. DEFINE THE TRANSITION FUNCTIONS

A transition function can be viewed as a procedure call to a system service routine requested by a subject, where the service desired is a specific change to the state variables. The parameters to the function are specified by the subject and must be checked by the system for validity before the system carries out any state change. This system-call view of transition functions is a bit simplistic—since state changes may occur that are not initiated by any subject (for example, asynchronous events and interrupts)—but the view is adequate for our purposes.

Table 9-1 summarizes the transition functions that we shall discuss in the remainder of this chapter. The first two will be introduced here, and the remainder will be covered in later sections.

1.	**Create_object** (o, c)	Create object o at class c.
2.	**Set_access** $(s, o, modes)$	Set access *modes* for subject s to object o.
3.	**Create/Change_object** (o, c)	Set class of o to c and create.
4.	**Write_object** (o, d)	Write data d into *contents*(o).
5.	**Copy_object** $(from, to)$	Copy *contents*$(from)$ to *contents*(to).
6.	**Append_data** (o, d)	Add data d to *contents*(o).

Table 9-1: Transition Function Examples. Listed are the transition functions used in our example of a state-machine model.

We define two simple functions: **Create_object** adds a new object to the set of known objects; and **Set_access** changes a subject's access to an object. In these examples we use the convention of placing the prime symbol ' in front of a state variable to refer to the new state. Unprimed variables refer to the value in the old state:

Function 1: Create_object (o,c)
    if $o \notin O$
    then $'O = O \cup \{o\}$ and
       $'oclass(o) = c$ and
       for all $s \in S$, $'A(s,o) = \emptyset$.

Function 2: Set_access $(s,o, modes)$
    if $s \in S$ and $o \in O$
    and if $\{[\mathbf{r} \in modes$ and $sclass(s) \geqslant oclass(o)]$ or $\mathbf{r} \notin modes\}$
               and
       $\{[\mathbf{w} \in modes$ and $oclass(o) \geqslant sclass(s)]$ or $\mathbf{w} \notin modes\}$
    then $'A(s,o) = modes$.

While these functions look like computer programs with mathematical operators, there are some important differences between the way a computer program is interpreted and the way these mathematical statements are expressed:

- The purpose of a function is to specify relationships between variables in the previous state and in the new state. The = sign in a function should be read as a statement of mathematical equality, and not necessarily as an assignment, even though an assignment to values in the new state might be implied.
- The function does not imply any specific ordering of statements (or

algorithm) for an operation. It should be viewed as a statement of what has happened to the state when the operation is completed.

- The function is *atomic*; that is, its effects are indivisible and uninterruptible. Specified state changes happen all at once, without the passage of any time "during" a state transition. This assumption of atomicity becomes important in modeling systems with multiple processors (see section 8.6). It also means that you have to be careful in multiprogramming systems (with single processors) not to ignore inadvertently the effects of asynchronous processes. These issues tend to involve detail in the formal specification more than in the model, but the conceptual problems are the same.

- Finally, the function is a description of all allowed state transitions. If the new value of a variable or element of an array is not explicitly forced to change, the value must not change. Thus, in an expression such as

if cond then . . .

if we omit the *else* clause and do not say what happens when *cond* is false, there must be no change to the state.[1]

The **Create_object** operation adds the requested object as a one-element set {*o*} to the set of current objects *O* (if that object is not already in the set) and sets the access class of that object equal to the requested value. It also sets the object's column of the access matrix *A* to null, so that no subject has access to the object. The **Set_access** operation sets new access modes in any element of *A*, as long as those new modes are consistent with the invariant. In keeping with our conventions, all other columns of $A(s,x)$, where $x \neq o$, remain unchanged.

Notice that both operations allow a subject to have less access to an object than the maximum permitted by the security properties. We might view the ability to reduce the access modes as a form of discretionary access control. Our policy says nothing about this discretionary access control, and therefore places no constraints on restricting access further than is required by the mandatory rules.

STEP 4. PROVE THE TRANSITION FUNCTIONS

Normally, once convinced that your functions are fairly simple and correct, you would define most of them before attempting to prove them rigorously. But it is always wise to try to prove the first few functions just to see if you are on the right track.

---

1. Some formal specification languages assume quite the opposite (see section 12.2).

For each function, you must prove the following theorem:

Invariant and **Function** imply 'Invariant.

where the prime symbol signifies that the invariant is being applied to the new state. In other words, the theorem says that each function must maintain the secure state.

Although we shall not go through the proof here, notice that **Create_object** would violate the invariant if it did not initialize to null the column of the access matrix corresponding to the new object. We could have initialized that column in any of a number of other secure ways, but this one allows maximum flexibility, since **Set_access** can later be called to set any access desired. Most systems in fact set some initial access modes on newly created objects, often to values specified by the caller. Because we initialized the mode to null, we can model a *create* function in our system as a sequence of calls—**Create_object,** followed by **Set_access.** Since the system is proved secure before, between, and after this pair of function calls, a system that carries out both functions as a single indivisible call is also secure.

STEPS 5 and 6. DEFINE AND PROVE INITIAL STATE

A last but very important item is the initial state. Mathematically, the initial state is expressed as a set of initial values of all the state variables in the system:

$$\{S_0, O_0, sclass_0, oclass_0, contents_0, subj_0\}.$$

In order to prove that this initial state is secure, we have to specify restrictions on these initial values.

The simplest initial state consistent with the invariant is one without any objects or subjects:

Initial State (1): $S_0 = \emptyset$ and $O_0 = \emptyset$

We do not have to define the initial values of any of the other state variables, since the state is secure regardless of their values. Eventually, of course, we must add to the model a function to create subjects as well as objects; otherwise, the system would never arrive at a state in which $S \neq \emptyset$.

Another, more realistic secure initial state allows for an initial (arbitrary) set of subjects and objects, all of the same initial (but arbitrary) access class c_0:

> **Initial State (2):** For all $s \in S_0$, $o \in O_0$
> $$sclass_0(s) = c_0$$
> $$oclass_0(o) = c_0$$
> $$A_0(s,o) = \{\mathbf{r},\mathbf{w}\}$$

The initial access matrix A_0 allows all initial subjects read and write access to all initial objects. This initial state is very general, because it places no constraints on the number of subjects and objects; it does, however, require all the subjects and objects to be of the same access class.

9.5.2 Adding Constraints to State-Machine Access Models

A key element of the philosophy underlying the state-machine models we have discussed so far is the concept of a *secure state*, where the definition of *security* is completely embodied in an invariant: you can take a snapshot of the system at any time and determine whether the system is secure based on the invariant, without regard to what happened in previous states. Nonetheless, an invariant alone does not quite specify all the security properties you may have intended. This is because security is not only a property of the current state of the system, but a property of sequences of states. Hence, we need a revised definition of *security* that covers relationships between variables in two successive state transitions, as well as within individual states. In this revised model, though each transition function may obey the invariant, a function may not be secure because the specific transition from the previous state was not permitted.

Specifying properties about transitions requires adding constraints to the definition of security in the model. In terms of proof, a constraint is handled just as the invariant is: you must prove that the constraint is satisfied by each function. A constraint differs from an invariant because it talks about the relationships between values in two consecutive states—before and after each transition function.

Constraints on transitions are needed for several reasons:

- Nonsecure transitions: the old and new values of variables must maintain a "secure" relationship (as we shall see below).

- Controls on subjects: subjects should not be allowed to invoke certain operations under certain conditions.
- Controls on information: a model that talks about information contents must control transitions that modify information.

Nonsecure Transitions

We now rewrite function 1, **Create_object,** slightly, so that it allows the access class of an existing object to be changed:

> **Function 3: Create/Change_object** (o,c)
> $'oclass(o) = c$; and
> if $o \notin O$ then $'O = O \cup \{o\}$; and
> for all $s \in S$, $'A(s,o) = \emptyset$.

As before, access to the changed or created object is removed for all subjects, so the function satisfies the invariant. But the function now allows what we would normally consider a severe security violation: the possible downgrading of the access class of an object.

The reason for this problem is that the original set of security properties said nothing about the possibility that access classes of objects might change. Suppose, however, that the properties are augmented with the additional statement:

Property (c): *The access class of an object cannot decrease.*

The **Create/Change_object** is now clearly in violation of the new property. Because the concept of downgrading involves a particular type of state transition, converting property (c) into a mathematical statement requires a constraint rather than an invariant:

Constraint 1: For all $o \in O$, $'oclass(o) \geq oclass(o)$

This constraint states that the access class of an object can only increase or stay the same in the new state.[2] Notice the use of the ' symbol in the constraint to distinguish between the new and old states.

2. Of course, a function that obeys this constraint must also obey the secure state invariant, so that the access matrix reflects allowed accesses based on the object's new access class. In a system obeying a multilevel security policy, such a change to the access matrix can result in a covert channel between the subject that invokes the function and other subjects whose access to the object was removed. One way to avoid this complication is to enforce a *tranquility* constraint, as is done in the Bell and La Padula model (section 9.5.3), where access classes cannot change at all.

Controls on Subjects

Other constraints on transitions restrict the operations that subjects may invoke. A commonly needed constraint prevents subjects from changing the access attributes of objects to which they have no access. It would not be proper, for example, to allow an operation that enabled a subject to give itself access to any object. As in the previous example, the security properties must be augmented, this time to constrain the modification of access modes:

Property (d): *A subject may modify another subject's access to an object only if the first subject can read the object.*

In the constraint that follows, we for the first time use the state variable *subj*, which is the identity of the active subject:

> **Constraint 2:** For all $o \in O$,
> if $r \notin A(subj,o)$
> then for all $s \in S$, $'A(s,o) = A(s,o)$.

Of course, **Set_access** does not satisfy this constraint, and a proof would therefore fail.

Since our simple model has only one function that changes access modes, we could have written a simpler constraint that applies only to the one object referenced by the **Set_access** function, but the above constraint is more sound because it prevents any operation of the model from violating the security properties. It is important to write constraints in as general a manner as possible, without reference to the specific operations in the model. If you include operation-specific information in a constraint, you are likely to miss some cases where the intent of your requirement is violated—especially if you later enhance the model and forget why the original constraints are there.

Controls on Information

One limitation of the state-machine access model and its rules and constraints is the fact that only changes to access rights (and not to information itself) are constrained. This is acceptable in many cases because the purpose of the model is to formalize the security policy, rather than the functions of the system. But suppose that we do want to model an operation on data contents, such as:

> **Function 4: Write_object** (o,d)
> if $o \in O$ and $w \in A(subj,o)$
> then $'contents(o) = d$.

Since **Write_object** does not change any variables mentioned in the invariant or in any of the constraints we have specified so far, it is secure according to our model. This operation also intuitively appears to obey the security properties, because it prevents you from writing into an object unless you have explicit write access, and because you can only get write access if the proper access class relationship is satisfied (as enforced by the invariant) at the time the access matrix is modified. Still, there is nothing in any of our formal statements (invariants or constraints) that justifies our confidence that this function satisfies the security properties. If we remove the important check for $w \in A(subj,o)$, the function still obeys the invariant and constraints but clearly violates property (b) about writing into objects.

The model (but not the policy) is insufficient because it only expresses the *potential access* of subjects to objects (as represented by the access matrix), and does not consider whether information is actually read or written. We have chosen to interpret the phrase "may write" in property (b) as "has write access to," as reflected in the access matrix. If you want to model the functions that read and write information, then *information* must be mentioned in the definition of the secure state.

We can fix the problem by changing the mathematical interpretation of property (b), but another way to achieve the same result is to add an explicit property statement:

Property (e): *A subject may modify an object only if the subject has write access to the object.*

This property translates into the statement:

Constraint 3: For all $o \in O$,
if $w \notin A(subj,o)$
then $'contents(o) = contents(o)$.

This constraint is sufficient to satisfy property (e) but is very restrictive, inasmuch as it allows no change to an object if the object is not writable—even as a side effect of an operation. Nonetheless, it expresses a useful property that allows us to prove the security of **Write_object.**

If you want to carry out a similar enhancement to the model to specify a **Read_object** function you must add yet another state variable—this time one that models the place where the contents of an object are read into. (Without such a variable, you would not be able to express **Read_object** as a state transition.) However, you will not be able to express any useful constraints on the reading of information (try it). Such constraints can only be addressed through a flow model (see section 9.6).

Since including functions that reference the contents of objects complicates the model and its proof, what would motivate us to try to do so? Historically, the contents of objects have not been included in functions of models because the secure state definition does not mention them. Where the intent of the model is to address the access policy, and not implementation details, it is undesirable to clutter the model with such operations as **Write_object** and **Read_object** that trivially obey the access matrix A, given that it is just as easy to show during correspondence proof that the implementation of such functions in the system obeys the constraints of the matrix. For example, it may be adequate to show how the read and write restrictions in the matrix map onto the read and write bits in memory descriptors, and how all machine instructions are constrained by the modes in the memory descriptors.

As abstract modeling has been used in more and more systems, however, it has become evident that information can be read and written in a real system in many ways—some by software, and some by hardware—that do not obey the access matrix in any obvious manner. People are uncomfortable when their system has numerous functions that manipulate information not represented by state variables in the model. Consequently, there is a temptation to add this information (and additional rules about operations on this information) to the model, so that some meaningful properties of these operations can be stated and an attempt can be made to prove them.

You will have to decide for yourself how far you want to go, but be warned that each additional state variable and its attendant operations will significantly complicate the model and its proof. Demonstrating correspondence of the implementation to a simple abstract model may be far more convincing than mapping to a very detailed complex model. Remember that a security model is supposed to represent only the security-relevant behavior of the system, not all variables and all operations in a system. If you want more detail, you should write a formal specification.

When to Use Constraints

A security model might need constraints as part of its security definition for any of several reasons; and just as you cannot prove that your invariant is an adequate statement of the policy, you cannot prove that you have all the necessary constraint. The adequacy of the constraints has to be accepted on faith.

In a typical model it is possible to come up with a large number of interesting constraints, many of which the functions trivially satisfy. It is also possible to define constraints that are true but have very complex proofs. Most constraints, however, merely express facts about the functions you have chosen to represent in the model, and so are not security-relevant. The best way to determine whether a constraint is necessary is to judge whether it is an obvious extension of the security properties. If it is not, leave it out—unless you have reason to believe that its omission might leave a security loophole. There is no formal way of determining whether a flaw is possible (other than proof by existence: finding and demonstrating a specific flaw), but the simpler your model is, the easier the task of anticipating flaws becomes.

It is most important to realize that formulating constraints on state transitions is an integral part of defining a system's security requirements.

9.5.3 The Bell and La Padula Security Model

One of the first security models—and by far the most often used—was developed by David Bell and Leonard La Padula to model the operation of a computer that obeys the military security policy (Bell and La Padula 1973; Bell and La Padula 1973–74). The work by Bell and La Padula grew out of earlier work at Case Western Reserve University (Walter et al. 1974). The goal of the model is to specify rules for multilevel operation of a computer; the precise description of the military security policy that permits such an operation is called the *multilevel security policy* (see section 6.4).

Because the Bell and La Padula model became the best-known formalization of the multilevel security policy, the concept of multilevel security is often equated with the Bell and La Padula model. In fact, however, several other models also satisfy a multilevel security policy. Each tends to express the policy in different ways, but the same policy is used by all. We shall consider the Bell and La Padula model in this section and a related class of information-flow models in section 9.6.

Models such as the noninterference model do not express a multilevel security policy directly; instead, they employ a more general policy, of which multilevel security is a special case. In the future, people may actually favor these more general models because they can be used to support other kinds of specialized models (multilevel security is often viewed as being overly restrictive for many applications).

In formalizing the multilevel security policy, the Bell and La Padula model defines a structure of an access class (with classification and category set as components) and establishes the partial ordering relationship between access classes that we call *dominates*. Section 6.4 discusses the meaning of *dominates* and the structure of an access class.

In mathematical notation, we write the *dominates* operation as a simple $\geq$ symbol, although in this instance the symbol does not indicate a numerical comparison. Thus, "A dominates B" is written $A \geq B$. To avoid confusion, we do not reverse the symbol and write $B \leq A$ ("B is dominated by A"), nor do we write $A > B$ ("A dominates but is not equal to B"). We shall use the conventional meaning of = to indicate equality in comparisons of two access classes.

The operation $\geq$ is described as a *partial ordering* on access classes. A partial ordering relation $\geq$ has the following mathematical properties between two access classes B and C:

Reflexive: $A \geq A$
Antisymmetric: if $A \geq B$ and $B \geq A$, then $A = B$
Transitive: if $A \geq B$ and $B \geq C$, then $A \geq C$

The biggest mistake you might make is to assume that

$$\text{if } A \neq B, \text{ then } B \geq A$$

This shows that it is not always possible to compare two access classes using a *dominates* relationship. Speaking loosely, people say that A and B are *disjoint* in such a case; but because A and B may have elements of their category sets in common, a more mathematically correct term is *incomparable*.

Besides defining a partial ordering, the *dominates* relationship has two properties that make it a lattice. Given any two access classes A and B (whether or not they are comparable):

- In the set of all access classes dominated by both A and B, there is a unique *greatest lower bound* that dominates all the others.
- In the set of all access classes that dominate both A and B, there is a unique *least upper bound* that is dominated by all the others.

You need not be concerned with the question of why such a partial ordering is called a *lattice*, but you should understand that the ability to express a security policy as a lattice is a fundamental requirement of many models of security.

Given a finite set of access classes, we can use the lattice property to define two important unique access classes: SYSTEM HIGH, which dominates all other access classes; and SYSTEM LOW, which is dominated by all other access classes. It is easiest to think of SYSTEM HIGH as an access class that contains the highest possible security level and all possible categories, and to think of SYSTEM LOW as an access class that contains security level zero and no categories. However, nothing prevents us from defining other values. For example, in a system that contains no information classified less than SECRET, the value of SYSTEM LOW is SECRET with no categories.

The security policy of the Bell and La Padula model has mandatory and discretionary components. The discretionary component is represented in an access matrix that is structured much as the access matrix $A(s,o)$ is in our example model. In addition to having read and write access modes, the discretionary component includes append, execute, and a control modes—the last of which indicates whether a subject can pass to other subjects the access rights it has to the object. The mandatory component of the policy, consisting of the simple security property and the confinement property that were introduced in section 6.4, is enforced by restricting the accesses that are granted, based on a comparison of the access class attributes of subjects and objects.

Unlike our example model, the Bell and La Padula access matrix models a discretionary policy only, not the mandatory constraints. This means that changes to the access matrix are constrained exclusively by control mode and not by access classes. At the time that access to an object is granted, both the discretionary check and the mandatory check are made.

There are about twenty functions or rules of operation in the Bell and La Padula model, having to do with modifying components of the access matrix, requesting and obtaining access to an object (as when opening a file), and creating and deleting objects; and each function is proved to preserve the definition of the secure state. No functions explicitly read or write the contents of objects: the model implicitly assumes, in an implementation, that, all access to objects is preceded by the appropriate access request and that reads and writes take place in accordance with the access that was granted. In a typical operating system, for example, the act of requesting access may take place at the time a file is opened for reading or writing, and subsequent reads or writes are limited to the modes of access granted at the time of opening.

In addition to proving the mandatory security policy, the functions obey a rather severe constraint of *tranquility* that prevents the access classes of objects from changing. This constraint is necessary because, if the access class of an object can change, accesses that have already been granted may no longer obey the secure state definition. If already-granted accesses are removed, a covert channel might result. A gross complication to the model is avoided by requiring tranquility.

Bell and La Padula developed their model based on Multics concepts and have provided a "Multics interpretation" of the model (Bell and La Padula 1975), but people soon realized that the model was generic enough to apply to many systems. The thinking was that, since the proof that the functions in the model preserve the security properties need be done only once, each new system thereafter could merely map its functions onto the model's generic functions. But few secure system developments have chosen to use the Bell and La Padula functions, opting instead for their own functions based on the Bell and La Padula security policy. As a result, when people talk about the Bell and La Padula model, they usually refer only to the simple security and con-finement property conditions, not to the functions that constitute the bulk of the model and its proofs.

One primary reason why the functions of the model have been ignored is that performing the system-specific mapping was perceived to rep-resent at least as much effort as rewriting and proving a new set of functions specific to the system. Furthermore, security models today are written in specification languages that are processable by machine (Bell and La Padula's was written and proved by hand), and the act of transcribing the Bell and La Padula functions into the specification lan-guage can be as much work as writing new functions. Machine pro-cessing is the most reliable way to carry out an error-free proof (although the machine does not actually save much manual labor).

The Bell and La Padula model, in attempting to be as applicable as possible to real systems, introduced the concept of *trusted subjects*—subjects for whom the confinement property checks that are prescribed in the rules of operation (and the tranquility constraint) do not nec-essarily apply. Remember that the confinement property's control over write-downs serves mainly to prevent accidents and to defeat Trojan horse attacks. In the real world, we can view trusted subjects as special processes or users that are trusted not to violate security even without enforcing confinement. Trusted processes are used for various system functions (such as backup) and to carry out the direct wishes of users and system administrators who want to be sure that no untrusted software is interfering. (See section 10.5 for an explanation of trusted processes for security kernels.) Among practitioners, there has probably been more controversy and misunderstanding about the notion of trusted subjects than about any other single aspect of secure systems.

Should you decide to study the Bell and La Padula model in more detail, bear in mind that terminology in the fast-moving field of computer security has changed significantly. Most of the terms used in this chapter and in this book (except for *access class*—see section 6.4.2) are commonly used today but were not in use at the time the Bell and La Padula model was developed. To make matters worse, terms originated by Bell and La Padula have come to mean different things over the years. In particular, the *-property defined by Bell and La Padula includes the read-up restriction as well as the write-down restriction— even though today it is almost exclusively applied to the write-down restriction.

9.6 INFORMATION-FLOW MODELS

One deficiency of the classical proof techniques used for state-machine models cannot be addressed by adding invariants or constraints. This deficiency involves the flow of information, rather than the control of security attributes of subjects and objects. We touched indirectly on the topic of information flow in section 9.5.2, when we talked about proving the security of information modification; in general, however, constraints on information flow can be expressed only by information-flow models. Many people consider information-flow models useful only for finding covert channels, because with suitable constraints on information modification (as in our example) there are no information channels via normal objects of the system. For this reason, *information-flow analysis*—the act of analyzing a system for adherence to the information-flow model—is often equated with *covert channel analysis.*

With most systems, in the absence of some kind of information-flow analysis, you have no assurance that your proved model represents a secure system. For example, a system adhering to the Bell and La Padula model may be riddled with covert channels. It is in fact possible to locate covert channels directly in the Bell and La Padula model, despite strict adherence to the confinement property designed to thwart Trojan horse attacks.

Meaningful flow analysis requires a detailed formal specification, not an abstract state machine model. This is because the variables that participate in covert channels are not necessarily represented in an abstract model. Section 12.7 discusses the flow analysis of formal specifications in detail. Flow analysis has also been attempted directly on computer programs (Tsai, Gligor, and Chandersekaran 1987), but such work is in its early stages. The complexity of flow in programs is usually such that the analysis requires excessive manual effort.

Although flow models require detailed specifications, our abstract model offers the readiest example to demonstrate why flow analysis is needed. Consider the following operation:

> **Function 5: Copy_object** *(from,to)*
>> If *from* $\in O$ and *to* $\in O$ and $\mathbf{w} \in A(subj,to)$
>> then '*contents(to)* = *contents(from)*.

This function copies the contents of one object into another, if the subject has write access to the destination object. The function is not secure because, in failing to check for read access to the *from* object, the *to* object may be written with information to which the subject has no access, and the subject might later read the object. What is missing from the "If" expression is the condition $\mathbf{r} \in A(subj,from)$.

It is impossible to write a constraint or invariant capable of detecting such an omission. While we were able to write a constraint to prevent illegal modification to information (see constraint 3 in section 9.5.2), there is no general way to express a constraint on the illegal reading or transfer of information as done by **Copy_object.**

You might argue that, mathematical difficulties aside, it is a simple matter to scan all functions and check for references to *contents(o)* not qualified by $\mathbf{r} \in A(subj,o)$. In general, however, such a constraint is unrealistic. For example, there is nothing wrong with the following function

> **Function 6: Append_data** *(o,d)*
>> If $o \in O$ and $\mathbf{w} \in A(subj,o)$
>> then '*contents(o)* = *contents(o)* $\cup \{d\}$

which adds data d to the contents of an object. The proper test is made to see that the subject can write the object; yet no security reason exists to require that the subject have read access to the object. A constraint that prevents unqualified references to *contents(o)* would prevent us from including this legitimate function in the model.

In a real system, many objects (such as buffer pools, quota variables, and global counters) are modified by all subjects (and need to be read in order to be modified, as in **Append_data**), despite not being directly visible to the subjects. Distinguishing between such legitimate read references to objects and references that do violate the security requirements (as in **Copy_object**) is very difficult, requiring a thorough analysis of each function in which such references occur.

Flow analysis can be meaningfully applied only to operations in a system that are used by untrusted subjects, such as processes possibly containing Trojan horses that violate the confinement property. Trusted subjects are specifically trusted not to exploit covert channels and are therefore not restricted by the confinement property. As was stated in section 3.3, users are trusted not to give away their own data; and so they, too, constitute trusted subjects in this sense. Therefore, functions in a model that are intended to be invoked directly by users, and not by potentially untrusted software, are not subject to flow analysis. (A user who does decide to give away data is not likely to bother with a low-bandwidth covert channel when there are far easier ways to do it.)

In carrying out flow analysis on a model or some level of specification, you have to be very careful that the more detailed specification or implementation does not introduce flows not identified at the level at which the analysis was carried out. Most correspondence-proof techniques do not specifically look for additional flows, because they are more concerned with proving that the invariants and constraints still hold at the lower level. For this reason, flow analysis has been criticized as giving users a false degree of confidence in the security of their system. If you fail to recognize the possibility of additional flows at the lower level, the flow analysis of the upper level represents nothing more than a safety check to show that you have not introduced insecure operations at that upper level. The only way to be absolutely sure that your system is free from nonsecure flows is to do the analysis on the code, but (as was stated above) this is often impractical.

9.7 INFORMAL MODEL-TO-SYSTEM CORRESPONDENCE

In this section we shall discuss the informal correspondence arguments in steps (a) and (b) of the development alternatives illustrated in figure 9-2. The concepts presented here are a prerequisite to understanding the formal paths (c) and (d) that will be covered in chapter 12.

The security model describes a state machine equipped with a small set of primitive operations that manipulate a small set of security-relevant state variables. A real system (also a state machine) has hundreds of operations and thousands of state variables. The task of proving that the variables and functions in a real system correspond to, or map into, those in the model is clearly formidable. Since an informal correspondence effort cannot achieve mathematical perfection, there is no point in trying. But you can carry out the correspondence to any intermediate level of detail, depending on the degree of assurance you seek.

The biggest payoff in confidence for a given amount of effort is achieved simply by having all key designers of the system understand the model and its rules, before any high-level design of the system is begun. With security foremost in their minds, the designers will be unlikely to violate the security requirements in any fundamental way.

If the system is designed in a pure top–down manner, the first stage of design is to identify the interface functions (without discussing the internal details of their implementation) and the principle objects that those functions manipulate. At a high level of design, where the functions and objects are described in general terms, it is possible to carry out a cursory model correspondence. More detailed mapping requires a detailed functional description of each operation, including all parameters that are passed through that interface, and a precise description of the changes made to objects and variables in the system.

9.7.1 Mapping the Functions

It would be nice if you could produce a straightforward one-to-one correspondence between operations in the system and operations in the model. But in general the system will have more complex functions that map into sequences of model functions. For example, a `create_file` function of the system may have the same effect as consecutive calls to **Create_object** and **Set_access** in the model. Such a mapping is permissible because our inductive proofs tell us that any sequence of transitions is secure.

You will also encounter many cases where several functions in the system map into the same operation in the model. In our example, `give_access` and `delete_access` both correspond to **Set_access**, but with different parameters. Another case of many-to-one mapping arises when the system has several functions that deal with similar operations on different types of objects: `delete_file`, `delete_directory`, `delete_device`, and so on. Of course, you do not need to implement every type of operation for every type of object permitted by the model.

You must be careful when a function in the model is implemented with a sequence of functions in the system. Proofs of the model assume that operations are atomic, and consequently they say nothing about the state of the system "in the middle of" an operation. If a function in the implementation only partially completes an operation in the model—carrying out only some of the required state changes—then the subsequent state of the system is not defined in the model and may not be secure. You can safely split an operation into pieces only if you can demonstrate that the pieces always occur in sequence, that they are always completed, and that no other operation of the system can take place in the middle of the sequence.

9.7.2 Mapping the Variables

State variables in the system will not map one-to-one with those in the model because the model has simple generic variables such as subjects and objects, whereas the system has several types of subjects and objects. Typically, you have to identify the key subjects and objects of the system, as well as the variables that contain their security attributes. You must also show how subject and object existence is expressed in terms of variables in the system. If you have an access matrix, you must identify how it maps onto the system's access control mechanism. For example, each column in the access matrix corresponding to an object of type *file* might be represented in the system by a file header containing an access control list. The access control bits in the per-process descriptor segment used by hardware in section 8.3.5 are a low-level manifestation of a portion of a row of the access matrix.

9.7.3 Unmapped Functions and Variables

Probably the biggest problem in showing the correspondence between a system and a model involves functions and variables in the system that do not manipulate security-relevant information and therefore do not correspond to anything in the model.

For example, functions such as `write_file` and `rename_file` might not reference state variables in the model. In such cases you have to judge whether the variables mentioned in the functions are in fact security-relevant. If you decide that they are, and you have no way to map them into the model, then the model is lacking a security-relevant aspect of the system and must be changed. If you decide that they are not, then you still have to make sure that any access to subjects or objects made by the function obeys all implied access rules of the model. In our model we did not originally have a **Write_object,** because we assumed that any function writing into an object would obey the access modes in the access matrix A. Without a **Write_object** function in the model, we would have to show that a `write_file` operation in the system checks the proper access rights.

You should resist the temptation to beef up your model with additional functions that only serve to make the mapping more nearly complete. Any increase in confidence that you gain by having a fuller mapping is offset by the increased complexity of the mapping and of the proofs of the model. You cannot escape the fact that the informal correspondence process is manual and subjective: adding excessive detail in an attempt to achieve perfection merely increases the chance for error and confusion. Using a formal specification technique (figure 9-2(c) or (d), discussed in chapter 12) will bridge the code–model gap more soundly than adding detail to the model will.

REFERENCES

Bell, D. E., and La Padula, L. J. 1973. "Secure Computer Systems: Mathematical Foundations and Model." M74-244. Bedford, Mass.: Mitre Corp. (Also available through National Technical Information Service, Springfield, Va., NTIS AD-771543.)
Highly mathematical description of the original Bell and La Padula model.

————. 1973–74. "Secure Computer Systems." ESD-TR-73-278, vols. 1–3. Hanscom AFB, Mass.: Air Force Electronic Systems Division. (Also available through National Technical Information Service, Springfield, Va., NTIS AD-780528.)
A further description, also highly mathematical, of the original Bell and La Padula model.

————. 1975. "Secure Computer Systems: Unified Exposition and Multics Interpretation." ESD-TR-75-306. Hanscom AFB, Mass.: Air Force Electronic Systems Division. (Also available through National Technical Information Service, Springfield, Va., NTIS AD-A023588.)
Provides a Multics interpretation of the Bell and La Padula model.

Biba, K. J. 1977. "Integrity Considerations for Secure Computer Systems." ESD-TR-76-372. Hanscom AFB, Mass.: Air Force Electronic Systems Division. (Also available through National Technical Information Service, Springfield, Va., NTIS AD-A039324.)
The Biba integrity model.

Boebert, W. E.; Kain, R. Y.; Young, W. D.; and Hansohn, S. A. 1985. "Secure Ada Target: Issues, System Design, and Verification." In *Proceedings of the 1985 Symposium on Security and Privacy*, pp. 176–83. Silver Spring, Md.: IEEE Computer Society.

The Secure Ada Target is a research project to use a capability-like mechanism for building a secure operating system that supports Ada programs.

Denning, D. E. 1983. *Cryptography and Data Security*. Reading, Mass.: Addison-Wesley.
A thorough study of cryptographic techniques, access controls, and database security, presented in textbook format with many exercises, examples, and references.

Goguen, J. A., and Meseguer, J. 1982. "Security Policy and Security Models." In *Proceedings of the 1982 Symposium on Security and Privacy*, pp. 11–20. Silver Spring, Md.: IEEE Computer Society.
An approach to modeling a secure system based on the noninterference principle; a version of this model is employed in the Secure Ada Target research project.

Haigh, J. T., and Young, W. D. 1986. "Extending the Non-Interference Version of MLS for SAT." In *Proceedings of the 1986 Symposium on Security and Privacy*, pp. 232–39. Washington, D.C.: IEEE Computer Society.
The technique used by the developers of the Secure Ada Target to apply a noninterference model to a capability-style protection mechanism.

Harrison, M. A.; Ruzzo, W. L.; and Ullman, J. D. 1976. "Protection in Operating Systems." *Communications of the ACM* 19(8):461–71. Reprinted in *Advances in Computer System Security*, vol. 1, ed. R. Turn, pp. 81–91. Dedham, Mass.: Artech House (1981).
A formal mathematical description of an access matrix model.

Landwehr, C. E. 1981. "Formal Models for Computer Security." *Computing Surveys* 13(3):247–78. Reprinted in *Advances in Computer System Security*, vol. 2, ed. R. Turn, pp. 76–107. Dedham, Mass.: Artech House (1981).
An overview of formal modeling techniques that have been applied to secure systems; contains many references.

Millen, J. K., and Cerniglia, C. M. 1984. "Computer Security Models." MTR-9531. Bedford, Mass.: Mitre Corp. (Also available through National Technical Information Service, Springfield, Va., NTIS AD-A166920.)
A summary of sixteen specific models, intended to guide the developer in making a selection.

Tsai, C-R.; Gligor, V. D.; and Chandersekaran, C. S. 1987. "A Formal Method for the Identification of Covert Storage Channels in Source Code." In *Proceedings of the 1987 Symposium on Security and Privacy*, pp. 74–87. Washington, D.C.: IEEE Computer Society.
Describes use of the Shared Resource Matrix (see section 12.7.2) to find covert channels directly in source code.

Walter, K. G.; Ogden, W. F.; Rounds, W. C.; Bradshaw, F. T.; Ames, S. R.;

and Shumway, D. G. 1974. "Primitive Models for Computer Security." ESD-TR-74-117. Hanscom AFB, Mass.: Air Force Electronic Systems Division. (Also available through National Technical Information Service, Springfield, Va., NTIS AD-778467.)
An early discussion of a multilevel security model, interesting for historical reasons.

Chapter *10*

Security Kernels

The security kernel approach is the single most often used technique for building a highly secure operating system. However, it does not follow that you can buy one easily, that you can build one easily, that most secure systems are based on a security kernel, or even that most people agree that the security kernel is the right way to go. Indeed, many researchers believe that the security kernel is the wrong approach and are working on alternatives. But to date, for the highest-security systems, the security kernel has shown more promise than any other single technique.

The security kernel concept was developed by Roger Schell in 1972 and has commonly been defined (Anderson 1972; Ames, Gasser, and Schell 1983) as the hardware and software that implements the reference monitor abstraction we introduced in section 4.2. Sixteen years after the idea was first proposed, only a handful of security kernels have been implemented, few are commercially available, and rarely are they being used for practical applications. This seeming lack of progress is due not to a problem with the kernel approach, but to a lack of interest in security on the part of vendors, as we discussed in chapter 2. With today's heightened interest in security in both industry and the government, you can expect additional commercially developed kernel-based systems to emerge in the next few years.

The first security kernel, developed by MITRE as a government-sponsored research project to prove the concept, ran on a DEC PDP-11/45 (Schiller 1975). Another notable research security kernel is the UCLA Data Secure Unix for the PDP-11/45 and 11/70 (Popek et al. 1979). The Department of Defense, under a project called Guardian, sponsored the design and formal specification of a security kernel for Multics (Schiller 1977), but the kernel was never implemented. Government-sponsored developments that led to functioning systems (which have seen limited use) include KVM—an enhanced version of IBM's VM/370, developed by System Development Corp. (now part of Unisys) (Gold et al. 1979)—and KSOS—a kernel intended to support Unix that was developed by Ford Aerospace and Communications Corp. to run on the PDP-11/70 (McCauley and Drongowski 1979; Berson and Barksdale 1979). Two commercial-grade security kernels are available: Honeywell's STOP, which runs on the SCOMP, an enhanced version of the company's Level 6 minicomputer (Fraim 1983), and the Gemini Computers' GEMSOS, which runs on the Intel iAPX 80286 microprocessor (Schell, Tao, and Heckman 1985).

10.1 THE REFERENCE MONITOR

In section 4.2 we introduced the abstract concept of the *reference monitor*, whereby all accesses that subjects make to objects are authorized based on information in an access control database (fig. 10-1). The specific checks that are made and all modifications to the access control database are controlled by the reference monitor in accordance with a security policy. The multilevel security policy implemented by most reference monitors is discussed in section 6.4.4, and an example of a model of a policy is provided in section 9.5.1.

In the early days of computing, we used the term *monitor* to identify the program in the system that controlled the actions of other programs. As these monitors became bigger, they began to be called *operating systems*, and the term *monitor* was relegated to the most primitive types of operating systems. The reference monitor is a special-purpose monitor that deals only with access control to resources. Usually, other security-relevant functions of the system lie within the security perimeter but are not part of the reference monitor (these are often called *trusted functions*—see section 10.5). All non-security-relevant functions of a system (functions that lie outside the security perimeter) are managed by the operating system.

The concept of the reference monitor would merely be academic without having a practical way to implement one. The security kernel was the proposed approach. While there may be other ways to build

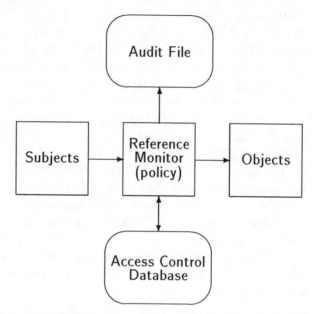

Figure 10-1. Reference Monitor. *All attempts made by subjects to reference objects are monitored and constrained in accordance with a security policy embodied in the reference monitor, using access control information stored in a database. Important security events are stored in the audit file.*

systems that satisfy reference monitor concepts, no other approach is as well-developed. For this reason, people tend to equate the reference monitor concept with the security kernel approach, and—particularly in discussions of principles, rather than of implementation details—the terms are often used interchangeably. You should try to keep an open mind, however, and be willing to accept the possibility that other types of reference monitors may someday exist.

10.2 THE THREE PRINCIPLES

The reference monitor and the security kernel must satisfy three fundamental principles:

- *Completeness:* it must be impossible to bypass.
- *Isolation:* it must be tamperproof.
- *Verifiability:* it must be shown to be properly implemented.

We shall examine each of these principles in detail, focusing on their design implications.

Realistically, no large system is likely ever to satisfy all three principles fully. The goals of the security kernel approach are to follow these principles as closely as possible—nobody would claim that a large system based on a security kernel guarantees perfect security.

10.2.1 Completeness

The principle of completeness requires that a subject not reference an object without invoking the reference monitor. It implies that all access to information must be mediated by the kernel. At first, you might think that this principle is quite reasonable, and that most operating systems today probably attempt to adhere to it. There are, however, a number of important differences between the unequivocal demand made by the completeness principle and the way operating systems are generally implemented.

An operating system usually considers the information in a system to lie in obvious places such as files, memory, and I/O buffers; and the operating system makes reasonable attempts to control access to these objects. The completeness principle is not satisfied with an ad hoc definition of the objects. Any repository of information, regardless of its size or intended use, is a potential object.

Among the additional objects where information can be stored are file names (which themselves constitute information), directories (which may include information about files), status registers, and active dynamic data maintained by the operating system and containing information about logged-in users, processes, resources consumed, and so on. You might recognize some of these items as potential covert channels (see section 7.2). The completeness principle insists that you make an explicit decision as to how the kernel will enforce access to each of these objects.

The completeness principle also places requirements on the hardware that supports a kernel-based system. If the kernel is to permit efficient execution of untrusted programs without checking each machine instruction, the hardware must ensure that the program cannot bypass access controls specified by the kernel. All references to memory, registers, and I/O devices must be checked for proper access through mechanisms such as memory management with access control (section 8.3). The kernel must be able to isolate processes from each other (section 8.2), and to ensure that the processes cannot communicate without kernel mediation. A computer that allowed all processes unconstrained access to a common page of physical memory, for example, would not be a suitable base for a security kernel.

10.2.2 Isolation

The isolation principle—which states that the kernel must be tamperproof—is, like the completeness principle, a common-sense goal for most systems. Even the most primitive operating systems make a reasonable effort to protect themselves, at least against most accidental and casual attempts at break-in.

Enforcing the isolation principle in a practical way requires a combination of both hardware and software. The primary hardware feature that enables the kernel to prevent user programs from accessing kernel code or data is the same memory management mechanism that the kernel uses to prevent processes from accessing each other's data. User programs must also be prevented from executing privileged instructions that the kernel uses to control the memory management mechanism. This requires some type of domain control, such as protection rings (section 8.4).

In a system equipped with the necessary hardware features, there is little chance that a user program could succeed in a direct attack on the kernel by writing the kernel's memory, executing a privileged instruction, or modifying the kernel software. While you might be tempted to provide additional isolation by fixing the kernel code in hardware read-only memory, direct writing of the kernel software is rarely a profitable route to penetration. A far more common penetration technique involves tricking the system into running your (the penetrator's) own program in privileged mode, thereby giving you control of the system without your having to touch either the kernel or any of its data (Karger and Schell 1974).

10.2.3 Verifiability

The principle of verifiability is addressed through relentless devotion to a number of design criteria:

- Employing state-of-the-art software engineering techniques, including structured design, modularity, information hiding, layering, abstract specification, and the use of appropriate high-order languages
- Emphasizing simplicity of functions at the kernel interface
- Minimizing the size of the kernel by excluding functions not related to security

If you keep these goals in mind while building a kernel, you will be able to convince yourself and others that the kernel is correct by using a combination of techniques:

- Code inspection
- Thorough testing
- Formal mathematical specification and verification

It is important to understand that the kernel approach does not require the use of a specific verification technique. Your choice depends on the degree of assurance you seek. If you do not intend to devote any appreciable effort to demonstrating its correctness, however, then developing a kernel is a waste of time.

Code inspection and thorough testing are of course commonly used for most systems, yet most systems are replete with bugs. Unless we do something different with these techniques, we have little reason to expect that they will work better for a security kernel.

The primary technique that supports the verifiability argument for a security kernel is the development of a mathematical model of security. The model precisely defines *security*, and the functions in the model are formally proved to be consistent with this definition. The model must be structured in a way that lends itself to some kind of correspondence demonstration—that is, to an argument that the kernel implementation adheres to the model. Chapter 9 discusses security models in detail, and section 9.7 provides guidelines for demonstrating this correspondence informally.

When the reference monitor approach was first proposed, it was thought possible to build a kernel that would be small enough to be verified by exhaustive testing. Model-to-implementation correspondence in such a case would consist of testing all possible security states of the system as defined by the model—or at least enough states to satisfy the tester that a security bug would be highly unlikely, given the designer's dedication to structuring and simplicity in the kernel's design. But except with respect to experimental kernels having limited functions, exhaustive testing is out of the question. While testing is certainly important, few people now believe that testing alone can provide enough assurance: some additional model-to-code correspondence work is required.

For a time, people had the dream of formally verifying (mathematically proving) this correspondence by relating the bits in memory to the abstract model. A number of formal specification languages, proof techniques, and automated tools were developed to help bridge the huge gap in level of detail between model and code. Some of these techniques, already under development for other reasons, were adapted to security correspondence. It quickly became evident, however, that, (like exhaustive testing), complete formal correspondence would not be practical for a long time, and that less-than-perfect assurance would have to suffice. Formal specification and verification are discussed in chapter 12.

If you are using state-of-the-art software engineering techniques, the process of developing and proving a model, writing an informal system specification, and informally showing correspondence between the code and the model will get you at least 80 percent of the way to full assurance. Writing a formal specification will get you another 10 percent of the way there, and all the known formal verification techniques will add at most another 5 percent. While many may quarrel with these percentages, few will argue that the effort to do formal verification is only justified in the highest-security environments.

Rather than trying to develop your own security model from scratch, you should seriously consider using or building upon an existing model—either the Bell and La Padula model discussed in section 9.5.3 or one of the handful of others discussed in section 9.3. If you decide to write a formal specification (an entirely feasible and useful exercise), use one of the specification languages discussed in chapter 12, and look at examples of secure systems specified in that language (Landwehr 1983). If you decide to go all the way and do proofs of your specification, you must obtain the automated processing tools appropriate for the verification system you have selected. It is useless to try to prove a specification by hand, without having a tool to check your proof (specific tools are listed in section 12.1).

If you want to go one step further and verify the code, stop and think again. There are no practical tools for proving a complete code correspondence of a large system or for checking the correctness of such a proof, so a proof of this kind would have to be supported by a huge manual effort. You are exceedingly unlikely to be able to do a convincing manual proof, given that the proof would have to be many times larger than the code and the specification combined. Section 12.8 gives you some feel for this process, though most of it is theory since only small examples have been carried out in practice. While people are still working on developing practical code proof techniques, your best bet for code correspondence is to carry out an informal demonstration, using systematic code review in conjunction with the formal specifications. Such an effort need not be greater than that required for any good code review process, but the use of a formal specification to guide your review will add credibility and objectivity to the process. Code correspondence can and should be used to guide system testing as well.

10.3 VIRTUALIZATION AND SHARING

In the face of a mandatory security policy, the kernel must be able to isolate subjects (processes) from one another so that, where the policy requires, it can prevent the actions of one subject from influencing another subject—even if the subjects want to communicate. This would be easy to do if processes had no way of interacting, but in most real-world systems such physical resources as memory, I/O devices, I/O media, and communications lines cannot be permanently allocated to individual processes without considerable cost or inconvenience. These resources must be shared among processes—carved up into portions that are dynamically assigned to processes as the need arises. Processes must then be prevented from accessing each other's resources. The easiest way to control resource access is to *virtualize* the resources. This means that a process accesses a resource by using a virtual name or virtual address that the kernel maps into a physical name. Because the mapping is under control of the kernel, the kernel can prevent two processes from sharing a portion of a resource that should not be shared. In chapter 8 we discussed ways by which hardware can manage a virtual address space for both memory and I/O devices. Physical regions of secondary storage media (disks) are virtualized using a file system, where processes use file names or virtual disk addresses rather than physical addresses. Section 11.4 discusses some issues in the design of secure file systems.

In addition to having the kernel control access to the resources, complete isolation requires that the kernel prevent a process from knowing the physical addresses and physical identifiers of its portions of dynamically allocated resources, because any dynamic resource allocation mechanism is a potential path for a covert storage channel. For example, in a system that swaps processes between memory and disk, revealing to a process the physical location of its memory might allow the process to infer something about the activities of other processes, especially if the process knows the memory allocation algorithm. A covert channel is possible if one process can modulate its usage of memory in a way that another process can observe. The kernel could try to hide such channels on a case-by-case basis, but the best general solution is to avoid the problem by only revealing virtual information to processes.

There are a couple of cases where the virtualization principle need not apply. First, when a resource is statically allocated to a number of processes and is not dynamically reallocated, the shared resource is equivalent to several unshared resources (one per process). Identifying physical locations or other information about the resource only reveals static information that cannot be used as a basis for covert communication. Second, if the resource is allocated by the direct actions of users (who do not originate covert communication), the principle again does not apply. As an example, revealing to a process the physical address of a terminal from which a user logs in is not a source for a covert channel (and is not a security problem, unless the policy states that the user's physical location or terminal line is sensitive information). But if a process can reserve a terminal line on its own and can either choose the line number or find out the line number that it has been given, then another process can determine that the line was reserved, and a covert channel between the processes is possible.

As we discussed in section 7.2.1, completely eliminating covert channels introduced by dynamically shared resources is probably impossible. The simplest way to avoid such channels is to minimize dynamic reallocation. In view of the declining cost of memory and hardware, it might be more feasible (and certainly it is easier and more secure) to allocate memory and disk space statically, than to go to great lengths to hide storage channels.

Of course, you do not want to eliminate interprocess sharing completely, or you might as well use an array of isolated microcomputers, one per process. No matter how cheap hardware becomes, you still want to be able to share data (as permitted by the security policy). Keep in mind that information sharing, as opposed to physical resource sharing, is the real goal of a multiuser computer system. Physical resource sharing is a practical necessity (or necessary evil) that the security kernel must manage in order to provide a secure information-sharing environment.

10.4 TRUSTED PATH

Figure 4.3 showed a clean, layered structure in which all trusted code is contained in the kernel, while users interact with the system through untrusted applications and the operating system. In practice, this structure does not work out perfectly. Users and system administrators must carry out a number of functions in any system through direct interaction with the kernel, without intermediate layers of untrusted software. These include the login function, specification of an access class (on a multilevel system), and administrator functions such as changing security attributes of users and files.

We must prevent a Trojan horse in the user's process from being able to mimic the login sequence, thereby tricking the user into giving away his or her password (one of the examples we discussed in section 7.1.1). In a multilevel system, users must be able to determine, from a trusted source, the access class of the process with which they are interacting. For certain functions, administrators must be able to verify the correctness of the output they receive on their terminal to make sure that it did not come from a Trojan horse. For all of these situations, we need a mechanism that effectively authenticates the kernel to the user (in addition to the usual mechanism that authenticates the user to the kernel).

Such a mechanism is provided by some form of *trusted path* or *secure path*, whereby the user has a direct communications link to the kernel or to trusted software. An easy, but costly way to provide a trusted path is to give each user two terminals—one for normal work, and one hardwired to the kernel. A more realistic technique is for users to establish the trusted path through their normal terminal, by causing an event that signals the kernel to grab the terminal away from untrusted software. This *secure attention* signal must be one that untrusted software cannot intercept, mask, or fake. On an asynchronous ASCII terminal line, the signal might be an out-of-band condition (such as a BREAK that is entered at the keyboard) or a line condition caused by momentarily turning terminal power off. If the kernel is able to intercept all characters entered at the terminal, any character can be chosen as a secure attention character.

Depending on the characteristics of the hardware, the kernel may have to go to great lengths to ensure that the user's process cannot place the terminal or line controller in a mode where the secure attention character might be missed. Early attempts at implementing a trusted path consisted of special lights on the terminal controlled by the kernel, or a special area of the screen reserved for kernel communications, but the flexibility of most terminals today is such that the kernel would have an extremely hard time preventing such a mechanism from being spoofed by a Trojan horse.

The requirement for a trusted path presents a serious problem when the user's terminal is in fact an intelligent device or a personal computer. The trusted path must persist from the user's keyboard, through any software in the terminal or PC, to the kernel in the host. Likewise a trusted display must persist from the kernel to the user's screen. The only way to ensure the integrity of such paths is to verify the trustworthiness of the software in the terminal or PC, and to ascertain that the software cannot be modified or adversely influenced by commands from the user's process in the host. For a PC, such assurance may only be obtainable by implementing a security kernel or other form of trusted software in the PC. Although there is no technical reason why a PC with the appropriate hardware architecture cannot run a security kernel—and, in fact, security kernels have been built for microprocessors (Schell, Tao, and Heckman 1985)—these difficulties have led to the requirement in some applications that only dumb terminals be used with kernel-based systems.

In a high-security environment where mandatory controls are present, a personal computer must always be treated as a computer and not as a terminal. Even if the PC is a single-user computer and the user owns all the data in the PC, mandatory security rules require that the PC protect the user's data from improper modification or disclosure that might result from malfunctions and Trojan horses in applications running on that PC. A PC that interacts with a host kernel-based system, even if only through a terminal-emulator program, does so as a host on a network and must face scrutiny regarding network security issues that go far beyond those of a single computer system—whether or not the PC has a security kernel. See chapter 13, particularly section 13.5, for a discussion of network security issues as they pertain to security kernels.

10.5 TRUSTED FUNCTIONS

In addition to the trusted path, *trusted functions* are needed on most systems, and the difficulty of integrating these trusted functions is another reason why the ideal layering of the kernel-based system is often violated. The administrator interactions and user logins that we discussed in section 10.4, plus a number of administrative functions such as backup, are functions that must be trusted to maintain the security of the system but that are usually carried out by autonomous processes rather than by the kernel layer running in an inner domain protected by the hardware. Logically, such functions are part of the trusted software, and therefore they should be considered part of the kernel; but architecturally they run as processes outside the kernel and use services of the kernel just as though they were untrusted processes. The only difference between trusted processes and untrusted processes is that the former may be privileged to modify kernel databases and to bypass certain requirements of the security policy.

Trusted functions, also called *trusted processes*, are controversial because early kernel-based systems had nearly as much software running in the form of trusted processes as they had running in the kernel, substantially increasing the quantity of trusted code. Nobody could come up with a good reason why trusted code running outside the kernel should be subject to less scrutiny than code in the kernel, yet it was difficult to come up with a rigorous definition of what these processes were supposed to do: the security policy for trusted processes is not as obvious and straightforward as are the simple security and confinement properties. Moreover, some of the verification tools did not permit proofs of trusted process properties. Trusted processes were viewed suspiciously as a catch-all category for software that is needed to maintain the security of the system but that nobody wants to verify.

Today the tools are a little better, and proofs of properties of trusted processes are feasible, but some of the controversy remains. Some people view the interface between trusted processes and the kernel as a special kind of interface for *trusted subjects*—processes that do not need to be constrained as much as untrusted processes. The kernel provides most of the same functions for trusted processes as it does for untrusted processes, but it bypasses normal security checks if a process possesses trusted-subject privileges.

Other people assert that the only important interface is the external interface into the security perimeter. The trusted processes clearly run within the security perimeter and in a sense are just extensions of the kernel. The interfaces between the trusted processes and the kernel are no more special than other interfaces between portions of software within the kernel. There is one security policy, and it must be enforced consistently everywhere around the security perimeter; no special policy is needed for the interface between the kernel and trusted processes.

Operating-system designers are often faced with making a decision about whether to implement a function as an autonomous process or to implement it as part of the operating system that is distributed across all processes. Usually the function is more efficient when it is inside the operating system, but maintenance is far easier (and the design may be simpler) when it is outside. Kernel designers are faced with the same decisions. For example, the login function is often handled by a (trusted) process rather than directly by the operating system or kernel. But clearly that process must be trusted as much as the kernel and must enforce the same security policy. It is hard to make a convincing argument either that the policy enforced by the login process or its degree of verification should depend on a design or implementation detail.

From a purist's point of view, the only trusted subjects are people: users and administrators. Users are trusted to protect information to which they have access, and administrators are trusted to protect the kernel and to specify security attributes of users. Like other interfaces into the kernel, the interfaces for these trusted subjects (implemented through the trusted-path mechanism we discussed in section 10.4) must be constrained by the security policy, except that certain rules (specifically, the confinement property of the Bell and La Padula model) may not apply to people. Whether the software that implements such functions runs as a separate process or runs within a privileged domain is an implementation detail.

10.6 KERNEL SECURITY POLICIES

Almost universally, the security kernel approach has been applied to systems that enforce a multilevel security policy (see section 6.4). In particular, the mandatory and discretionary policies of the Bell and La Padula model (section 9.5.3) are the ones most commonly used. While few people doubt that the security kernel is a good place to enforce a mandatory security policy, a great deal of controversy has surrounded the discretionary policy.

We saw in section 6.2.5 that a Trojan horse can easily bypass discretionary access controls without violating any rules. This is true even if the controls are enforced in a security kernel. Nobody questions the usefulness of discretionary access controls; but many doubt whether, given this vulnerability to Trojan horses, it pays to go to the effort of implementing the controls in a kernel. After all, the kernel is supposed to be as small and simple as possible, and the cost to implement anything in a kernel is quite high because of the verifiability requirement. Discretionary access controls can easily be implemented in the operating system outside the kernel. Such controls can also be implemented within an expanded security perimeter that includes more than just the kernel.

The kernel typically provides two types of functions to support discretionary access controls. One function is an explicit kernel call that allows a user (or a process) to set the access rights to an object. The other function is the act of enforcing those rights on each access to the object (as part of the complete mediation principle). The kernel function that sets access rights on an object must of course check to make sure that the user or process has sufficient right to do so (for example, by ensuring that the user owns the object or that the object is contained in a directory that the user can modify), but the function places no constraints on the access rights that the user or process may specify. The definition of *discretionary access control* requires that a user be allowed to give away a file to anyone as a matter of discretion.

Thus, while the kernel faithfully enforces the access rights on an object, it does not restrict the values to which those rights may be set, thereby leaving discretionary access controls wide open to a Trojan horse attack.

It appears, at first, that the root of the vulnerability of discretionary access control is the fact that a program in the user's process can give away access rights. Consequently, it is occasionally proposed that this capability be eliminated by providing a trusted path such that only the user can set access rights. As we established in section 7.1.2, however, such a restriction is nearly useless—unnecessarily constraining the flexibility of the system, while doing nothing to defeat a Trojan horse.

You may conclude that, in order for the effort to implement discretionary access control in the kernel to be justified, you have to prove that you can prevent a Trojan horse from entering the system (or from entering a specific set of applications). In section 7.1.2 we discussed some ways to limit the occurrence of a Trojan horse through procedural controls. In a fairly closed system where no user programming is allowed or where the only users who are able to write programs are trusted, it is possible to increase your level of confidence that no Trojan horse can get into places where it would do much harm. You must be very careful, however, that you do not close the system to such a degree that your need for a security kernel is dubious. If you go so far as to require all your users to be cleared for access to all the information in the system, then you do not need much security.

Another way to minimize the occurrence of a Trojan horse is to use an integrity policy (see section 6.5) in which integrity access classes are assigned to subjects and objects based on some measure of their reliability. The kernel will prevent high-integrity programs and data from being contaminated (modified) by lower-integrity programs. If you login at a high integrity level, your process will only be able to run high-integrity programs, and you need not worry about accidentally using a low-integrity program that might contain a Trojan horse.

The integrity technique has a practical limitation: all programs used in a high-integrity process, including any that run in the operating system and all system applications needed by the process, must be of high integrity. This makes the use of normal-integrity tools such as compilers and text editors impossible in conjunction with these high-integrity programs. In general, using a level of integrity above that of the average system utility is practical only for very special cases.

In summary, the jury is still out on the usefulness of discretionary access control in the kernel. While most security kernels do implement a discretionary policy (because the government's *Criteria* (see section

1.2) requires that such controls lie within the security perimeter), you will have to judge for yourself whether it is appropriate for your kernel to do so.

10.7 KERNEL IMPLEMENTATION STRATEGIES

In general, a security kernel resembles an operating system and uses conventional operating-system design concepts. The hardware support required for a security kernel is also largely conventional. The kernel must control all subjects and objects within the security perimeter, and therefore it must provide support for processes, a file system, memory management, and I/O. Nothing in the three principles of the reference monitor approach inherently dictates an architecture fundamentally different from that of conventional operating systems. In fact, these principles are worthwhile guidance for the design of any operating system.

Most of the differences between a kernel and an operating system are quantitative and follow from the high priority given to the three principles in comparison to flexibility, functions, performance, cost of development, ease of use, and other factors that are normally more important to an operating system. The most direct quantitative impact is caused by the verifiability principle, which dictates that the kernel have a primitive interface and be much simpler and smaller than a full operating system, while at the same time insisting that it be closely scrutinized (and therefore more costly to build in relation to its size).

But if we look at the kernelized system as a whole, including the operating system and all the applications, the architectural aspect that differs most from conventional systems is the existence of an additional operating-system layer on top of the kernel that compensates for all the functions that the primitive kernel does not provide and so keeps the system running smoothly. The kernel approach does not require such an operating system, but a properly constructed kernel is, by definition, too primitive and inconvenient to use directly for an interface to applications. A kernel also does little to prevent denial of service unless denial of service is expressed as a security requirement.

Since few of us are in a position to build a complete system from scratch (including all hardware and software), we shall discuss in this section some of the early trade-offs you might make in planning to kernelize an existing system. Chapter 11 covers additional design topics pertaining to both kernels and conventional systems that are not covered here or in preceding sections.

Suppose that you are given an existing insecure operating system (ISOS) running on top of a reasonably modern computer (RMC). You will be subject to one of the following constraints (fig. 10-2), which are listed in order from most restrictive to least restrictive:

(a) *Identical operating system:* You must support the existing ISOS with minimal or no changes, and you must support all existing applications with no changes (object code compatibility). You must be able to support all future releases of ISOS with minimal effort on your part for each new release.

(b) *Compatible operating system:* You may completely redesign the existing ISOS, but you must support all existing applications with no changes to the applications.

(c) *New operating system:* You need neither retain the existing ISOS nor support existing applications. You are building a new secure operating system (SOS), and any resemblance to the original is incidental.

We shall now discuss implementation issues for each case.

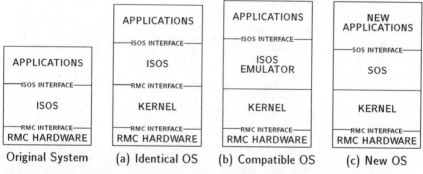

Original System   (a) Identical OS   (b) Compatible OS   (c) New OS

Figure 10-2. Kernel Implementation Strategies. There are three ways to incorporate a security kernel into an insecure operating system (ISOS) on given computer hardware (RMC): the first (a) retains most of the ISOS code and applications; the second (b) redesigns the operating system but retains the ISOS interface, thereby preserving the applications; and the third (c) is a completely redesigned SOS with a new interface and applications.

10.7.1 Case (a): Identical Operating System (Virtual Machine)

This case is at once the most restrictive and the most realistic. In most cases where security is the only motivation for improving a system, you are required to use as much of the code from an existing operating system as possible, and you must maintain full compatibility with existing applications. A further constraint may be that you must avoid the need to issue a new release of your system every time the original operating system is changed.

In this approach, the original operating system is used almost intact, and the kernel is implemented as a new layer within the existing system. The only practical way to implement this strategy is through a *virtual machine monitor* (fig. 10-3), such as IBM's VM operating system. In this case, the kernel is the virtual machine monitor, whose interface is nearly identical to that of the original hardware. The kernel supports multiple virtual machines (with a copy of the operating system running in each machine), in a manner analogous to the way in which an operating system supports multiple processes. The operating system, un-

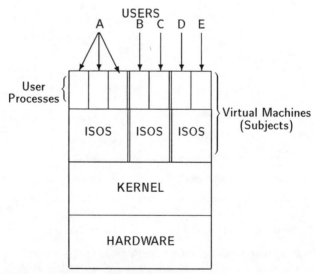

Figure 10-3. Virtual Machine Monitor Approach. In this architecture, the kernel supports multiple virtual machines, each of which runs a copy of the original operating system. Each operating system may service multiple applications and users. The kernel enforces the vertical isolation between virtual machines but not between processes on the same machine.

aware that it is being controlled by the security kernel, carries out its own functions of multiprocessing and memory management as if it were on the bare machine. In this structure, the virtual machines occupy isolated areas of memory; sharing memory is not usually possible because the operating systems, unaware of each other, do not have the necessary coordination mechanisms. With a few modifications, however, or with an operating system that is already able to run as a virtual machine, some sharing could be permitted (under control of the kernel, of course).

The virtual machine approach has been used quite successfully in KVM because both the hardware (the IBM 370) and the original operating system (VM/370) were already structured to support virtual machines. Certain hardware features are crucial to practical implementation of a virtual machine monitor, so this approach is not suitable for all systems.

In this architecture, the kernel's idea of a subject is in fact a virtual machine. Each virtual machine has a unique identifier and a set of security attributes on the basis of which the kernel makes its access decisions. Because the kernel does not manage (nor necessarily know about) the processes operating above that virtual machine, the kernel cannot perform any finer-grained access control over those processes. The kernel carries out actions requested by the operating system in each virtual machine and cannot trust the operating system to distinguish between the requests of different users. As far as the kernel is concerned, each machine is a single subject.

The operating system running in each virtual machine protects itself and the integrity of that machine, and the kernel protects itself and the integrity of the overall system. Such an architecture requires a hardware base with at least three states or domains, one for the kernel, one for the operating system, and one for all the application. Furthermore the architecture requires that the original operating system be able to run outside the most privileged state of the machine—something it probably is not accustomed to doing. It is unlikely that you will get away without making any changes at all to the original operating system; but if the operating system is well-structured to begin with, the changes may be very minor.

If we want each virtual machine to take on the role of a surrogate for a single user, the kernel must permit no more than one user to access each machine. The user may have multiple processes on that virtual machine, but all processes have the same access rights (enforced by the kernel) as the virtual machine. This single-user virtual machine is represented in the leftmost ISOS in figure 10-3. The kernel's enforcement of access control to the granularity level of the virtual machine is equivalent to enforcing access to the level of a single user.

On the other hand, it might be desirable to allow a virtual machine to be used by several users, as represented by the other two ISOS's in figure 10-3. Since ISOS is a multiuser operating system, this is a natural thing to do. In this case the kernel cannot distinguish between the actions of different users on the same machine. For access control purposes, the users must be considered as members of a group, and the kernel's access enforcement is to the level of granularity of a group of users.

Which of the two approaches—single- or multiple-user virtual machines—you adopt depends on your security policy and on pragmatic issues such as performance. "Sliding" a virtual machine monitor beneath an existing operating system is well-known to have an adverse impact on performance. If the hardware is optimized to support a virtual machine concept, however, the impact might not be too great. But in a system with a hundred simultaneously logged-in users, the overhead involved in maintaining a virtual machine per user could be intolerable. On the other hand, if the security policy requires the kernel to distinguish between the actions of programs run by different users, there is no secure alternative.

Even though the kernel's security policy cannot distinguish between the operating system and the applications, there is no reason why the operating system cannot continue to enforce its own security policy over the applications. While we cannot trust the operating system to enforce its security policy with the same level of assurance we have in trusting the kernel, that does not necessarily render the operating system's controls useless. In particular, conventional discretionary access control (already a feature of most operating systems) will continue to be enforced even if the operating system is running on top of a kernel. The kernel might enforce more stringent mandatory security controls that the operating system does not provide.

In a virtual machine architecture, the kernel can manage a file system on secondary storage in a number of ways. One way is to provide each virtual machine with a private area of disk in which the operating system manages its own file system. (In KVM each VM is given access to its own minidisk area of disk.) The kernel mediates the I/O to the disk but does not interpret the contents of a virtual machine's disk area. But in order to allow sharing of information, the kernel must allow two virtual machines to access the same disk area in accordance with the security policy. Whether this is workable depends on how easily the operating system is able to coordinate sharing a file system with another machine.

10.7.2 Case (b): Compatible Operating System (Emulation)

Even if you are lucky enough to be free to redesign the internals of the operating system, you will doubtless be constrained by existing applications. In figure 10-2(b), your constraints are to use the existing RMC computer and to implement the same ISOS interface (so that applications do not know the difference between the real ISOS and the ISOS emulator). You have complete freedom to define an interface between the ISOS emulator and the kernel. This approach was proposed for the KSOS project, where a Unix emulator was to run on top of the security kernel.[1]

The most straightforward way to realize this approach is to implement the operating system emulator as a program within each user's process, running in a domain outside the kernel but with more privileges than the user programs enjoy (fig. 10-4). In this case, unlike the situation in the virtual machine monitor approach, each subject is a process that operates as a surrogate for a single user. But like the virtual machine system, this architecture requires a machine that has at least three domains. In general, the emulator that runs in each process acts as a translator, rendering operating system functions into kernel calls, rather than as a complete operating system, because the emulator only controls a single user's process and cannot freely share information with its counterparts in other processes. Nonetheless, a properly constructed emulator can maintain a certain amount of global control over users in all processes. With some luck, sections of the code for the emulator can be obtained unmodified from the original operating system, because most operating systems are already built to distribute a portion of their outer layers among the processes in the system.

Since you are designing both the emulator and the kernel, and since you are constrained only by the ISOS interface at the top and the hardware at the bottom (and perhaps by the desire to use some existing code), you can make the optimum engineering choice of the split in functions between them. But some common problems arise in attempts to kernelize an operating system in this way, because of incompati-

---

1. The Unix emulator was later abandoned as a result of budgetary constraints.

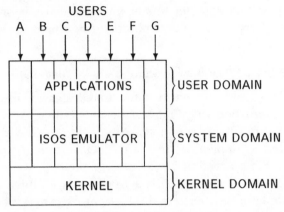

Figure 10-4. Operating-system Emulator. *A program running in an intermediate domain of each process emulates operating-system calls, using combinations of kernel calls.*

bilities between the security policy that the kernel must enforce and the characteristics of the interface to be emulated:

- Some functions of the interface are not secure according to the new policy and cannot be emulated.
- Some functions of the interface, though secure, are exceptionally difficult to emulate.

In section 5.2 we discussed some examples in which applications depend on functions of an operating system that are insecure. You are most likely to encounter such problems when you try to enforce mandatory controls on a system that depends on the ability to communicate or share information among many or all processes. In particular, you cannot emulate functions that reveal global dynamic status about the system if the kernel enforces mandatory controls. These functions are not a problem in the virtual machine approach because each machine runs its own complete operating system in its own security domain and can function quite well without being aware of other machines.

A function that is secure but difficult to emulate under mandatory access controls is one that maintains an interprocess synchronization mechanism, in the form of locks that are shared by several processes. On the "vanilla" system, there might be a system-wide database (in memory) containing information about locks, such as the list of processes waiting on each lock. The lock manager enforces access control on the locks, so that a process may only use a lock when permitted by the process that created the lock. But mandatory controls do not allow any single system-wide object to be read and written by all processes: the locking mechanism has to be redesigned to use multiple databases— one per access class. Because the system may support a huge number of different access classes, the databases must be dynamically created in memory (assuming that the kernel supports shared memory) each time a process of a new access class is activated, and they must be deleted when the last process of a given access class terminates. Reliably deleting objects, so as to avoid filling memory with thousands of unused lock databases, is a difficult design problem.

Another function—secure, but difficult to emulate—provides access control for small objects such as records or interprocess messages. A kernel with a primitive file system is unlikely to support many types of objects, so a simple way to manage small objects is to store one object per file. While such a scheme is not hard to implement, its performance implications and storage requirements might make it impractical. A much more complex scheme might be required, whereby multiple objects are stored on a per-access-class basis, as are the locks in the previous example.

Before undertaking a project to kernelize an existing operating system, you should carefully analyze each function to be emulated and determine exactly where the function might fail under the kernel's security policy. Most of the problems you identify will involve additional error conditions that can usually be implemented in a compatible way, or functions that do not work in quite the same way but are not used much anyway. You may however, run into a few show-stoppers, where fixing the problem nullifies so many applications that you must abandon hope of emulating the existing operating system.

If you find that a function will work but is very difficult to implement, you might decide to place part of it in the kernel. A locking mechanism, for example, is much easier to implement in the kernel, where it can know about all processes. But you should make such decisions carefully and with good reason, or before you know it the kernel will be as big as the original operating system, and the emulator will be little more than an empty shell.

10.7.3 Case (c): New Operating System

The third case arises when you are designing your own system from scratch, and thus have the rare freedom (within reason) to define your own operating system interface. This case of course assumes that you are designing a complete operating system and not just a kernel. In case (c) you are allowed to define an operating system interface that is compatible with the security policy enforced by the kernel. The interface might closely match the functions provided by the kernel, either on a one-for-one basis or through simple mappings of operating system functions to kernel functions. With the flexibility afforded by the freedom to choose an interface, you can probably design both a kernel of minimal size and an operating system that performs well. With appropriate hardware support (see chapter 8), your fully functional secure operating system need perform no worse than any insecure operating system that has similar functions.

The SCOMP is an example of a kernelized system with a specialized operating system. On top of the kernel is a simple operating system that provides more application-friendly features than the bare kernel does.

The structure of the system will resemble that in figure 10-4, with a portion of the operating system code running in each process under control of the kernel. But because there is no compatibility constraint on the type of sharing that the operating system must implement, you can design both the file system's and the operating system's internal databases to use kernel primitives to share information in accordance with the security policy. This flexibility minimizes the need to implement special-purpose functions in the kernel.

If you have a multilevel security policy, for example, a process running at SYSTEM LOW (see section 9.5.3) outside the kernel can write information readable by all other processes. Such a process can manage a large number of administrative functions affecting system databases that are read (but not written) by other processes. These include the user registration file, configuration information, *sysgen* parameters, and start-up procedures.

A SYSTEM HIGH process outside the kernel can handle functions that must be able to read system-wide information written by all processes. Such a process can read (but not write) any file in the system without special privileges. Examples of applications of this type are processes that handle audit or accounting logs or that monitor system usage.

You cannot go too far with this notion of untrusted processes for system functions. The system backup process, for example, only requires read access to files and might therefore seem to be a good candidate for a SYSTEM HIGH untrusted process. But if you ever want to restore the files you have backed up, you will be unable to believe any of the access class labels or kernel data written by backup. In general, backup and restore operations must be implemented within the kernel or as trusted functions (see section 10.5).

REFERENCES

Ames, S. R., Jr.; Gasser, M.; and Schell, R. R. 1983. "Security Kernel Design and Implementation: An Introduction." *Computer* 16(7): 14–22. Reprinted in *Advances in Computer System Security*, vol. 2, ed. R. Turn, pp. 170–76. Dedham, Mass.: Artech House (1984).
An overview of the reference monitor concept, security models, and kernel implementation issues.

Anderson, J. P. 1972. "Computer Security Technology Planning Study." ESD-TR-73-51, vols. 1 and 2. Hanscom AFB, Mass.: Air Force Electronic Systems Division. (Also available through Defense Technical Information Center, Alexandria, Va., DTIC AD-758206.)
The first study to document the government's computer security problem and the proposed solutions in the form of the reference monitor and the security kernel; now no longer useful as a primary technical reference, but historically important.

Berson, T. A., and Barksdale, B. L. 1979. "KSOS—Development Methodology for a Secure Operating System." *Proceedings of the NCC* 48: 365–71. Reprinted in *Advances in Computer System Security*, vol. 1, ed. R. Turn, pp. 155–61. Dedham, Mass.: Artech House (1981).
A description of the development and verification techniques used in the Kernelized Secure Operating System research project for the PDP-11/70.

Fraim, L. J. 1983. "SCOMP: A Solution to the Multilevel Security Problem." *Computer* 16(7): 26–34. Reprinted in *Advances in Computer System Security*, vol. 2, ed. R. Turn, pp. 185–92. Dedham, Mass.: Artech House (1984).
A minicomputer-based security kernel with sophisticated hardware protection controls; this system is a Honeywell product.

Gold, B. D.; Linde, R. R.; Peeler, R. J.; Schaefer, M.; Scheid, J. F.; and Ward, P. D. 1979. "A Security Retrofit of VM/370." *Proceedings of the NCC* 48: 335–44.
Describes the KVM security kernel.

Karger, P. A., and Schell, R. R. 1974. "Multics Security Evaluation: Vulnerability Analysis." ESD-TR-74-193, vol. 2. Hanscom AFB, Mass.: Air Force Electronic Systems Division. (Also available through National Technical Information Service, Springfield, Va., NTIS AD-A001120.)
A discussion of penetrations of Multics, pointing out several classic types of flaws in various areas; useful as a guide to detecting flaws in other operating systems.

Landwehr, C. E. 1983. "The Best Available Technologies for Computer Security." *Computer* 16(7): 86–100. Reprinted in *Advances in Computer System Security*, vol. 2, ed. R. Turn, pp. 108–22. Dedham, Mass.: Artech House (1984).
An overview of all past and ongoing secure system projects, with many references.

McCauley, E. J., and Drongowski, P. J. 1979. "KSOS—The Design of a Secure Operating System." *Proceedings of the NCC* 48:345–53. Reprinted in *Advances in Computer System Security*, vol. 1, ed. R. Turn, pp. 145–53. Dedham, Mass.: Artech House (1981).
A description of the design of the KSOS security kernel for the pdp-11.

Popek, G. J.; Kampe, M.; Kline, C. S.; Stoughton, A.; Urban, M.; and Walton, E. J. 1979. "UCLA Secure Unix." *Proceedings of the NCC* 48: 355–64.
The UCLA security kernel for the PDP-11.

Schell, R. R.; Tao, T. F.; and Heckman, M. 1985. "Designing the GEMSOS Security Kernel for Security and Performance." In *Proceedings of the 8th National Computer Security Conference*, pp. 108–19. Gaithersburg, Md.: National Bureau of Standards.
A description of a security kernel for the Intel iAPX 286 microprocessor offered by Gemini Computers.

Schiller, W. L. 1975. "The Design and Specification of a Security Kernel for the PDP-11/45." ESD-TR-75-69. Hanscom AFB, Mass.: Air Force Electronic Systems Division. (Also available through Defense Technical Information Center, Alexandria, Va., DTIC AD-A011712.)
Historically important as the first formal specification for a security kernel.

———. 1977. "Design and Abstract Specification of a Multics Security Kernel." ESD-TR-77-259. Hanscom AFB, Mass.: Air Force Electronic Systems Division. (Also available through Defense Technical Information Center, Alexandria, Va., DTIC AD-A048576.)
A worked example of a formal specification of a security kernel for a large operating system (though the system was never implemented).

Chapter *11*

Architectural Considerations

This chapter covers a number of miscellaneous topics pertaining to the design and development of secure systems, as well as to their applications. It applies to both security kernels and conventional designs.

11.1 OPERATING-SYSTEM LAYERING

Although the concept of layering is not unique to secure operating systems, it is particularly useful for them because it promotes a structured design that can help satisfy some assurance needs. A layered operating system is one whose internal structure looks like a stack of systems, each having an interface for use by the layers above (table 11-1).

Layers in a system are strictly hierarchical: the lower layers provide primitive functions, and the higher layers use the primitive functions to provide more complex functions. By employing the technique of *data hiding,* the software in each layer maintains its own global data and does not directly reference data outside its layer. Each layer knows only about its own data and about the set of functions available to it below; it knows nothing about higher layers except such information as can be deduced from interactions across the interface. The rule is "downward calls only."

One way we can view the functions of the layers resembles the way we view layers in a kernel-based system implementing a virtual machine (refer to figure 10-3), where each of the three layers is a complete

Layer	Function	
10	user applications	} Outside
9	command language interpreter	} Operating System
8	**operating system interface**	
7	device input/output	
6	high-level processes	
5	directories	
4	files	} Inside
3	segments	Operating System
2	pages	
1	low-level processes	
0	hardware	

Table 11-1. Operating-system Layers. *Each layer provides a set of functions for the layers above it, using functions available to it in the layers below. Everything at or below layer 8 in this example is within the operating system (or security kernel). This architecture resembles that of PSOS (Neumann et al. 1980).*

minioperating system providing functions in all necessary areas: object management, process management, I/O, and so on. The minioperating systems in the higher layers have more functions and are more complex than those in the lower layers. In such a structure, there is no reason why any layer need use functions belonging to a layer other than the one immediately below. The primary difference between the layering inside the operating system in table 11-1 and that in figure 10-3 is that inside the operating system there is no need to enforce vertical isolation between portions of the upper layers, as there is between processes or virtual machines. Performance of operating systems layered in this way tends to be poor because many of the frequently used simple functions that are implemented in the lower layers can be accessed only by a cascade of calls through multiple upper layers.

Another view constrains each layer to a particular subset of functions, as in the example in table 11-1. The hierarchical structure (downward calls only) is maintained, but no single layer provides enough interfaces to be usable as an operating system in itself. A layer may directly call functions several layers down, bypassing intermediate layers. In table 11-1, for example, a user application in layer 10 may be permitted to read and write a file by directly calling layer 4, without necessarily passing through intermediate layers.

The structure whereby a layer services a single functional area is more efficient, because the layer need not participate in functions of the lower layers; but it is also more error-prone, because software in a higher layer may be able to bypass intermediate layers and directly access objects that the intermediate layers should handle. In table 11-1, for example, layer 5 creates directories using the files provided by layer 4. If programs in layer 6 (or above) always call layer 5 before calling lower layers, the integrity of the directories can be maintained by layer 5. But if a program makes a direct call from layer 10 into layer 4, for example, that program might be able to write into a file containing a directory without the directory manager's knowledge. To handle this type of problem gracefully, each layer must provide pass-through interfaces to functions in layers beneath it, allowing lower-layer functions to be used only where the data-hiding constraints of the layer are not violated. In our example, the directory layer would provide pass-through calls for the open-file function in the file layer, but only after checking the arguments of the open-file call to make sure that files containing directories are not opened.

Regardless of how the layers are interpreted, security decisions usually must be made by most layers. Normally, having a single "security layer" is impossible because each layer has its own set of objects that require secure management. It would be nice if, for example, the operating-system interface layer in table 11-1 could validate the legitimacy of all system calls, since that would relieve the lower layers of the duty to check their arguments. But the ability to do so, especially for the pass-through calls, might require that the interface layer know about details of the lower-layer data structures, thereby violating the data-hiding principle of layering. If a whole operating system existed in each layer, with no pass-through functions, such knowledge would not be required because each layer would fully protect all its objects.

In most systems, the layering structure is enforced during development, rather than at run time, using design guidelines and development tools such as compilers that prevent out-of-layer references. When in execution, the entire operating system runs in one or two domains, and the hardware has little or no role in preventing erroneous software in the operating system from violating the layering. While the layering structure looks as though it could be handled by hardware that supports hierarchical domains, there is little security advantage in adopting this strategy because the entire operating system (or security kernel) is security-relevant. Once a system call passes through the operating system interface and satisfies the initial checks of its arguments, any lower layer can cause a security violation if it misbehaves.

In summary, layering supports design verification by promoting a clean architecture and reducing the chance for design and implementation errors. Some verification techniques model the layering structure (see section 12.6.2). Using hardware to enforce layering during execution may add robustness to the system in the face of programming errors, but it adds little measurable security.

11.2 ASYNCHRONOUS ATTACKS AND ARGUMENT VALIDATION

In section 8.4.2 we discussed hardware techniques for checking pointers passed as arguments between domains. Pointer validation is a special case of argument validation performed by all operating systems prior to carrying out a user's system call request. Where a system supports multiple processors and multiprogramming, there exists a class of problem referred to as the *asynchronous attack*, whereby one process passes pointers to parameters (residing in its virtual memory) to the operating system, and another process (with access to the same memory containing the parameters) modifies the parameters between the time the operating system validates them and the time they are used. The first process (the one making the system call) is suspended during the call so that it cannot modify the parameters, but any other process or processor may be able to run during the call. Another term that has been used to describe this problem is TOC/TOU ("time of check/time of use").

As we discussed in section 8.4.2, the safest solution to the TOC/TOU problem is for the operating system to copy the parameters to a location safe from asynchronous modification prior to validation. But it is also necessary for the operating system to prevent an asynchronous change to all information on which the validation depends, not just to the parameters themselves. We spoke earlier, for example, of a segment descriptor that is modified between the time access to the segment is determined and the time the segment is referenced. Another example, at a higher level, involves a system call to read a file. The operating system must first read a directory to find out the caller's mode of access and to obtain the location of the file on disk. By the time the file on disk is read, the file may have been deleted and a new file put in its place—a file to which the caller did not originally have access. Of course, operating systems can handle these cases through the use of appropriate locks, but each case must be handled in its own way: there are no generic solutions.

While locking helps avoid the TOC/TOU problem in situations where tables and operating-system databases are involved in checking access, a user's database that is randomly located somewhere in a process's address space cannot be locked by the operating system. In situations where such data take part in an access check, the data may have to be copied into the operating system in total.

Asynchronous actions that change the contents of memory can also occur as a result of I/O operations. A classic penetration of os/360 involves writing a channel program that is valid at the time it is checked by the operating system prior to the start of I/O, but causes itself to be modified (overwritten with the data being read) in a way that invalidates the prior check. Thus, you are not necessarily safe from the TOC/TOU problem even if your system runs on a single processor and your operating system prevents a process switch between time of check and time of use.

11.3 PROTECTED SUBSYSTEMS

A *protected subsystem* is an application program outside of the operating system that carries out functions for a group of users, maintains some common data for all users in the group, and protects the data from improper access by users in the group. The subsystem itself is protected from tampering. A database management system that maintains a database shared by a group of users is a protected subsystem. The operating system, via conventional access controls, prevents users from tampering with either the database or the DBMS itself. The database can only be accessed through proper calls to the DBMS. Most transaction monitors are also subsystems. A program such as a compiler is not a subsystem because the compiler runs with the access rights of the user that called it, operating on data accessible only to that user.

One key problem in supporting a protected subsystem is how to prevent user programs from accessing the subsystem's shared data directly, while allowing the subsystem access to the data. In most systems, the easiest way to implement such a scheme is to run the subsystem in its own process with its own access rights and its own files (fig. 11-1). User processes send requests to the subsystem via shared memory or interprocess messages. The subsystem remains permanently active, ready to process a request at any time.

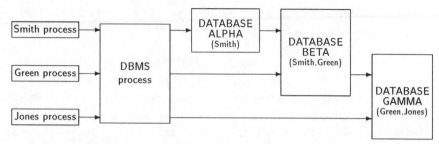

Figure 11-1. Protected Subsystem in an Active Process. *In this structure, the DBMS runs as a process that is inherently no different from a user process. The operating system's normal access-control mechanism prevents all but the DBMS process from accessing the database files. The DBMS must control individual users' access to different files and different portions of files.*

When subsystems are supported in individual processes, they tend to require centralized system management to ensure that they are always active. Users cannot write their own subsystems and change them as they see fit. But these management problems are not as important a consideration as a security problem: the operating system cannot tell on whose behalf the subsystem is working at any given time. The subsystem is responsible for enforcing access to data belonging to a number of users, even though the subsystem is apt to be far less trustworthy than the operating system. As far as the operating system is concerned, all files used by the subsystem belong to a single user (DBMS, in figure 11-1). The security controls in the operating system only keep the subsystem's database separate from other processes.

A related way to support subsystems, employed in Unix via its set-uid mechanism, involves activating a separate subsystem process on each request made by another process (fig. 11-2). The subsystem process runs with the identity of the subsystem and not with the user's identity. At any one time, multiple subsystem processes may be operating on common data. This technique has all the same security problems as the single process, because each of the multiple processes takes on the identity of the same user, but it does minimize the need for centralized management of subsystems.

In yet another approach, the subsystem runs as just another program in the context of each process that uses it, thereby taking advantage of the operating system's process isolation mechanisms to separate the actions of different users. In order to prevent the applications from damaging the subsystem's data, this approach requires a machine whose

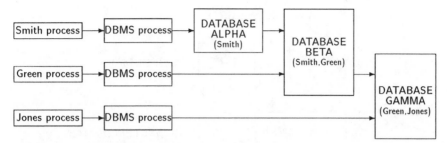

Figure 11-2. Protected Subsystem Activated on Request. *The subsystem is activated as a separate process each time it is needed, while retaining its own identity separate from that of the invoking process.*

hardware supports hierarchical domains (see section 8.4). The subsystem runs in an inner domain that is more protected than the user program but less protected and less trusted than the operating system. The subsystem must still be trusted to manage data shared among several users, but the operating system can enforce a certain degree of control over the data: the data can be protected from processes outside a given group of users as well as from programs running in domains less privileged than that of the subsystem.

The maximum number of domains in a system that contains hierarchical domains is usually limited to a small number such as 3, 4, 7, or 16. As illustrated in figure 8-5, domains tend to be reserved for specific functions—the innermost ones for the operating system, the outermost ones for users, and some intermediate ones for subsystems. Recall that access control to files is based on the user identifier of the process and on the domain in which the process is running; there is no further distinction among programs within the same domain.

This structure works very well when the system supports just one or two subsystems, since each can run in its own domain. But with a limited number of domains, the use of subsystems must be centrally managed; and in a large system with scores of subsystems, there are too few domains. If several subsystems are placed in the same domain and are used by the same process, the operating system or hardware cannot distinguish between the programs of one subsystem and those of another. In figure 11-3, both the MAIL and DBMS subsystems run in the same domain. If both subsystems are used by process P1, they share the same user identifier, SMITH; therefore, both have access to the same

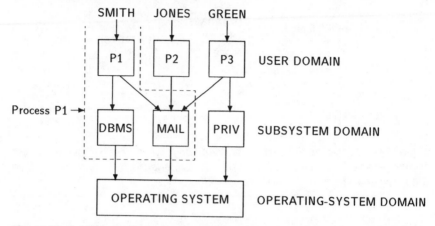

Figure 11-3. Mutually Suspicious Subsystems. *Process P1, with access rights of user SMITH invokes both the DBMS and the MAIL subsystems. The sub- systems run as part of process P1, but in a more privileged subsystem do- main. The access rights of a program in the subsystem domain run by P1 are based on the same identifier SMITH so there is no way for the DBMS subsystem to protect itself from the MAIL subsystem. This is a classic prob- lem with hierarchical domains.*

files. Where two subsystems are mutually suspicious this is a security problem. There are several ways around this problem (Schroeder 1972), but none is very attractive. While it nicely addresses the performance problems of the other approaches, the use of hierarchical domains for subsystems can only succeed in a few special cases and is not a general solution.

Hierarchical domains are poor vehicles for protected subsystems be- cause there is, in general, nothing hierarchical about access rights of different subsystems. We need a more generalized domain structure, where subsystems run in private domains that are isolated from each other and from their callers, and where no practical limit constrains the total number of domains on a system. This need has driven many researchers to design hardware that can support a generalized domain or capability architecture (see section 11.6), and a few commercial sys- tems have been built around this concept. The IBM System/38 and Intel iAPX 432 are examples. But the hardware designs are more radical, and little experience has been accumulated in building secure operating systems on these machines. Such *domain machines* are viewed in practice as offering a means to improve software reliability, because a software problem in one domain cannot affect software in another domain. Building a secure operating system or security kernel on such a machine remains an area of research.

11.4 SECURE FILE SYSTEMS

The file system is the primary focus of access control in an operating system. Following are some important aspects of file system design that affect the implementation of secure file systems.

11.4.1 Naming Structures

Early in the development of the first secure operating systems, certain file-system-naming structures were recognized to be better than others for secure sharing of files. The simplest structure is the *flat file system* wherein file names are maintained in a global name space stored in a single system-wide directory. Any process or user can ask for any file by name, and access to a file is determined by looking up information about the file in the directory.

Flat file systems make poor secure file systems because there is no way to hide the existence of a file from a user. Nobody has yet come up with a way to hide the file names in such a system. Even if the operating system refuses to tell you directly whether a file of a given name exists, you can always infer it by attempting to create another file of the same name and checking to see whether you get a "name duplication" error message. Some measure of security can be attained by forcing people to use mundane file names so that the name itself will not reveal any useful information, but in general the existence of the file (as well as the name of the file) must be hidden. This problem makes flat file systems particularly inappropriate for mandatory security controls, because the file name and file existence are ideal covert storage channels (see the example in section 7.2.1).

Most attempts to make flat file systems secure involve some type of qualifier (such as a mandatory access class) that is automatically attached to the file name and distinguishes between two files of the same name that were created by different processes having different security attributes. In effect, the system maintains two or more versions of the file, one for each access class at which the file is created. But the approach has serious functional (not security) problems, because it requires a process that wants to read a file to know which qualifier to use (when it has access to more than one version).

One way to prevent covert channels in a flat file system is to prevent processes from choosing file names. In this approach, each file is assigned a unique ID by the operating system at the time of its creation. A process can create a file whenever it pleases, but it cannot select the name; and all processes must use the unique ID for future access to the file. This approach is adopted by the KSOS security kernel. While it works well for files that are created and used by programs, users cannot be expected to remember system-generated unique IDs. In order to allow users to name files, the system must maintain a directory that maps user-selected file names to unique IDs. Such a directory is none other than a global name space, posing the same security problems as a flat file system.

The other file-naming structure is the *hierarchical file system*, wherein a collection of files is contained within a directory and directories are contained within other directories (fig. 11-4). The name of a file is specified as a *path name*—a series of directory names beginning at the root directory and ending with the file's parent directory, followed by the name of the file in the directory.

Access to directories, which contain names and pointers to files and other directories, is controlled in a manner similar to access to files, except that directories are readable and writable only indirectly through special system calls. When you create a file, you have to specify the directory in which it is to be created. If you want to create a file

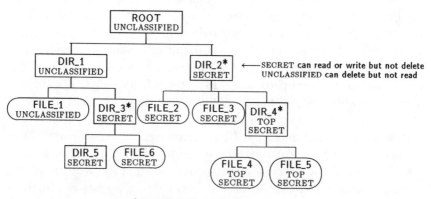

* Upgraded Directories

Figure 11-4. Multilevel Secure Hierarchical File System. Boxes represent directories, and capsules represent files. A directory contains a list of files and other directories, plus information on access control and file system management. Shown is one way to organize a multilevel file system so that the access classes increase as you go down the tree.

whose existence you want hidden from another user, you create the file in a directory that the user cannot read. A user without read access to a directory cannot infer anything about its contents or about the hierarchy below that directory.

To prevent covert channels in a multilevel secure hierarchical file system, we must avoid write-downs or confinement property violations (see section 6.4.1) in directories, by preventing a process from creating an object (a file or directory) in a directory unless the process has write access to the directory. This means that a TOP SECRET process cannot create a file in a SECRET directory. However, a SECRET process can create an object in a SECRET directory and then upgrade the object to TOP SECRET. The TOP SECRET process can thereafter write into the object. In this way, a tree of directories and files is created in which access classes stay the same or increase as you go down the tree.

In a multilevel hierarchical file system, an object whose access class is greater than its parent's is an *upgraded* object that cannot be deleted by a process running at the object's access class. The object can only be deleted by a process running at the parent's access class—even though that process cannot read the object. This causes some difficulties because a process at the parent's access class cannot find out (and cannot be permitted to determine) whether an upgraded directory is empty; the system must permit the directory to be deleted by that process even if the directory is full of files and other directories. Despite this difficulty, hierarchical file systems are far preferable to flat file systems when multilevel security is involved.

11.4.2 Unique Identifiers

A highly secure system needs an unambiguous way to identify subjects and objects uniquely for access control and administrative functions. Guaranteeing uniqueness of subject identifiers is a manual job, because subject unique IDs are based on user names assigned administratively and centrally. Object unique IDs present a more difficult management problem, because not all objects are manually created and because user-assigned object names cannot be trusted to be unique.

Ideally, the unique ID for an object is a number that is generated by the system when an object is created and is never reused for another object in the life of the system. Normally the user or process also specifies a human-readable name for the object, but the unique ID is the basis of access control decisions. It is important to avoid assigning two unique IDs to the same object. It is convenient—though not essential—to avoid changing the unique ID of an object unnecessarily.

You may notice that the unique ID name space appears to be the same global name space that we said was a bad idea in section 11.4.1. Because you do not specify unique IDs yourself when you create objects, however, and because you use the conventional (for example, hierarchical) name to access the object, using system-assigned unique IDs for ambiguity resolution and other functions listed below avoids all of the problems of a global name space.

One purpose served by the unique ID is to permit the system to determine whether two objects are the same. Without a unique ID, this is harder than you may think, because the same file may be identified in many different ways—especially where file names can change, where files can have multiple names, or where files are accessible through indirect links, as in Unix or Multics. Knowing whether two objects are the same is necessary in order to determine whether or not to revoke access when security attributes of object change.

Object unique IDs are also used for administrative functions, such as backup and retrieval. Without a unique ID, it is impossible to ascertain whether a backed-up image of a file written long ago is the same file that currently resides on the system or is a completely different file that just happens to have the same user-defined name. A security violation could result if the wrong file is retrieved.

Even if the contents of a file are completely erased and rewritten, its unique ID need not be changed, because it remains the same file for purposes of access control. If a file is deleted and a new one is created in its place with exactly the same access attributes, it can safely be assigned the same unique ID; but in general the operating system does not bother to keep track of the access attributes or unique IDs of deleted files. If the access attributes of a file change, the unique ID need not change, since the process that changed them possessed the right to access the file both before and after the change.

Unique IDs generated by the system have gained a reputation as a source of covert channels. In order to ensure uniqueness of IDs, one approach to generating unique IDs is to use the value of a counter that is advanced each time an object is created. But if a process can see the unique IDs of two successive objects it has created, it can determine whether another process has created an object in the interim. This results in a covert storage channel.

To counter this problem, a better source for unique IDs is a real-time clock whose resolution is sufficiently small that no two successive objects will have the same unique ID. This eliminates the covert storage channel but permits the exploitation of timing channels by providing, in effect, a process-readable system clock. While this timing channel may not be new (the system probably already provides a clock for user processes), the unique-ID clock may be more accurate than a low-resolution clock that processes need for their usual timing functions.

When a unique-ID generator is based on a clock that must be manually set each time the system is booted, the clock may be set wrong through human error. If the clock is set to a time in the past, unique IDs of previously created objects may be duplicated, and serious security problems can result. If the clock is set to a time in the future, no secure way exists to restore the clock to its proper value without finding and deleting all objects that have been created in the interim.

11.5 SECURITY GUARDS

The *security guard* is a low-cost add-on security mechanism that addresses a particular class of multilevel security problems. In many environments, users need to communicate with a system even though certain of those users cannot be allowed direct access to the system because of weaknesses in the system's security controls. The users may need access to a restricted set of data, and the system may not be strong enough to protect other highly sensitive data residing on that system.

Figure 11-5 shows an example of a guard that permits users logged into a system running at a LOW access class to submit queries to a database running on a system at a HIGH access class. The two systems are not allowed to communicate directly because neither is trusted. The guard is a trusted (usually kernel-based) system that is allowed to communicate with both systems simultaneously; it is trusted to prevent a nonsecure flow of information from HIGH to LOW. The guard accepts queries from the LOW system and passes them to the HIGH system unmodified: this is perfectly safe. The response to the query is received by the guard and displayed to a human reviewer to ensure that it contains no information above the LOW access class.

In a similar manner, a guard can be used for access to a LOW database by users on a HIGH computer. In this case the human reviewer must examine the queries, not because the HIGH user might try to disclose information but because the HIGH computer cannot be trusted to prevent disclosure.

Fully automated guards have been used for one-way traffic, such as sending mail from a LOW to a HIGH system. The only information that the LOW system needs to receive in response to a message it has sent is an acknowledgment that the message was accepted by the guard. The guard has enough store-and-forward capability to ensure that little

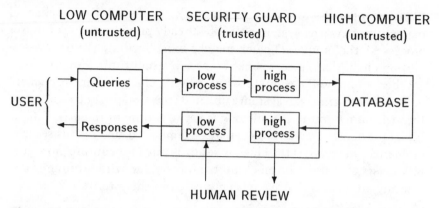

Figure 11-5. Security Guard. Queries from the LOW to the HIGH system are passed essentially unmodified, while responses are manually filtered for HIGH system data content. Where the guard computer enforces process isolation with suitable assurance (for example, if the guard is based on a security kernel) the low and high processes running on the guard need not be trusted.

or no information about the status of the HIGH system can be deduced by the LOW system, thereby minimizing the possibility that a covert channel will occur. Section 13.5 discusses why secure one-way traffic cannot generally be supported on a network.

Automated guards have also been implemented to handle database queries, where the queries and responses are highly structured and can be thoroughly checked so that the possibility of covert communications from HIGH to LOW is remote. For the most sensitive applications, however, you must assess the Trojan horse threat before deciding whether the automated guard approach is suitable (Denning 1984).

While the guard concept may seem "low-tech," it is the only practical way to carry out various applications on many existing systems. Without a guard, the function is carried out using pencil-and-paper messages.[1] The guard itself has to be developed using advanced computer security principles. The Department of Defense has developed several guards, one of which is based on a security kernel (Woodward 1979; Denning 1984).

---

1. In many environments a person reads messages on one terminal and retypes the message into another terminal, because the two systems cannot be trusted to be electrically connected.

11.6 CAPABILITY-BASED ARCHITECTURES

In section 6.2.2, we discussed the concept of a capability list for access control and noted that capabilities have enjoyed more success as a low-level mechanism than as a user-visible one. In section 8.4.2, we examined how to use capabilities, supported by hardware, as pointers to implement nonhierarchical domains. While researchers have always shown a great deal of interest in capabilities, most capability systems remain research systems; only a very few (such as IBM's System/38 and the Intel iAPX 432) have been built commercially.

Despite the fact that capabilities are touted as a protection mechanism, using them for secure systems raises a fundamental problem. As a key to an object, a capability can be passed freely between domains, and possession of a capability is sufficient to permit access. Indeed, a primary advantage of capabilities is their ability to be given away without the system's having to keep track of who has access to what. Each application can manage its own capabilities as it pleases.

The flexibility to pass a capability to someone else is acceptable if the capability is for an object that you own, but it is unacceptable if the capability is for an object that you do not own. For example, a subsystem that processes data on behalf of one user, and thereby receives some capabilities for the data, should not be allowed to pass those capabilities to other users. The opportunity for a Trojan horse to propagate capabilities in an unconstrained manner makes pure capabilities useless for enforcing mandatory access controls.

A number of researchers have addressed this deficiency, in various ways (Karger 1987; Boebert et al. 1985; Newmann et al. 1980; Rajunas et al. 1986). Some place controls over the propagation of capabilities by constraining the locations in which they can be stored. Others place additional constraints on access, beyond those specified in the capability. One approach is to use capabilities only as temporary keys for active processes and to redistribute the keys on each new access, in a manner similar to checking for access at the time a file is first opened.

Rather than being used as a mechanism by which users may control access, capabilities can act quite effectively as an underlying protection mechanism. Some of the efforts currently under way are likely eventually to give us a way to build a secure system with greater ease and flexibility than current approaches allow, but in the short run the conventional machine architecture with conventional mechanisms appears to be the most practical.

REFERENCES

Ashland, R. E. 1985. "B1 Security for Sperry 1100 Operating System." In *Proceedings of the 8th National Computer Security Conference*, pp. 105–7. Gaithersburg, Md.: National Bureau of Standards.
A description of mandatory controls proposed for Sperry (Unisys) operating systems.

Blotcky, S.; Lynch, K.; and Lipner, S. 1986. "SE/VMS: Implementing Mandatory Security in VAX/VMS." In *Proceedings of the 9th National Computer Security Conference*, pp. 47–54. Gaithersburg, Md.: National Bureau of Standards.
A description of the security enhancements offered by Digital Equipment to upgrade the security of its VMS operating system.

Boebert, W. E.; Kain, R. Y.; Young, W. D.; and Hansohn, S. A. 1985. "Secure Ada Target: Issues, System Design, and Verification." In *Proceedings of the 1985 Symposium on Security and Privacy*, pp. 176–83. Silver Spring, Md.: IEEE Computer Society.
The Secure Ada Target is a research project to use a capability-like mechanism for building a secure operating system that supports Ada programs.

Denning, D. E. 1984. "Cryptographic Checksums for Multilevel Database Security." In *Proceedings of the 1984 Symposium on Security and Privacy*, pp. 52–61. Silver Spring, Md.: IEEE Computer Society.
Discusses, among other things, the Trojan horse problem in an automated security guard.

Kahn, K. C.; Corwin, W. M.; Dennis, T. D.; D'Hooge, H.; Hubka, D. E.; Hutchins, L. A.; Montague, J. T.; Pollack, F. J.; and Gifkins, M. R. 1981. "iMAX: A Multiprocessor Operating System for an Object-Based Computer." In *Proceedings of the 8th Symposium on Operating System Principles, ACM Operating Systems Review* 15(5): 127–36.
Another capability-based system.

Karger, P. A. 1987. "Limiting the Potential Damage of Discretionary Trojan Horses." In *Proceedings of the 1987 Symposium on Security and Privacy*, pp. 32–37. Washington, D.C.: IEEE Computer Society.
Discusses a technique to limit discretionary Trojan horses on the basis of built-in knowledge of usage patterns; also provides a good overview of the problem and good references to related techniques.

Landwehr, C. E. 1983. "The Best Available Technologies for Computer Security." *Computer* 16(7): 86–100. Reprinted in *Advances in Computer System Security*, vol. 2, ed. R. Turn, pp. 108–22. Dedham, Mass.: Artech House (1984).

An overview of all past and ongoing secure system projects, with many references.

Neumann, P. G.; Boyer, R. S.; Feiertag, R. J.; Levitt, K. N.; and Robinson, L. 1980. "A Provably Secure Operating System: The System, Its Applications, and Proofs." Computer Science Lab Report CSL-116. Menlo Park, Cal.: SRI International.
The design and formal specification (using old HDM) of a capability-based operating system. The system was never implemented, but it evolved into the Secure Ada Target.

Rajunas, S. A.; Hardy, N.; Bomberger, A. C.; Frantz, W. S.; and Dundau, C. R. 1986. "Security in KeyKOS." In *Proceedings of the 1986 Symposium on Security and Privacy*, pp. 78–85. Washington, D.C.: IEEE Computer Society.
A capability-based operating system for IBM mainframes.

Schroeder, M. D. 1972. "Cooperation of Mutually Suspicious Subsystems in a Computer Utility." Ph.D. dissertation, MIT. Project MAC Report #MAC TR-104. DARPA Order #2095. (Also available through National Technical Information Service, Springfield, Va., NTIS AD-750173.)
Discusses mutually suspicious subsystems and proposes a way to use the Multics ring-based architecture to support them.

Woodward, J. P. L. 1979. "Applications for Multilevel Secure Operating Systems." *Proceedings of the NCC* 48: 319–28.
A discussion of various applications for security kernels, with a specific discussion of security guards.

Chapter *12*

Formal Specification and Verification

In section 4.3 we looked at an overview of the typical informal system development process and saw how that process is supplemented by formal techniques. The *formal specification* and *formal verification* phases of the formal system development paths (fig. 12-1) are used to increase the level of assurance that a system will meet its security requirements.

In chapter 9 we discussed mathematical concepts for defining a security model of a system, and in section 9.1 we summarized several paths—formal and informal—for demonstrating correspondence of the system to the model (illustrated in figure 9-2). Section 9.7 discussed specific techniques for following the informal paths without having to use a formal specification. The formal techniques for showing correspondence covered in this chapter closely follow the philosophy of the informal techniques, and reviewing section 9.7 will help you put these formal techniques into perspective.

Despite the similarity in some of their formal methods, you should distinguish between the process of writing a formal model and the process of writing a formal specification. Formal specifications are only useful for systems that must maintain the highest degree of security, whereas models have a much broader applicability. You need to have a model in order to write a specification, but the converse is not true.

The purpose of formal specification is to describe the functional be-

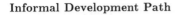

Informal Development Path   Formal Development Path

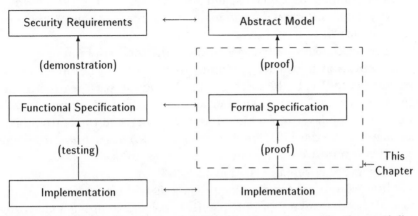

Figure 12-1. System Development Paths. *The formal specification satisfies the phase of system development corresponding to the informal functional specification.*

havior of the system in a manner that is precise, unambiguous, and amenable to computer processing. The purpose of the computer processing is to carry out various forms of analysis on the specification with minimal chance of human error. The primary goal of the analysis is to prove properties about the specification. The computer processing does not help you design and build the system: designers and implementers must read the formal specification and manually develop the software (and hardware) that satisfies the intent of the specification, much as they would use a natural-language specification.

A formal specification can be used to prove many properties about the design of a system, but our primary concern is the correspondence of the specification to the security model. Proving that the specification conforms to the functions, invariants, and constraints of the model is one step in the formal verification of a system.

Another step in the verification consists of proving that the implementation adheres to, or corresponds to, the formal specification. Unlike the specification proof, a complete formal implementation proof of a large system is but a dream with today's technology, although a great deal of research is in progress and the theory is well-understood. We may have to await much more advanced tools (perhaps even artificial intelligence) before we see a fully verified operating system. But even if we cannot formally verify all the code, the formal process gives us the advantage of a precise (and verified) specification from which to carry out an informal (largely manual) argument to support that correspondence.

When we think of formal specification, the concept of multiple layers of specification is usually predominant (fig. 12-2). The intent of the layering is to divide the large gap in abstraction between the model and the code into several smaller and (it is hoped) more manageable steps. The top layer looks most like the model, and the bottom layer looks most like the code. Proofs between the layers ensure correspondence from top to bottom. The various ways to decompose a system into layers are covered in section 12.6.

While we discuss formal specification as if the goal were to verify formally the accuracy of the specification and to prove code correspondence, a formal proof of the specification is not a mandatory part of the development process. The discipline of formally specifying a sys-

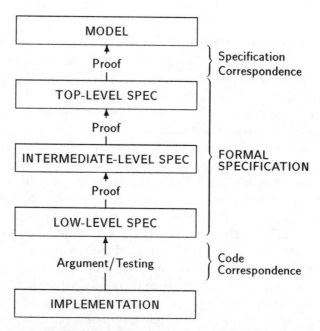

Figure 12-2. Specification Layers. *A formal specification may consist of several layers—the top layer most resembling the model, and the bottom layer most resembling the code. If verification is to be performed, the formal proof takes place between each pair of layers except with respect to the code.*

tem can be of significant benefit even if no formal verification is carried out; however, if you do not follow through and invest some substantial effort in showing specification and code correspondence, writing a specification will be a waste of time. It is particularly common to see formal specifications, written early in the design of a system and proved to be secure, lying on a shelf gathering dust as the system is implemented because nobody has taken the time to keep the specifications up to date.

12.1 FORMAL SPECIFICATION TECHNIQUES

Doing a credible job of specifying and/or verifying a system requires a collection of languages and automated tools. Only a handful of formal specification languages have been applied to sizable systems. The following four are the most popular of these:

- Gypsy Verification Environment (GVE), developed by the University of Texas (Good, Akers, and Smith 1986)
- Formal Development Methodology (FDM), developed by the System Development Group of Unisys (formerly System Development Corp.) (Scheid et al. 1986)
- Hierarchical Development Methodology (HDM), developed by SRI International (Crow et al. 1985)[1]
- AFFIRM, developed by the Information Sciences Institute at the University of Southern California (Thompson and Erickson 1981)

These systems are large and complex and differ greatly from one another. Each has notable strengths and weaknesses, and none is entirely free of problems (Cheheyl et al. 1981; Kemmerer 1986). The field of formal specification and the tools developed to handle specifications are by no means mature. These systems are called *methodologies* because they not only incorporate a specification language and related tools but prescribe a way of designing a system. While you can accomplish a great deal using only the specification language, you will obtain the greatest benefit if you adopt the design approach that these systems recommend.

The most common way to view a system (and the way employed by FDM and HDM) is as an abstract state machine—the same approach

---

1. The new, enhanced version of HDM is under development. The old HDM (Robinson, Silverberg, and Levitt 1979), though now obsolete, is the source of many concepts on which new HDM and other work in the field is based; and the old tools, particularly the MLS flow-analysis tool, are still in use.

that is used for an abstract model. This means that the system has state variables and state transition functions. In fact, to a large extent, state machine specifications are no more than complex models. The difference between a state-machine model and a state-machine specification lies in the degree of detail; the latter looks far more like a description of a real system than like an abstract statement of rules and relationships.

Gypsy specifications are significantly different from those written in FDM or HDM. Instead of modeling an abstract state machine with state variables, Gypsy employs specifications of the inputs and outputs of the individual procedures in the implementation, modeling a system in a manner that closely resembles the way it is written as a hierarchy of nested procedure calls. This technique has enjoyed some success as being the one most amenable to code proofs.

AFFIRM uses a form of specification called *algebraic* that describes the functions of a system by specifying the cumulative effect of a sequence of nested function calls. Algebraic specifications have not yet received much use for secure systems, so we shall not dwell on them in detail.

12.2 PROPERTIES OF FORMAL SPECIFICATIONS

At first glance a formal specification looks much like a computer program, with its logical and arithmetic statements, but the notation is quite different. Figure 12.3 is an example of a formal specification. The language of this example specification is not an existing language, but it resembles the style of Ina Jo (the language used in FDM) and Special (the language used in old HDM). The notation of a formal specification language is much richer than that of a programming language and allows you to express logical operations and relations not possible in a computer program—especially those involving set theory. The following will help clarify some of the notation used in the example:

`type1: SET_OF type2`	type `type1` is a set with elements of type `type2`
`var:typename`	identifier `var` is of type `typename`
`'var`	value of `var` in new state
`{var1,var2}`	set of elements
`var1 U var2`	set union
`var1 IN var2`	TRUE if `var1` is an element of set `var2`
`exp1 exp2`	boolean OR of two expressions

The functions in the specification are equivalent to function or procedure calls in a system; but unlike a computer program, the body or effect of the function is a nonprocedural description of the function and not an algorithm. The effect asserts what is true after the function completes, without saying how the function is implemented.

The statements in the functions are mathematical expressions and should not be read as if they were assignment statements in a computer program. For example, the two statements

$$`var = var + var2$$
$$var2 = `var - var$$

```
TYPES
    process                            Process name
    file                               File name
    class                              Access class
    mode: "r" | "w"                    Possible modes
    modes: SET_OF mode                 A set of modes

CONSTANTS
    init_procs (p:process): boolean    Arbitrary constants
    init_files (f:file): boolean       used for initial state
    init_class: class

VARIABLES
    proc_class (p:process): class      Access class of process p
    file_class (f:file): class         Access class of file f
    access (p:process, f:file): modes  Access modes for p to f
    file_exists (f:file): boolean      TRUE if file f exists
    proc_exists (p:process): boolean   TRUE if process p exists
    cur_proc: process                  Current process

AXIOM                                  Partial ordering of class
    FOR_ALL (c1:class, c2:class, c3:class)
        (c1 >= c1)
      & (IF c1 >= c2 & c2 >= c1 THEN c1 = c2)
      & (IF c1 >= c2 & c2 >= c3 THEN c1 >= c3)

INITIAL
    proc_exists = init_procs &
    file_exists = init_files &
    (FOR_ALL (p:process, f:file)
            SUCH_THAT (proc_exists(p) & file_exists(f))
        (proc_class (p) = init_class) &
        (file_class (f) = init_class) &
        (access (p, f) = {"r","w"}))
```

Figure 12-3. Formal Specification of Security Model. *The variables* proc_ class *and* file_class *are arrays indexed by parameters identifying processes and files, respectively. Each element of the two-dimensional* access *matrix is a set that contains zero or more of the values* "r" *or* "w"*. While all data types used in this specification are listed, most do not need to be elaborated.*

```
/* Create file f with access class c */

FUNCTION create_file (f:file, c:class)

   IF NOT file_exists (f)                        File must not already exist
   THEN 'file_exists (f)                         Make it exist
      & 'file_class (f) = c                      Set its access class
      & FOR_ALL p:process SUCH_THAT proc_exists (p)
            'access (p, f) = NULL                Give nobody access

/* Give process p access mode m to file f */

FUNCTION give_access (p:process, f:file, m:mode)

   IF (proc_exists (p) & file_exists (f))        Process and file must exist
      & ( (m = "r" &                             Mode requested is r and
            proc_class (p) >= file_class (f))      file is readable or..
       |(m = "w" &                               Mode requested is w and
            file_class (f) >= proc_class (p)))     file is writeable
   THEN 'access (p, f) = access (p, f) U {m}     Add mode to access rights

/* Rescind process p access mode m to file f */

FUNCTION rescind_access (p:process, f:file, m:mode)
   IF (proc_exists (p) & file_exists (f))        Process and file must exist
      & (m IN access (p, f))
   THEN 'access (p, f) = access (p, f) - {m}     Take away requested mode
```

Figure 12-3. Formal Specification of Security Model (continued). *Shown are functions to create a file, give a single access mode, and rescind an access mode.*

are equivalent expressions, stating a relationship between the old and new values of var and the old value of var2. The two statements

$$('var2 = 'var + 5) \ \& \ ('var = 3)$$
$$('var = 3) \ \& \ ('var2 = 8)$$

are also equivalent. No order of evaluation is implied by an ordering of expressions.

It is easy to write an expression that cannot be true:

$$'var = 3 \ \& \ 'var = 4$$

If this is the sole expression in the effect of a function, the function is attempting to force the new value of var to two different values, rendering the function inconsistent and any proof of the specification invalid. Nonetheless, although it is useless to do so, there is no harm in writing a false expression as a condition, as in:

```
IF `var = 3 & `var = 4 THEN . . .
```

Effects of functions state what must be true after a function is invoked; consequently, if the effect of a function can never be true, the function is inconsistent. For example, assume a function has the following statement as its sole effect:

```
IF a = b THEN var = 6 ELSE `var = 7
```

This says that old value of var is 6 when a = b. If a is not equal to b, the new value of var is set to 7. Because an effect of a function must always be true, this function can be inconsistent if it can be called when a = b and var does not equal 6. Placing undue constraints on the old values of variables is dangerous unless the specification shows that the function is not called under circumstances where the effect cannot be true. Some languages allow you to specify preconditions that state when the function can be called.

This last example shows that determining the inconsistency of a function depends on other functions of the specification. In general, it is meaningless to write an effect that constrains the old value of a variable to a specific value or values unless you can guarantee that the constraint will always be true. In general there must be some way to force an effect to evaluate to true through assignments of values to variables in a new state.

A specification may be *nondeterministic* in several ways:

```
`var > 3
`var = 3 | `var = 4
`var1 = `var2
```

The first statement says that the new value of var is greater than 3. A function with such a statement is nondeterministic unless another statement in the function further constrains var. The second statement allows var to have one of two possible values. The last statement says that the new values of two variables are equal. It is nondeterministic if no other statement in the same function specifies a value for one of them, but it is inconsistent if the function constrains the new values to be different.

The ability to make nondeterministic statements is of great benefit when you are writing formal specifications, because it allows you to say what is allowed without constraining the implementation and without forcing you to include unnecessary detail. One of the common forms for a function in a secure system is as follows:

> **if** *security checks fail*
> **then** *return "security error"*
> **else** *(perform function* **or** *return "other error")*

This effect prevents the function from being performed if the security checks fail, but it does not specify under what other conditions it may not be performed. The nondeterministic **else** clause allows for optional completion of the function under conditions not specified. Because a function that has no effect when it is invoked is as secure as it would be if it never were invoked, this function is just as secure as if it had been written without the **or** *return "other error"* clause or if it had been written with a detailed description of the conditions that cause *"other error"*. Since detailed descriptions just add clutter to a specification and do nothing to help prove the security of the functions, the detail can be omitted.

One final important convention applies to our specification: if a variable or array element is not specifically shown to change in a function or in one branch of a conditional (**if** statement), it is assumed to remain unchanged; and when we specify a new value for one element of an array, the other elements must not change. Though this no-change convention may seem intuitively obvious (it is clearly the convention used in programming languages), most verification systems must be told explicitly when variables do not change. This is because verification systems take the mathematical view that a function specification is like a theorem that must be proved true under the assumption that variables not specifically constrained can take on any possible values. This mathematical view of specifications, which conflicts with the programming view, is a source of some frustration and requires the user to insert numerous no-change statements throughout the specification. These no-change statements may increase the size of a specification by as much as 50 percent. In general, developing a tool that views a specification as resembling a program (and so figures out when variables mentioned in one part of a function do not change in another part) is a difficult theoretical problem.

12.3 EXAMPLE OF A FORMAL SPECIFICATION

Our example of a formal specification applies to a system that satisfies the formal model discussed in chapter 9. The variables and rules of the model are repeated in figure 12-4 for convenience. The definition of the secure state and any other constraints of the model will be addressed later, when we discuss proving the specifications.

The model has two functions: one to create an object, and one to specify access modes in the access matrix. While we could have translated the model directly into a formal specification (as you might do if you were going to write the highest of several levels of specification), it is more informative here to show a specification for a slightly more concrete system and then illustrate how that specification maps to the

---

State variables:

$$S = \text{set of current subjects}$$
$$O = \text{set of current objects}$$
$$sclass(s) = \text{access class of subject } s$$
$$oclass(o) = \text{access class of object } o$$
$$A(s,o) = \text{a set of modes, equal to one of:}$$

$\{r\}$	if subject s can read object o
$\{w\}$	if subject s can write object o
$\{r,w\}$	if both read and write
$\emptyset$	if neither read nor write

$$contents(o) = \text{contents of object } o$$
$$subj = \text{active subject}$$

Rule 1. Create_object (o,c):
  if $o \notin O$
  then $'O = O \cup \{o\}$;
    $'oclass(o) = c$;
    $'A(s,o) = \emptyset$.

Rule 2. Set_access $(s, o, modes)$:
  if $s \in S$ and $o \in O$
  and if $\{[r \in modes$ and $sclass(s) \geq oclass(o)]$ or $r \notin modes\}$
              and
    $\{[w \in modes$ and $oclass(o) \geq sclass(s)]$ or $w \notin modes\}$
  then $'A(s,o) = modes$.

Figure 12-4. Example of Formal Model. *This example is identical to the one discussed in detail in chapter 9.*

model. The specification in figure 12-3 is a partial description of a system that uses an access matrix (as in the model) but has processes and files instead of generic subjects and objects. The create_file function is similar to the **Create_object** function of the model. The give_access function is different from **Set_access,** in that it adds a single access mode (either "r" or "w") to a set of modes for an entry in the access matrix, rather than resetting the entire entry with a new set of modes. The function rescind_access takes away an access mode.

The data types of the file, class, and process identifiers are not defined in this specification. Just as nothing in the model nor in its proofs depends on how subjects, objects, or access classes are represented, the functions in this specification and proofs of this specification do not depend on the data types of these items. You might be tempted to assign names or numbers to files, but it is better to eliminate such detail in the specification.

While it is not necessary to say how the types are represented, it is often necessary to state certain properties that apply to the types. For example, we have included an AXIOM stating that the >= relation on data items of type class defines a partial order. Without this axiom, the system that processes this specification would not know how to interpret the >= operator on variables of the unspecified data type class.

All of the parameterized variables (arrays) in figure 12-3, such as file_class and file_exists, appear to be of infinite extent. Clearly the implementation must have an upper bound on the number of files, but this limit is unimportant in our specification, as in many others: it is far easier to prove properties about a specification if such limits are omitted, in all but the most detailed specifications.

12.4 SPECIFICATION-TO-MODEL CORRESPONDENCE

Proving that a specification corresponds to a model amounts to proving that the specification is one example of a system that obeys the model. If the variables and functions in the specification map one-to-one with the variables and functions in the model, little more than inspection should be required to prove the correspondence. But in general it is necessary to write *mappings* between the model and specification.

Figure 12-5 describes these mappings in mathematical terms, using the example specification and the model. The mappings for types, parameters, and variables are nearly one-to-one with those in the model. The purpose of the parameter mappings is to show how dummy variables used in the mapping translate into variables in the specification.

Mappings for Types

subject	process
object	file
access class	class
access mode	mode

Mappings for parameters

s:subject	p:process
o:object	f:file
c:access class	c:class
m:access mode	m:mode

Mappings for variables

O	SET_OF {f:file SUCH_THAT file_exists(f)}
S	SET_OF {p:process SUCH_THAT proc_exists(p)}
$olev(o)$	file_class(f)
$slev(s)$	proc_class(p)
$A(s,o)$	access(p, f)

Mappings for Functions

Create_object(o,c)	create_file(f,c)
Set_access($s,o,modes$)	if r ∈ *modes*
	then give_access (p, f, "r")
	else rescind_access (p, f, "r")
	and
	if w ∈ *modes*
	then give_access (p, f, "w")
	else rescind_access (p, f, "w")

Figure 12-5. Mappings between Specification and Model. The variables and rules of operation in the model depicted in figure 12-4 are mapped onto the variables and functions in the specification of figure 12-3.

Since arrays in both the model and the specification are of infinite extent, it is acceptable to map *slev(s)*, for example, onto proc_class(p) without bounding the value of *s*. If proc_class were finite, containing only access classes of processes that exist, the mapping would have to be qualified to constrain *s* to values that are elements of *S*. Expressing the mapping of a finite subset of values of *s* onto values of p would also be quite complicated. The only difficult mapping in the example is that of **Set_access.** This function of the model maps to a combination of calls to give_access and rescind_access (no ordering implied).

Since we are mapping this specification to the model, we must prove that the specification adheres to the same definition of the secure state and to any additional constraints that we have proved about the model.

The mappings for the variables and functions in figure 12-5 allow us to translate the definition and constraints of the model into terms of the specification, by simple substitution (figure 12-6). It is necessary to prove the following theorem for each function in the specification:

if INVARIANT and *body of function*
then ' INVARIANT and CONSTRAINTS

where ' INVARIANT represents the INVARIANT with all references to variables replaced by their new values.

The mapping for **Constraint 1** in figure 12-6 is trivially satisfied by our specification, because file_class never changes for any file that

---

MODEL

Invariant: The system is *secure* if and only if, for all $s \in S, o \in O$,
    if $r \in A(s,o)$ then $sclass(s) \geq oclass(o)$,
    if $w \in A(s,o)$ then $oclass(o) \geq sclass(s)$.

Constraint 1: For all $o \in O$,
    $'oclass(o) \geq oclass(o)$.

Constraint 2: For all $o \in O$,
    if $r \notin A(subj, o)$
    then for all $s \in S$, $'A(s,o) = A(s,o)$.

SPECIFICATION

INVARIANT

```
FOR_ALL (p:process, f:file) SUCH_THAT (file_exists (f) AND proc_exists (p))
    (IF "r" IN access (p,f)
        THEN proc_class (p) >= file_class (f))
    & (IF "w" IN access (p,f)
        THEN file_class (f) >= proc_class (p))
```

CONSTRAINTS

```
FOR_ALL f:file SUCH_THAT file_exists (f)
    'file_class (f) >= file_class (f)

FOR_ALL f:file SUCH_THAT file_exists (f)
    IF NOT ("r" IN access (cur_proc, f))
    THEN FOR_ALL p:process SUCH_THAT proc_exists (p)
        'access (p, f) = access (p, f)
```

Figure 12-6. Mappings of Secure State and Constraints. The definition of the secure state and the constraints of the model map directly to an INVARIANT *and* CONSTRAINTS *by simple variable substitution from the mappings in figure 12-5.*

already exists. For purposes of illustration we have also included **Constraint 2** and its mapping, even though it is not satisfied by our specification (nor by the model, as we discussed in section 9.5.2): both give_access and rescind_access fail to check for "r" access by the current process before modifying the access matrix.

12.5 TECHNIQUES FOR PROVING SPECIFICATIONS

Proving specifications is so complex and error-prone that nobody trusts manual proofs; an automated tool is needed. These tools, called *theorem provers*, vary in sophistication from proof checkers that ensure the correctness of manual steps to artificial intelligence aids that grind away for hours on their own. Integrated specification and proof systems automatically generate the necessary theorems, based on the axioms, functions, invariants, constraints, and other elements of the specification.

The current state of the art in proving specifications has advanced sufficiently to make it feasible to prove constraints and invariants on large specifications containing thousands of lines, with reasonable confidence that the specification is indeed secure. ("Reasonable confidence" is the best we can achieve because theorem provers cannot detect all possible inconsistent ways to write a specification. If you work at it, you may be able to make the system prove false theorems—that is, formulas that are not true.) You can expect to expend far more effort in doing the proof than in writing the specification, however, so you should not take the decision to do proofs lightly. Again, there is value in writing a specification even if no proofs are done. Furthermore, proofs of specifications rarely detect true design errors: by the time you get to the proof stage, you will have manually caught most such errors. The inability to prove a portion of a specification is usually attributable to a typographical error or to a specification that was written in a legitimate and secure form that the proof system nonetheless cannot handle. Still, a proof does give you confidence that your specification (on which, presumably, you are basing the design of the system) does not have a serious security flaw.

12.6 METHODS OF DECOMPOSITION

At one extreme, you can have a specification that is very abstract and closely resembles the model (as does our example); in such instances you must deal with the difficult task of convincingly demonstrating the correspondence between the code and the specification. At a much more detailed level, the specification might closely match the operations visible at the interface to the system—function for function, and parameter for parameter. Such a specification will be very complex and unreadable, and a formal proof that it corresponds to the model may be impractical. These alternatives are shown qualitatively in figure 12-7. At an even more detailed extreme, the specification represents the internal procedures of the system rather than the visible interface. The correspondence proof to the model may be extremely difficult (or at least no easier than the second case), but the correspondence to the code may be close enough to permit a partial proof.

Several specification techniques deal with these large differences in levels of abstraction in various ways. They correspond, roughly, to the techniques used in FDM, old HDM, and Gypsy, although some techniques are used by more than one methodology.

12.6.1 Data Structure Refinement

The *data structure refinement* method, used in our example and in FDM, employs a refinement of detail at different levels of abstraction. Each layer of specification is a state machine that completely describes the system. The top layer is highly abstract and combines multiple data types, variables, and functions into a few simple functions. The second layer adds more detail, possibly dividing generic functions about subjects and objects at the top layer into specific functions about specific types of objects. Once the second layer is written and has been shown to map into the upper layer (in the sense that we mapped the specification into the model in our example), the upper-layer specification is no longer needed. The second layer is a more concrete description

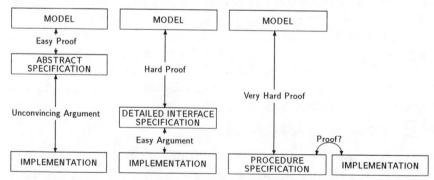

Figure 12-7. Extremes of Specification Detail. *A detailed specification will make the code correspondence simpler but the formal proof harder (and maybe impractical), whereas a highly abstract specification will make the code correspondence impractical or unconvincing.*

of the system and, when proved to satisfy the mapped invariants and constraints, satisfies the same security properties as the top layer.

Similarly, we can add more detail at the next-lower layer and have yet more functions. Once we add a layer, do the mappings to the upper layer, and complete the proofs, we no longer need the upper layers (unless we someday need to modify and re-prove the lower layer). The bottom layer (the one closest to the implementation) may closely correspond to variables and functions in the code, making it a very precise and detailed description of the interface to the system and a specification from which designers can implement a system.

The data structure refinement technique does not provide you with any clues for designing the internals of the system. The lowest level of specification only describes the system interface; it says nothing about the design. Making a credible code correspondence argument that the underlying software accurately implements this specification requires traditional software engineering techniques such as code inspection and testing.

12.6.2 Algorithmic Refinement

In contrast to the data structure refinement technique, whose lowest-layer specification presents the external view of the system, the *algorithmic refinement* technique, used in HDM and illustrated in table 12-1, allows you to specify some of the internal structure of the system. The technique most directly applies to systems designed with internal layers, as discussed in section 11.1. The technique views a system as a series of layered abstract state machines. Each machine makes available a set of functions for use by the machine above. The implementation of each function in a machine consists of an abstract program that calls functions in the machine below. (For simplicity, only call statements are shown in the programs in the table, but in general the programs may contain the usual semantics of programming languages.) The lowest-level machine provides the most primitive functions of the system—those that cannot be further decomposed.

The abstract machine concept is best illustrated with an example of a three-layer machine implementing a file system (table 12-2). The bottom, most primitive machine (machine 0) knows only about disks, disk blocks, and memory. It provides a few primitive functions, such as

```
disk_block_read(disk_name,block_address,
            buffer_address)
```

and knows nothing about the concept of files or access control.

Layer	Formal Specifications	Abstract Programs		
	interface to system ↓			
N	top-level machine (interface specification) func A func B	proc A_N call A_{N-1} call C_{N-1} return	proc B_N call B_{N-1} call A_{N-1} return	
$N-1$	intermediate machine func A func B func C	proc A_{N-1} call A_{N-2} call C_{N-2} return	proc B_{N-1} call B_{N-2} call A_{N-2} call A_{N-2} return	proc C_{N-1} call C_{N-2} return
$N-2$	intermediate machine	proc A_{N-2}	proc B_{N-2}	proc C_{N-2}
⋮	⋮	⋮	⋮	⋮
1	intermediate machine	proc A_1	proc B_1	
0	primitive machine	proc A_0	proc B_0	⋯

Table 12-1. Algorithmic Refinement. The approach of specifying layered abstract machines allows the internal structure of a system (below the top-level interface) to be modeled. The top-level machine provides the functions visible at the interface to the system.

Machine 1 provides a primitive flat file system, with functions typical of a file system manager:

```
file_descriptor = open(file_index)
file_read(file_descriptor,offset,buffer)
```

where `file_index` is simply an integer pointing to the file on disk. The implementation of functions in machine 1 consists of abstract programs that use the functions of machine 0 to create a file system out of disk blocks, using file indexes (stored on disk blocks) to keep track of multiple files and using file descriptors stored in memory to keep track of open files.

Machine 2 implements a hierarchical file system containing directories and files within directories. It provides file names as strings of characters and functions for access control to files. It implements directories (using files in machine 1) that store names of files and access control information.

In the algorithmic refinement technique, the highest-layer machine implements the interface to the system as it appears to users. Each

Abstract Machine	Data Structures	Functions
Machine 2	Files Directories	Create/delete files/directories Read/write files Access control functions
Machine 1	Files File descriptors	Create/delete files Read/write files
Machine 0	Disk blocks	Read/write disk blocks

Table 12-2. Example of Three-Machine System. *The higher-level machines provide increasingly more complex file system functions.*

function call at the interface results in a possible cascade of calls to lower-layer machines.

When you write a specification using this technique, you write two things for each abstract machine: a formal state-machine specification that resembles a single-layer specification of the sort used in the data structure refinement technique; and an abstract program for each function in the machine, providing an algorithmic description of the function in terms of calls to functions in the lower-layer machine. Code correspondence proofs using a specification such as this require proving that the abstract programs at all layers correspond to the real programs in the system.

Proof of a specification developed with these techniques first requires proving that the highest-layer machine specification corresponds to the model, in a manner identical to the one used to prove a specification in the data structure refinement technique. Then, in a manner analogous to (but mechanically quite different from) proving the consistency of mappings between layers, we must prove that the abstract program for the highest-layer machine correctly implements its specification, given the specification of the functions of the next-lower-layer machine. The process is repeated down to the lowest layer, at which point we must assume that the specification of the lowest layer primitive machine is implemented correctly. In the overall proof, it is necessary to specify how data structures in each machine are mapped onto data structures in the next-lower machine.

Each layer in the real system corresponds to a layer of the specification, with functions that closely match the functions in the abstract programs. As a result, it should be much easier to argue for correspondence between the specification and the code in this case than if you had only an interface specification, as in the data structure refinement technique. In fact, it has been proposed (but never proved) that someday it might be possible to write a translator that converts an abstract program into a computer-language program.

Unfortunately, the algorithmic refinement technique suffers from several drawbacks that make its use a bit more theoretical than practical (though pieces of practical systems have been developed using this technique and show promise for the near future). The primary drawback is the difficulty involved in carrying out proofs of the abstract algorithms. It is much more difficult to prove an algorithm than to prove a mapping, and such a proof becomes intractable for all but fairly small algorithms. Abstract program proofs differ little from concrete program proofs; the only reason there is greater hope of proving abstract programs is that these programs can be written in a highly restricted language that need not deal with many details of real programming.

Another drawback—this one far from fatal—is that the top-level specification is quite complex because it represents the real interface to the system. Because the specification is so close to the real system, proving its correspondence directly to the model has all the same problems with level of detail that we faced with the data structure refinement technique, where we proposed a single very detailed specification between the model and the code (the leftmost extreme of figure 12-7).

The reason this second drawback is not fatal is that nothing restrains us from applying the multiple levels of the data structure refinement technique above the top-level abstract machine (fig. 12-8). Using this method, we can have the best benefits of both worlds; do not go to your corner software store looking for an off-the-shelf system that implements this combination of techniques—at least for a few years.

12.6.3 Procedural Abstraction

Gypsy's specification technique might be called *procedural abstraction.* Gypsy directly models the way a system is implemented: as a set of nested procedure calls. As in the algorithmic refinement technique, each function in a Gypsy specification is equivalent to a function in the implementation, but Gypsy does not require the system to be built in layers, as does HDM. The specification of a Gypsy function describes how the function manipulates its arguments, not how the function affects a global state of the system. Gypsy goes further than HDM and FDM in allowing you to specify the functions of every internal procedure in the system, not just the interface to the system or to each layer.

Because Gypsy specifications are so closely aligned to the code (in

Data Structure Refinement

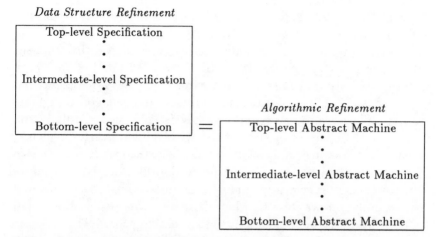

Figure 12-8. Combination of Specification Techniques. *Though not yet demonstrated in practice, a merge of both the data structure refinement and algorithmic refinement techniques can achieve the benefits of both.*

fact, the Gypsy language includes a PASCAL-like programming language),
Gypsy might be viewed as more a program-proving system than a specification system. But Gypsy does permit you to write specifications
without code and to prove abstract properties about those specifications
without writing the programs. When used in this manner, the specification for the set of top-level procedures accessible from outside the
system resembles the specifications for the top-layer interface machine
in HDM and for the bottom-layer interface in FDM.

12.7 INFORMATION-FLOW ANALYSIS

The concept of information flow was introduced in section 9.6 as a
way of addressing deficiencies in the state-machine modeling technique—where the concept of a secure state and constraints on state
transitions are insufficient to prevent certain nonsecure information
flows, such as covert channels—while permitting legitimate functions.
Information-flow analysis is a general technique for analyzing leakage
paths in a system (Lampson 1973; Denning 1983); it is applicable to
any security model. The technique can be applied to programs or to
specifications, although the rules governing the two applications are
different. At present, we shall discuss how to apply information-flow
analysis to nonprocedural formal specifications, in order to support the
proof that a specification meets a mandatory multilevel security policy.

Later, in section 12.7.2, we shall briefly discuss the use of flow analysis with programs.

Before beginning any flow analysis effort, you must realize that the flow analysis of the specification—like any other proof of the specification—is only meaningful to the extent that the implementation corresponds to the specification. While this should be an obvious point, many people seem to focus on flow analysis as being particularly vulnerable to deficiencies in state-of-the-art of proving correspondence, when in fact flow analysis is no more vulnerable than other techniques.

You might convince yourself of the need for flow analysis by noting that our example specification in figure 12-4 has several covert channels. The example allows for a number of write-downs (see section 6.4.4), by permitting the actions of a process at a high access class to be detected by a process at a lower access class. One such case is in the file_exists array, where a high process can create a file and a lower process can determine that the file already exists by trying to recreate the file and noting that the access array did not change. (Although they are not shown, we presume that the complete system has functions that return information about what accesses are allowed, either by asking directly or by attempting an access and getting a failure.)

Using the multilevel security policy as our requirement, we find that the complete statement of an informations flow policy is very obvious:

Flow Policy: *If information flows from object A to object B in a state transition, the access class of B must dominate the access class of A.*

It seems apparent that this policy fulfills the intent of the multilevel security policy.

In theory, if you can eliminate all *flow violations* in a system (or in a model of a system), the system (or model) has neither covert nor overt channels, and there is no need to perform any of the invariant or constraint proofs about secure states and state transitions.[2] Unfortunately, deciding what is and what is not a flow is not always easy; and tools that perform flow analysis, because they are ultraconservative in finding flows, are usually insufficient to justify our declaring a specification completely clean. You usually have to carry out an error-prone informal analysis to vindicate the apparent flow violations. For these practical

2. As we shall see later, sometimes the proof of a flow formula requires you to write and prove an invariant as a lemma. Such an invariant might closely resemble the secure state invariant that you would prove about the model.

reasons, the invariant and correspondence proofs add considerably to the assurance in the security of the specification, even though flow analysis theoretically might be sufficient. (Real systems are also never completely free of real flow violations, so the manual analysis would be required even if the tools were perfect.)

An information flow can be viewed as a cause-and-effect relationship between two variables w and v. In any function where v is modified and w is referenced, there is flow from variable w to variable v (written $w \rightarrow v$) if any information about the value of w in the old state can be deduced by observing the value of v in the new state. For simplicity, we do not explicitly show the new value in the notation (as in $w \rightarrow 'v$), but the understanding is that the flow always moves from a variable in an old state to a variable in a new state.

When analyzing functions in a model or specification, if we cannot tell ahead of time whether a particular function will result in a flow, we play it safe and flag it anyway. Such is the case when the flow occurs only under certain conditions that are not explicit in the definition of the function being analyzed. In fact, when looking at isolated functions, we can never tell whether a potential flow is an actual flow. Only by looking at the system as a whole can we identify the real flows. Thus, when we talk about a flow in a function, we almost always mean a potential flow. Sometimes it is possible to rewrite the function or specification so as to eliminate the potential flow. In such a case, the potential flow is called a *formal flow* because it appears only as a result of the form in which the specification is written.

The process of flow analysis includes both finding the flows and proving that they do not violate flow policy. The functions are observed one at a time, each expression in the function is analyzed, and each flow between a pair of variables is written as a flow statement. (Rules for finding the flows from expressions are covered in section 12.7.1.) A given function may yield many flow statements. A flow may occur only under certain conditions, depending on the values of other variables, so in general a flow statement has the following form:

Flow Statement: If *condition*, then $A \rightarrow B$

where *condition* is some expression, and A and B are variables.

To decide whether a flow expressed in a flow statement is safe according to the flow policy, we generate from each flow statement a flow formula having the following form:

Flow Formula: If *condition*, then *class(B)* $\geq$ *class (A)*

where *condition* is the same as in the flow statement, *class(x)* means "the access class of *x*," and $\geq$ is a symbol meaning *dominates*. Proving that there are no flow violations in a function requires proving that each flow formula is true. If the formula cannot be proved, it may represent a real or formal flow violation that must then be justified. To assist you in proving the flow formulas, you may use invariants or constraints in the specification (provided that the specification has already been proved to satisfy the invariants and constraints), or you may write new invariants that you subsequently have to prove.

Notice that the flow formula is defined in terms of the access classes of variables. Probably the most restrictive aspect of information-flow analysis for multilevel security is the need to define an access class manually for every variable in the specification—even for internal state variables that are not objects according to the security policy. If you choose the wrong access class, a flow violation will show up, so you do not have to worry about introducing an undetected error in this process. But in many cases, no matter what access class you pick, a formal flow violation will be committed in some function somewhere, even though the specification may be secure and may exhibit no covert channels. Sometimes you can eliminate a flow by rewriting the specification, but that may make the specification so obscure that correspondence to the code is extremely difficult to demonstrate.

Information-flow analysis is something of an art. The rules for deciding when information flow is possible are complex and difficult to apply by hand. In practice, flow analysis is rarely done on a system at the level of an abstract model. While a flow analysis of a model can indeed catch many potential flow violations, it will also miss most of the interesting ones. This is because a model leaves out many details of a system, such as state variables and functions that do not affect the security state of the system as represented in the access matrices. Yet it is precisely these internal state variables that provide the paths for covert channels. Flow analysis on a model can catch these only if the operations on such variables are represented in the functions of the model.

12.7.1 Flow Rules

At the current state of the art, automated flow tools work syntactically. Semantic assumptions that the flow tool makes about a specification are based solely on the syntactic style in which the specification is written, not on what the specification says: if you write the same secure function in two different ways you may get different flow formulas, some of which are true and some of which are false. The false formulas are due to the ultraconservative nature of the analysis, which finds all possible flows but also flags many formal flows.

Syntactic flow analysis is based on a number of simple rules. Given a form of expression in a specification, a *flow rule* specifies the potential flows. Following are examples of two simple flow rules:

Flow Rule 1. In the equality statement with a single new-value operator,

$$'v = expression$$

where *expression* is an arbitrary expression containing no new values, there is an unconditional flow from all variables mentioned in *expression* to v. This includes all variables appearing as parameters of functions and indices of arrays in *expression*.

Flow Rule 2. To find the flows in the statement,

$$\textbf{if } condition \textbf{ then } statement\text{-}1 \textbf{ else } statement\text{-}2$$

where *statement-i* are of the form of the statement in flow rule 1, analyze *statement-1* and *statement-2* for flows according to flow rule 1. When *condition* is true, all the flows in *statement-1* occur; when *condition* is false those in *statement-2* occur. There are also unconditional flows from all variables mentioned in *condition* to all variables that are the target of flows in *statement-1* and *statement-2*.

The preceding rules, though too simple to take care of all cases (especially those where the new value of a variable appears in the expression), can be used to analyze some of the expressions in the examples in table 12-3.

Examples 1 and 2 illustrate flow rule 1, where a flow occurs from any variable in an expression—even when it is in a parameter of a function in an array index—to the new value of the variable. We do not bother with flows from constants: constants are considered to have SYSTEM LOW access class, so any flow from a constant is safe. In the example, the function *f(x)* is a constant function of the variable x. In example 2, we have an array *var* that is a variable; consequently, we have to show that a flow occurs from the specific array element to the new value, as well as from the variable used as the array subscript. Example 3 illustrates flow rule 2, where the flows in each branch of a

Example	Flows	Rationale
1. $'v = w + f(x) + 5$ $[f(x)$ is a constant$]$	$w \rightarrow v$ $x \rightarrow v$	Flow from old values to new values in expression; no flows from constants.
2. $'v = var(w)$	$w \rightarrow v$ $var(w) \rightarrow v$	
3. if $a = 1$ then $'v = w$ else $'v = x$	if $a = 1$ then $w \rightarrow v$ if $a \neq 1$ then $x \rightarrow v$ $a \rightarrow v$	Unconditional $a \rightarrow v$ because $'v$ depends on w.
4. if $w = 1$ then $'v = 5$ else $'v = 6$	$w \rightarrow v$	
5. if $w = 1$ then $'v = 2$ else $'v = w$	$w \rightarrow v$	

6.   if $w = 1$ then $'c = 1$ and
                  $'v = x$
      else $'c = 3$ and
                  $'v = x$
	$w \rightarrow c$
	 $x \rightarrow v$
		No $w \rightarrow v$ because $'v = x$ unconditionally.

7.   if $w = 1$ then $'c = 1$ and
                  $'v = 'c$
      else $'c = 3$ and
                  $'v = 'c$
	$w \rightarrow c$
	 $w \rightarrow v$
		No $c \rightarrow v$ because old value of c is irrelevant.

8.   if $w = 1$ then $'c = 2$ and
                  $'v = 'c + 1$
      else $'v = c - 1$
	if $w \neq 1$ then $c \rightarrow v$
	 $w \rightarrow v$
	 $w \rightarrow c$	

9.   if $w = 1$ then $'c = a$ and
                  $'v = 'c + 1$
      else $'c = a$ and
                  $'v = 'c - 1$
	$a \rightarrow c$
	 $a \rightarrow v$
	 $w \rightarrow v$
		No $w \rightarrow c$ because $'c = a$ unconditionally.

10. $'v = a$	$a \rightarrow v$	
11. $'a = c$	$c \rightarrow a$	
12. if $a = b$ then $'w > v$	"everything" $\rightarrow w$	Nondeterministic assignment is flow from all variables.

Table 12-3. Examples of Flow Analysis. *This table illustrates the flows that result from various types of expressions that might appear in a specification.*

conditional statement are conditional and where an unconditional flow occurs from the variable a mentioned in the condition. The latter flow occurs because the value of w can be deduced from the new value of v. You may argue that, if in example 4 we end up with $'v = 6$, we do not know much about w, but information flow analysis does not try to quantify the amount of flow: that is a job for a covert channel analysis of the resultant system, which serves to determine the bandwidth of any covert channels revealed by information-flow analysis (see section 7.2).

In example 6, a flow tool operating according to our rules would indicate a flow that was not there. According to flow rule 2, we should indicate the flow $w{\rightarrow}v$; but no such flow exists, since v is set to the same value regardless of w. By moving the assignment to $'v$ outside the **if** statement, we can make the formal flow disappear.

Example 7 contains statements in which the new value of a variable appears in places other than on the left-hand side of an $=$ sign, making our flow rules inappropriate for such cases. The example illustrates that flows only originate from old values of variables, not from new values. It also shows that, even though v is not the target of any flows according to flow rule 1, it still is the target of a flow from w, thereby violating flow rule 2. Syntactically, examples 6 and 7 are nearly identical, yet the flows they exhibit are different.

The rules for finding flow depend not only on the specification language but on the specific security properties that the flow analysis is intended to support. In particular, net flow after a succession of state transitions depends on the order in which the functions are invoked. For example, if our specification has two functions—one whose effect is example 10 in the table, and the other whose effect is example 11— the net flows for 10 followed by 11 are as follows:

$$a{\rightarrow}v \text{ and } c{\rightarrow}a$$

just as indicated in the table. But if 11 is followed by 10, the new value of v depends on the original value of c, and the original value of a is irrelevant. (The new value of a after the first statement serves as the old value of a for the second.) The net flow is thus

$$c{\rightarrow}a \text{ and } c{\rightarrow}v$$

apparently indicating that there is a flow $c{\rightarrow}v$ that we did not find when we analyzed the statements in the table independently. (The flow from a has also disappeared).

In general, this omission of a flow would indicate a fatal flaw in the flow analysis technique by which you examine functions individually; but if we look at the flow formulas that we have to prove for multilevel security, such an omission can introduce no new flow violations. While the net flow depends on the order of the functions, the security relationship we want to prove about the flows does not. The two flows $a{\rightarrow}v$ and $c{\rightarrow}a$ require us to prove that

$$class(v){\geqslant}class(a) \text{ and } class(a){\geqslant}class(c)$$

Transitivity allows us to conclude that

$$class(v) \geq class(c)$$

which is exactly the same formula that we would need to prove if we had detected the flow $c \rightarrow v$. While order of statements affects the flows, order has no effect on the multilevel security analysis of the flow formulas. The transitivity of the multilevel security relationship we have termed *dominates* permits us to use flow analysis to determine whether individual functions are secure and allows us to declare an entire specification secure if all the individual functions are. If we were to use flow analysis to prove a nontransitive security relationship that depends on the order of function calls, we would have to worry about all possible sequences of functions and would have little hope of analyzing a specification for flow in a practical manner.

Another important note about flow analysis relates to nondeterminism. If a function contains a nondeterministic expression involving a new value of a variable, the variable may take on any of several values, and the selection of the new value may depend on any other state variable in the specification. Hence there is a potential flow from all variables in the specification to the new value—even from variables not mentioned in the function. Unless you have an invariant or constraint that limits the new value to one specific value, or unless the variable's access class is SYSTEM HIGH, it will be impossible to prove that the function is secure. You would have to supplement the flow analysis with some type of informal argument that the nondeterminism is secure. Thus, while nondeterminism is an important convenience in writing formal specifications, it should not be used (except to a very limited extent) in specifications that are subjected to flow analysis.

One way out of this dilemma is to write two or more levels of specification, where the top level is very general and nondeterministic and the lower level is fully deterministic. The flow analysis need (and should) only be performed on the lowest level. Another trick is to write a deterministic expression that sets the new value to some unspecified, but constant, function of other variables:

$$'w = f(x,y,z)$$

For flow analysis purposes, it does not matter what the constant function f is, so no elaboration on the definition of f is needed. You only need to list all the variables that might be input as parameters to that function. If the flows $x{\to}w, y{\to}w$, and $z{\to}w$ are secure, and if the statement accurately represents all possible dependencies on the new value of w, the nondeterminism is eliminated with little adverse impact on the generality of the specification.

12.7.2 Flow Analysis Process

Because the syntactic flow analysis technique only flags potential flow violations, additional covert channel analysis is required to determine whether the violations are real. There are no tools that help you do this, since it requires looking at the specification as a whole and deducing or proving additional properties. A typical argument to support the contention that a flow is not real would be based on the fact that the specification lacks certain functions that could exploit the flow. If the function is later added to the specification, the violation could become real even though no existing function changes.

As a very simple example, consider example 8 in table 12-3, and assume that the flow $c{\to}v$ is a violation. If we can prove that w is always 1, we will establish that this flow never occurs, but doing so requires that we examine the entire specification for places where w is set. Even if we prove that $w \neq 1$, we risk reintroducing the flow each time we add a new function that might affect w. Thus, when we add a function to the specification, we do not have to re-prove the flow formulas for existing functions; but we do have to rejustify all the failed proofs that depended on knowledge of other functions.

Formal flow analysis is ruthless, requiring you to look at every reference to every state variable of the system. In fact, flow analysis is not valid unless every variable is involved, because it is all too easy for a covert channel to sneak in via a variable that has not been examined. Because flow analysis of a specification only tells you whether or not the specification is secure—and nothing about the security of the implementation—it would be best to do flow analysis on the code. But, though the state of the art of flow analysis seems to work fairly well with detailed formal specifications, it does not work well with code. (Some effort with respect to code flow analysis has shown promise (Tsai, Gligor, and Chandersekaran 1987).)

Finding flows by hand is hard and tedious, although it has been done on fairly large specifications. It is best done with one of several automated flow analysis tools (sometimes called *flow table generators*) that perform a simple syntactic analysis of a machine-readable specification and generate tables of potential flows with the proper conditions. The flow tables are examined either manually or with the aid of another tool that attempts to prove that each flow is allowed. Flow analysis tools are available for old HDM (called the MLS *formula generator*) (Feiertag 1980), FDM (Eckmann 1987), and Gypsy (Haigh et al. 1987).

Because flow tools require that you assign access classes to all variables, they flag many internal flows as potentially insecure even though the net effect may be secure. Therefore a flow tool works best on a specification whose internal variables are largely segregated according to access class. For example, if all variables referenced in functions available to a process are treated as arrays indexed by process ID, a great many potential flows will be avoided. Whether such a specification accurately reflects the implementation depends on the underlying architecture.

Another technique for covert channel analysis—the *Shared Resource Matrix* (SRM) (Kemmerer 1983)—is very similar to flow analysis in the way it which it detects covert channels. In addition to looking at each function individually, however, the SRM requires a process called *transitive closure* that analyzes the specification as a whole. The SRM technique does not require you to assign access classes to all internal variables, thereby eliminating a significant source of frustration in flow analysis, and does not require determinism. But as a result it cannot prove that individual functions are secure in isolation. Transitive closure takes into account interactions between functions, and detects cases where adding a seemingly secure function to an existing secure system renders the result insecure. The SRM technique has been used successfully on several projects, but the analysis has been largely manual: tools to support the technique simplify the matrix generation but do not assist in any proofs. All potential channels, even trivial ones, have to be manually examined and justified. Because you do not have to specify access classes of internal variables, the SRM technique is much better suited to examining code than is flow analysis, although experience in using it for this purpose has been minimal (Tsai, Gligor, and Chandersekaran 1987).

12.8 CODE CORRESPONDENCE PROOFS

The theory for proving programs correct has been around for many years (Floyd 1967; Hoare 1978), but practice lags far behind and will remain so for the foreseeable future. There are a number of reasons for this lag:

- The proofs become exceedingly complex as programs become larger, so that the proof effort is many times greater than the effort to write the program.

- Popular high-order programming languages are not designed for provability, making proofs hopeless without severe programming restrictions.
- The few languages that were designed for provability suffer from inefficiencies that make them unsuitable for many applications.
- Tools to assist program proofs (either to check the correctness of proofs done manually or to carry out proofs on their own) and proof techniques are in their infancy. Theorem provers designed for specification proofs are not suitable for programs.

Nobody doubts that it is possible to prove the correctness of programs, but few people believe that it is practical or cost effective to do so, even for the most highly secure systems. The largest high-order language program ever proved was on the order of 1,000 lines.

Unlike specification proofs, for which it is only necessary to prove fairly simple selected properties related to security, proving that a program satisfies its specification entails proving the complete correctness of the program. This is because there is no a priori way to determine whether any aspect of a program will affect its specification. Some researchers have concentrated on proving programs directly, using flow analysis (and without using a specification), thereby minimizing the need to do correctness proofs of the system. Such techniques are in their infancy, however.

Even though we cannot do the proofs of a program formally, we can talk about the process as if it were possible, use formal techniques when practical, and use informal demonstration when proofs are infeasible. Regardless of the specification technique we are using, program proof means showing that a procedure meets its formal specification—one procedure at a time corresponding to one function in the specification. In the algorithmic refinement technique in table 12-1, we have top-level procedures that implement the functions in the interface specification and lower-level procedures that implement functions in intermediate abstract machine specifications. If we use only the data structure refinement technique, we do not have the benefit of internal layers of specification to break the proof into smaller pieces, and therefore we must prove that the entire implementation corresponds to the lowest-level (interface) specification. But with either specification technique, the proof approach is the same.

The initial steps in the proof of a procedure require mapping variables, parameters, and types in the formal specification of the function onto global variables, types, and parameters used in the procedure—much as we mapped the top-level specification into the model, or levels of hierarchical specification into each other. In the Gypsy system, the specification language is integrated with an implementation language, so the specification already uses the same data types and variables as are used in the program. But if your program is written in PL/I, C, or PASCAL, there will be no obvious correspondence, and a mapping will be required.

The technique of program proof requires the programmer to write down entry assertions and exit assertions for each procedure in the system. *Entry assertions* state relationships between all global variables in the system and parameters to the procedure that are true upon entry to the procedure. *Exit assertions* state properties that are true upon return from the procedure (fig. 12-9). Proving that a program is correct involves proving that it meets its exit assertions. The following formula is to be proved:

> Entry assertions **and** effects of code **imply** exit assertions.

The *effects of code* are the accumulated sequential effects of all the statements in the procedure. In general, though, you cannot do a proof of a procedure in one fell swoop. Instead, the procedure is divided into sections of code, and a *verification condition* is written that states the formula to be proved for each section.

Program	Assertions
procedure	$\longleftarrow$ entry_proc1
s1	
s2	
s3	
call proc2	$\longleftarrow$ entry_proc2
	$\longleftarrow$ exit_proc2
s4	
s5	
call proc3	$\longleftarrow$ entry_proc3
s6	$\longleftarrow$ exit_proc3
return	
	$\longleftarrow$ exit_proc1

Verification Conditions
1. *entry_proc1* & *S1* & *S2* & *S3* → *entry_proc2*
2. *entry_proc1* & *S1* & *S2* & *S3* & *exit_proc2* & *S4* & *S5* → *entry_proc3*
3. *entry_proc1* & *S1* & *S2* & *S3* & *exit_proc2* & *S4* & *S5* & *exit_proc3* & *S6* → *exit_proc1*

Figure 12-9. Use of Entry and Exit Assertions. *It is necessary to prove that, given the entry assertions for* proc1, *the statements in the procedure satisfy the entry assertions for all called procedures, as well as satisfying the exit assertion for* proc1.

If the procedure is a simple function that executes an in-line sequence of statements based on its parameters and then returns, the *effects of code* may be easy to determine. If the procedure calls nested procedures, the entry assertions for the nested procedures must be proved to be satisfied by the program at the point each procedure is called. Then the exit assertions for the nested procedure can be taken as the *effects of code* for the procedure call statement.

Through the use of entry and exit assertions, each procedure can be proved in isolation—looking only at the assertions, and not at the body of any other called procedure. If a procedure is modified but its entry and exit assertions remain the same, the proofs of procedures that call it need not be redone. In fact, a primary benefit of this approach is that you can design a system as a tree of procedure calls with only entry and exit assertions and no code. You can then implement and prove the procedures in any order, redoing a proof only when an assertion used in that proof changes. Gypsy benefits greatly in this respect because the programs and assertions are integrated, and it is easy to track when a procedure changes that might affect assertions used elsewhere.

As you can see in figure 12-9, the verification conditions get quite large as you accumulate statements and exit assertions from called procedures, even if many of the statements and assertions are irrelevant to subsequent assertions. A way to reduce these is to insert *intermediate assertions* manually at various points in the program; these assertions must be proved true upon reaching the points at which they appear, after which they can be used as given for proofs beyond that point. The intermediate assertions leave out details that are not necessary for further proofs. Nothing prior to an intermediate assertion need be examined to prove subsequent assertions. You cannot introduce an error with an incorrect intermediate assertion, because the proof of a false assertion will fail. If the intermediate assertion contains insufficient detail to prove subsequent assertions, the proof of a verification condition will fail. In practice, the only places where intermediate assertions are useful are at branches and loops. A *loop invariant* is an assertion that states properties that are true each time through a loop. If the loop can be shown to terminate (another hard problem), the *effects of code* for the loop are represented by the loop invariant.

The entry and exit assertions for a procedure that implements a function in the formal specification are taken from the formal specification of that function. The entry assertions come from invariants, axioms, and other criteria in the specification, and the exit assertions include the specified effects of the function. Automated tools (called *verification condition generators)* that understand program semantics and can create these assertions from specifications and programs have been developed in experimental examples, but tools to generate these conditions for practical use with sizable programs are still a long way off. Because the verification condition generator must be intimately familiar with the semantics of the language, and because most popular programming languages do not have formally defined semantics, such tools have only been developed for certain languages designed for provability. Of course, each combination of a programming language and a specification language requires a different tool. The tool that is closest to practical application is in the Gypsy system, where proofs of small programs have been successfully carried out.

REFERENCES

Boebert, W. E.; Franta, W. R.; Moher, T. G.; and Berg, H. K. 1982. *Formal Methods of Program Verification and Specification.* Englewood Cliffs, N.J.: Prentice-Hall.
A mathematical text on formal program verification and specification that offers in-depth study of the topic.
Cheheyl, M. H.; Gasser, M.; Huff, G. A.; and Millen, J. K. 1981. "Verifying Security." *Computing Surveys* 13(3):279–339.
An overview of four popular specification verification systems: Gypsy, old HDM, FDM, and AFFIRM.
Crow, J.; Denning, D.; Ladkin, P.; Melliar-Smith, M.; Rushby, J.; Schwartz, R.; Shostak, R.; and von Henke, F. 1985. "SRI Verification System Version 1.8 User's Guide" and "Specification Language Description." Drafts. Menlo Park, Cal.: SRI International Computer Science Laboratory.
These references for enhanced HDM are still in draft form, and the system itself is still under development.
Denning, D. E. 1983. *Cryptography and Data Security.* Reading, Mass.: Addison-Wesley.
A thorough study of cryptographic techniques, access controls, and database security, presented in textbook format with many exercises, examples, and references.
Eckmann, S. T. 1987. "Ina Flo: The FDM Flow Tool." In *Proceedings of the 10th National Computer Security Conference*, pp. 175–82. Gaithersburg, Md.: National Bureau of Standards.
A flow tool for the Ina Jo language.
Feiertag, R. J. 1980. "A Technique for Proving Specifications Are Multilevel Secure." Computer Science Lab Report CSL-109. Menlo Park, Cal.: SRI International.

A mathematical description of a flow model and of a flow-analysis technique implemented in a tool to find covert channels in HDM *specifications.*

Floyd, R. 1967. "Assigning Meaning to Programs." In *Mathematical Aspects of Computer Science,* ed. J. T. Schwartz, pp. 19–32. Washington, D.C.: American Mathematical Society.
A description of the assertion technique for proving program correctness.

Good, D. I.; Akers, R. L.; and Smith, L. M. 1986. "Report on the Language Gypsy: Version 2.05." Report #48. Institute for Computer Science and Computing Applications, University of Texas at Austin.
The Gypsy reference manual.

Haigh, J. T.; Kemmerer, R. A.; McHugh, J.; and Young, W. D. 1987. "An Experience Using Two Covert Channel Analysis Techniques on a Real System Design." *IEEE Transactions on Software Engineering,* SE-13(2):157–68.
A comparison of the Shared Resource Matrix methodology and the Gypsy flow-analysis tool.

Hoare, C. A. 1978. "An Axiomatic Basis for Computer Programming." *Communications of the ACM* 12(10):576–81.
A theoretical description of the use of a verification condition generator to produce theorems for proving programs.

Kemmerer, R. A. 1982. *Formal Verification of an Operating System Kernel.* Ann Arbor, Mich.: UMI Research Press.
The full details of the UCLA security kernel research project's verification.

———. 1983. "Shared Resource Matrix Methodology: An Approach to Identifying Storage and Timing Channels." *ACM Transactions on Computing Systems* 1(3):256–77.
The major alternative to flow analysis for identifying covert channels in a specification.

———. 1986. "Verification Assessment Study." C3-CR01-86, vols. 1–5. Ft. Meade, Md.: National Computer Security Center.
A massive study of four verification systems (Gypsy, enhanced HDM, FDM, *and* AFFIRM) *using several large common examples, complete with critiques and comments by users and developers.*

Lampson, B. W. 1973. "A Note on the Confinement Problem." *Communications of the ACM* 16(10):613–15.
One of the first papers to discuss covert channels (called confinement or leakage paths) and techniques to close them.

Robinson, L.; Silverberg, B.; and Levitt, K. 1979. "The HDM Handbook." Vols. 1 and 2. SRI Project 4824. Menlo Park, Cal.: SRI International.
Describes old HDM *and the Special specification language.*

Scheid, J.; Anderson, S.; Martin, R.; and Holtzberg, S. 1986. *The Ina Jo Specification Language Reference Manual—Release 1.* TM 6021/001/02. Santa Monica, Cal.: System Development Corporation (now Unisys). *The Ina Jo specification language is used in FDM.*

Thompson, D. H., and Ericksen, R. W., eds. 1981. "AFFIRM Reference Manual." Marina Del Rey, Cal.: USC Information Sciences Institute. *This document can be read as both a description of AFFIRM and a reference manual.*

Tsai, C-R.; Gligor, V. D.; and Chandersekaran, C. S. 1987. "A Formal Method for the Identification of Covert Storage Channels in Source Code." In *Proceedings of the 1987 Symposium on Security and Privacy,* pp. 74–87. Washington, D.C.: IEEE Computer Society. *Describes use of the Shared Resource Matrix to find covert channels directly in source code.*

Chapter *13*

Networks and Distributed Systems

Most books and reports on network security focus on encryption. To many people—including some experts—network security *is* encryption, and the sole purpose of network security is to prevent wiretapping. But the total network security problem is far more than the wiretapping threat, and encryption is just part of the solution.

Understanding network security entails understanding network architectures, from the standpoints of protocol design and of physical construction and topologies. It also entails understanding how encryption techniques can be applied to solve part of the network security problem. In the first two sections that follow, we shall develop some terminology important to network security and some fundamental concepts of networking and encryption; then we shall undertake a detailed discussion of network security architectures.

13.1 OVERVIEW OF NETWORKING CONCEPTS

This section gives you a quick overview of various salient characteristics of network architectures. This overview assumes that you have some prior knowledge of networking concepts and that you understand the reasons for the various types of network architectures; it concentrates on presenting facts and terminology and is not intended to be a tutorial on networking.

13.1.1 Protocol Hierarchies and Models

The purpose of a network is to provide a mechanism for two peer communicating entities to exchange information. The entities—which may be computers, operating systems, programs, processes, or people—are the users of the network's services. The network provides an interface composed of a set of functions, much as an operating system provides an interface consisting of system calls (fig. 13-1). The description of this interface is the functional description of the network. Typical functions in a network interface enable the entities to send and receive messages, to obtain status information, to identify remote peer entities with which to communicate, and so on.

In order for two entities to understand each other they must agree on a common *protocol*. The definition of a protocol includes data formats of messages and sequences of messages. A protocol definition must take into account the types of functions provided by the interface to the network service on which that protocol depends: the protocol description is specified in terms of the generic function calls to that interface.

A network is constructed as a hierarchy of layers, each of which im-

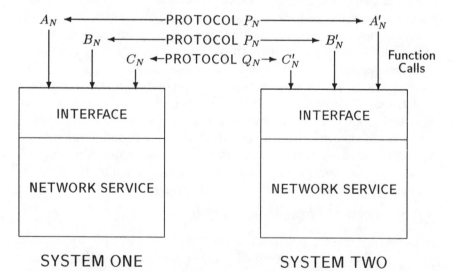

Figure 13-1. Use of Protocols. The pairs of communicating entities, $\{A_N, A'_N\}$, $\{B_N, B'_N\}$, and so on, use the network service to implement protocols P_N and Q_N. Several sets of entities may obey the same or different protocols using the same network service. The network service is accessed via function calls through an interface.

plements a specific type of network service. If we look inside the network service in figure 13-1, we see that the service itself is composed of communicating entities that exchange information with their remote peers, implement their own protocols, and use services of a lower-layer interface (fig. 13-2). The layer $N-1$ entities constitute the network service for layer N. Notice that A_N can choose from among several lower-layer entities, thereby forcing its communication with A'_N to employ a specific lower layer protocol.

The purpose of a protocol model is to provide a framework for describing the layered services of a network in a manner independent of the specific protocols that are used within the layers. Each layer of a model provides a network service to the layer above, and within each layer reside the communicating entities that implement one or more protocols appropriate to the layer. The *ISO Reference Model*, illustrated in figure 13-3 as it might be employed in a packet-switched network, is a familiar example. (ISO is the International Standards Organization.) Another notable model is the *Arpanet Reference Model*, used by the Department of Defense. A model does not prescribe any specific protocols; it defines only the general characteristics of protocols in each layer.

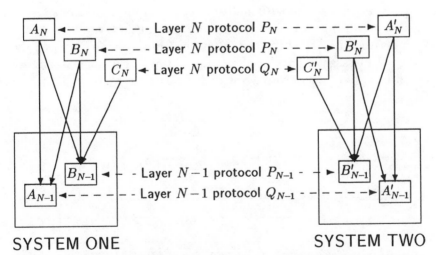

SYSTEM ONE   SYSTEM TWO

Figure 13-2. Communicating Entities. Within layer N, A_N communicates with its remote peer A'_N by means of a common protocol P_N, employing services of layer $N-1$ through an interface to entities A_{N-1} or B_{N-1}. The layer $N-1$ entities likewise communicate with their peers by means of lower-layer protocols P_{N-1} and Q_{N-1}.

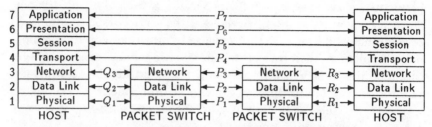

7	Application			P_7				Application
6	Presentation			P_6				Presentation
5	Session			P_5				Session
4	Transport			P_4				Transport
3	Network	Q_3	Network	P_3	Network	R_3	Network
2	Data Link	Q_2	Data Link	P_2	Data Link	R_2	Data Link
1	Physical	Q_1	Physical	P_1	Physical	R_1	Physical
	HOST		PACKET SWITCH		PACKET SWITCH		HOST

Figure 13-3. ISO Open Systems Interconnection Reference Model. A protocol is used within a layer by a pair of peer communicating entities. Protocols in layers 4–7 are end-to-end or host-to-host; lower-layer protocols are used for individual physical links. Not all lower-layer protocols need to be alike: only communicating pairs within a layer must use the same protocol.

The primary function of a protocol layer is to transmit and receive data on behalf of the communicating entities in the layer above. The entities pass messages across the interface to a lower layer, along with control arguments. A layer treats the messages passed to it as data and wraps the data with header and/or trailer information (such as destination address, routing controls, and checksum) that is needed by the layer to process the message as requested through the control arguments from the layer above. These wrapped messages are then passed into the layer below along with additional control information, some of which may be forwarded or derived from the higher layer. By the time a message exits the system on a physical link (such as a wire), the original message is enveloped in multiple nested wrappers—one for each layer of protocol through which the data have passed (fig. 13-4).

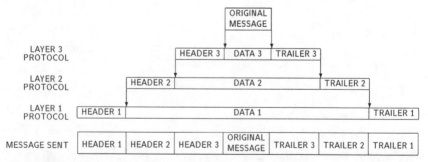

Figure 13-4. Nested Headers on a Message. Each protocol layer wraps its own header and trailer around the data passed to it from above. The data field of protocol layer N contains a complete message received from protocol layer N+1.

Good protocol layering requires that a layer not look at or depend on the contents of the data field that it receives from the layer above: communication of control information between layers (for example, requests to open and close connections, specifying source and destination addresses) should be done through function calls and arguments, and not by reference to the data contents of the messages.

13.1.2 Characteristics of Protocols

Security issues tend to center on four of the layers in the ISO model, allowing us to view protocols in terms of a four-layer model in which several of the ISO layers may be collapsed into one:

- Application (ISO 5,6,7)
- Transport (ISO 4)
- Network (ISO 3)
- Data link (ISO 1,2)

This view is not universal. On occasion, the session layer (layer 5) might need to implement certain security services offered by an application or transport layer; and at times, we need to distinguish between the physical layer and the data link layer. But for our purposes it is easiest to focus on these four layers. Please note that what we say here about protocols is merely typical of existing protocols operating at given layers: it is not a hard and fast requirement of all such protocols.

Both the data link and network protocol layers provide a datagram network service. *Datagrams* are packets of information composed of a header, data, and a trailer. The header contains information (such as destination address) needed by the network to route the datagram, and it may also contain other information (such as source address and *security labels*). The trailer contains little more than a checksum.

HEADER					TRAILER
DESTINATION	SOURCE	SECURITY LABEL	OTHERS	···DATA···	CHECK

The communicating entities that make use of a datagram service must specify the destination address (via control information) and the data for each message to be transmitted. The data link and network protocols package the message in a datagram and send it off. The datagram service does not support any concept of a session or connection, and it maintains no memory of whom it is talking to once a message is sent or received. Such memory, if needed, is the responsibility of the user of the datagram service (the next-higher protocol layer). Retransmission and error checking are minimal or nonexistent. If the receiving datagram service detects a transmission error (through a checksum, perhaps), the datagram is usually ignored, without notifying the receiving higher-layer entity.

The transport layer provides a highly reliable communications service for entities wishing to carry out an extended two-way conversation. The service employs the concept of a *connection* or *virtual circuit*, with *open* and *close* commands to initiate and terminate the connection, in addition to the usual transmit and receive functions. Information is accepted by the transport layer for transmission as a stream of characters and returned to the recipient as a stream.

The application layer provides functions for users or their programs and is highly specific to the application being performed. A single exchange at the application layer (called a *session*) might include an electronic mail message transfer, a file or database copy, or a user's query/response transaction with a database management system. A session can be very short or can last for days. A given application layer protocol may employ multiple connections at the transport layer to accomplish its job.

13.1.3 Network Topologies and Components

Today's network topologies are designed to handle two distinct needs: *wide-area* and *local-area* communications. A common wide-area network technology is based on packet switching. The physical structure of a packet-switched network, illustrated in figure 13-5, resembles a random sprinkling of nodes or packet switches interconnected in an arbitrary fashion. A packet switch is connected to neighboring packet switches and may be the point of entry into the network for one or more hosts. The software in the host communicates with its adjacent packet switches by means of a network-layer protocol, sending datagrams (packets) into the network that are routed to the destination host—via multiple intermediate destinations if necessary—in a manner determined by routing algorithms in the packet switches. These routing algorithms are adaptive to a limited extent: they take the dynamics of the network into account, altering the path taken by successive packets between two hosts depending on the network load and the status of the communications lines.

A local-area network (LAN) has a number of characteristics that dis-

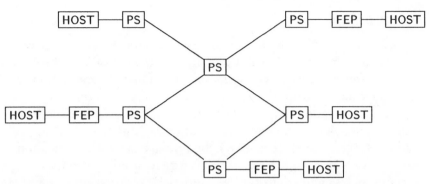

Figure 13-5. Packet-switched Network. *The packet-switching nodes (PS) are usually small dedicated computers, interconnected by high-speed long-distance telephone lines. Hosts may connect directly to the packet switches or via front-end processors (FEPs).*

tinguish it from a wide-area network. These include throughput that is several orders of magnitude higher, extremely short delay, and large total carrying capacity (bandwidth). The most common LAN topologies employ a *broadcast* medium, in which a datagram transmitted by one host to another host is in fact received by many or all hosts, with the understanding that only the intended recipient will bother to read the datagram. There is no routing in a broadcast medium. Figure 13-6 shows a typical picture of a broadcast local-area network using a bus topology, where hosts are linked to the bus through interface units that contain varying amounts of intelligence and may be integrated as I/O controllers into the hosts themselves.

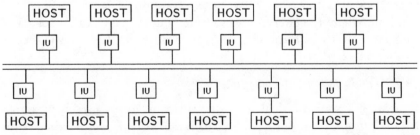

Figure 13-6. Local-Area Network. *The popular* Ethernet *has this bus architecture, whereby each host (connected to the network via an interface unit), has the ability to receive all the traffic on the LAN.*

13.2 ENCRYPTION

Though not a solution in itself, encryption is an important component of most network security solutions. In order to devise a security architecture for a network, you must understand where encryption can help and where it cannot. We shall review here some of the fundamentals of encryption that pertain to networking (we are not concerned with techniques that are only useful for encrypting files on disks, for example), and we shall then cover the primary network applications. Fortunately, you do not have to be an expert in cryptography to understand these applications: unlike section 13.1, this section is a brief tutorial and does not require much prior knowledge of the topic. Several books offer more detailed coverage of encryption (Denning 1983; Meyer and Matyas 1983). A good survey of network security and encryption is provided in an article by Voydock and Kent (1983).

We have not yet talked about what it means to have a secure network (that is the topic of section 13.3), but we can make some general statements about the purpose of encryption in order to give the techniques discussed here their proper perspective. The primary goal of encryption is to allow peer entities to communicate by using their common protocol over an unprotected path in a manner that is as secure as if the path were physically protected. Depending on your definition of *security* (that is, depending on how you define the threats), encryption may achieve that goal quite satisfactorily or may not help at all. For example, a goal of protection from eavesdropping by a wiretapper is readily satisfied by encryption, but a goal of preventing denial of service—where the threat is someone cutting an unprotected wire—cannot be addressed by encryption. Encryption between two entities can be implemented at any protocol layer, but for present purposes it is easiest to think of encryption as taking place between two computer systems over a physical link, where the encryption is implemented in a box that serves as each computer's link interface. We shall discuss later what it means to encrypt at other protocol layers.

13.2.1 Fundamentals of Encryption

A *cipher* is a mathematical algorithm that transforms a string of source data *(plaintext)* into unintelligible data *(ciphertext)*, and vice versa, in a way that uniquely depends on the value of a cryptographic variable or *key*. If you do not have the key, you cannot carry out either transformation.

A *secret key cipher* is one for which both encipherment and decipherment require the same key; consequently, the sender and the receiver must share secret information.[1] The most popular secret key algorithm (besides various classified algorithms used by the Department of Defense) is the Data Encryption Standard (DES) specified by the National Bureau of Standards (1977). This algorithm is available from several vendors in the form of an integrated circuit chip that is used in a number of commercial encryption products. Secret keys are also called *symmetric keys.*

A *public key (asymmetric key) cipher* always has two different keys: one private, and one public. A message enciphered with either key can be deciphered only with the other key.[2] The public key is easily calculated from the private key via a simple mathematical transformation, but it is not possible (or more precisely, it is computationally infeasible) to determine the private key from the public key. Each user has a unique private key, which is kept secret and from which the user calculates a public key to be distributed to others. In a typical application, the sender enciphers a message with the receiver's public key, and only the receiver can decipher the message. Only the receiver (not the sender) possesses secret information. In contrast to DES, there is no one generally accepted public key algorithm, and hardware is not readily available; but the RSA algorithm has a number of useful properties (Rivest, Shamir, and Adleman 1978), in which there is a considerable interest today. Because public key algorithms (even the hardware implementations) are computationally very slow (tens of characters per second), their use is limited to selected applications such as key management (section 13.2.4).

For communications we are particularly interested in *stream ciphers,* which are able to transform a message in serial fashion as characters or blocks of data enter a communications network. Either public or secret key ciphers can be used in the streaming mode.

Encryption Modes

Ciphers for serial encryption have several modes of operation, each providing certain capabilities for communications. We shall look briefly at the modes defined for DES. Similar modes are used by other algorithms.

---

1. Strictly speaking, the two keys need not be the same, but it must be possible to derive either key from the other.
2. This concept of enciphering with either key is somewhat simplistic and applies only to certain public key ciphers, but it is sufficient for this discussion.

In the simplest *block mode*—also called *electronic code book*— a block of plaintext (64 bits or 8 characters in DES) and a key are combined to yield a block of ciphertext (fig. 13-7a). Every block of plaintext is encrypted independently of preceding blocks. This mode is unsuitable for most communications applications because transmission of repetitive plaintext blocks will yield repetitive ciphertext, permitting easy cryptanalysis via a one-for-one substitution or *known plaintext attack*.

This problem of repetitive plaintext is addressed through the use of a *chaining mode* (fig. 13-7b). Encryption still takes place in blocks, but the calculation of the ciphertext for a block uses three inputs: the plaintext block, the key, and a feedback value based on the previous block of information. Even with highly repetitive sequences of plaintext, the ciphertext has the appearance of being a random stream. A single-bit change in one block of the plaintext propagates indefinitely into the subsequent ciphertext. To start out the process, an initialization vector (IV) is used in place of a feedback value, as input to the first block.

Because chaining modes have distinct starting points where the IV is fed into the calculation, some means of synchronization between sender and receiver is essential. The sender and receiver must agree

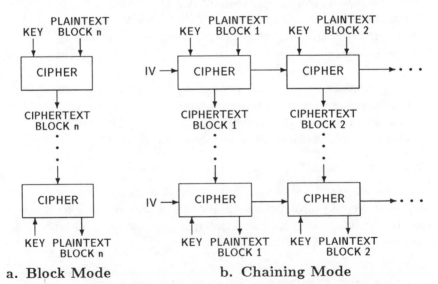

a. **Block Mode**   b. **Chaining Mode**

Figure 13-7. Encryption modes. In block mode (a), each block is independently encrypted. In chaining modes, (b), the ciphertext for a block depends on the previous blocks in the message.

on the IV as well as on the key, and they must have a way to signal the start of a new message. They must also be able to determine block boundaries. The design of chaining modes addresses various types of synchronization problems that could be introduced by errors during transmission: errors where bits in the ciphertext change, and errors where there are extra or dropped bits. Without synchronization, the received plaintext stream would be continuously unintelligible.

Two types of chaining modes use different approaches in addressing the synchronization problem. In *cipher block chaining*, where the ciphertext for each block is used as the feedback value into the next block, a bit error in the ciphertext propagates no more than two blocks into the deciphered plaintext. But cipher block chaining does not deal well with lost or extra bits or characters in the ciphertext where block framing can be lost. Once framing is lost, it can only be restored by some out-of-band technique (unencrypted signal) that resynchronizes the blocks. Thus, block chaining is suitable only for applications where dropouts are unlikely and where framing can be maintained: in synchronous lines at the data link layer, and in protocols that use frames, packets, or datagrams. On synchronous lines, the encrypted data stream is constantly changing—even when the sender is transmitting nothing but continuous synchronization (SYNC) characters.

Cipher feedback mode deals with dropped or extra characters or bits (which are most prevalent on asynchronous lines) by means of a combination of chaining and shifting of characters within a block. An extra or lost character in transmission affects no more than the next block or two of characters in the plaintext because framing is restored on each character boundary through use of unencrypted start and stop bits. The disadvantage of this technique is that only one character (rather than a whole block) is transmitted for each pass through the encryption algorithm, slowing down the encryption by a significant factor. Fortunately, asynchronous lines do not usually operate at high enough speeds for performance to be a problem.

Because it is relatively simple to implement, single-bit cipher feedback is common on synchronous lines, where the encryption device ignores character boundaries and cycles single bits through the encryption algorithm.

Link and Packet Encryption

Encryption is employed in different ways in different protocol layers, but these ways break down into two main types: *link encryption* and *packet encryption.* Link encryption is restricted to physical-layer and data-link-layer protocols in which the information is transferred in a continuous stream of bits or characters and where there is no concept of a message. In most protocols above the data link layer, communication takes place in the form of distinct packets or datagrams. Many data-link-layer protocols, such as HDLC and CSMA/CD, also use packets called *frames*. From an encryption standpoint, these frames must be treated as packets and not as bit or character streams.

Link encryption is the simplest (and safest) form of encryption and is the preferred method when the only needed security is protection of the physical wire or radio link. It is commonly used on point-to-point synchronous or asynchronous lines. In link encryption, the encryption boxes on the ends of the link synchronize at a well-defined point and then employ a chaining mode to encipher all the data between them indiscriminately. If there are no data to transmit, the transmitting box sends continuous fill characters that are enciphered as if they were data; as a result, an observer of the traffic on an encrypted link sees random characters or bits, whether or not any information is being transmitted. If cipher block chaining is used, a means must be provided for the transmitter and receiver to resynchronize if an error occurs. This is accomplished by sending an out-of-band signal (such as a BREAK) or a unique bit pattern (such as a stream of zeros or ones). In cipher feedback mode, with character framing on the line, synchronization is automatic.

On links that are shared by multiple nodes—especially local area networks composed of rings and buses—and in all higher layer protocols, information is transmitted in frames or packets of fixed or variable sizes. Packet encryption avoids synchronization problems because the chaining process is restarted on each packet. If a receiver misses or ignores some packets, subsequent packets can still be deciphered without error because each packet is independent of previous packets from the point of view of the encryption mechanism: a transmission error in one packet will not propagate to subsequent packets. Packet encryption is often called *end-to-end encryption*, because it was first employed at the network or transport layers between end host systems on a wide-area network; but packet encryption is also needed at the data link layer, if the information is processed in frames.

Packet encryption differs substantially from link encryption because a part of the packet header is not encrypted. Parts of the header must remain unencrypted because the header contains information needed by the recipient in order to decipher the message. (For example, a recipient communicating with a number of systems may need to see a source address in order to determine which of several keys to use for decryption.) Moreover, if encryption occurs at a higher-layer protocol, any additional headers appended by lower-layer protocols will be (and must remain) unencrypted. If the destination address of a datagram in a packet-switched network were encrypted, for example, the packet switches in the network (which do not know the key) would not be able to route the datagram to its proper destination.

13.2.2 Security Services

Although we have talked so far about encryption as a way of preventing an observer or wiretapper from reading traffic on a communication path, encryption can address various other threats, and it has a number of vulnerabilities to those threats. Somewhat unconventionally, we shall consider security concerns as classified into the following categories:

- *Confidentiality* – ensuring that the information is not subject to un-authorized disclosure (is not readable to the wiretapper through passive wiretapping or eavesdropping)
- *Integrity* – ensuring that the information is not subject to unauthorized and undetected modification (selective modification by the wiretapper through active wiretapping or tampering)
- *Inference* – ensuring that the wiretapper is not able to deduce anything about the information (by means of traffic analysis)
- *Authentication* – ensuring that communicating entity that receives a messages knows the peer entity that originated the message
- *Denial of service* – ensuring that the wiretapper is not able to destroy information

As has already been noted, encryption is not a general solution to denial of service, and we shall not cover denial of service here as a security threat. The other four categories are discussed in the subsections that follow.

Confidentiality

Stream ciphers are very safe against eavesdropping if used properly, but some residual vulnerabilities remain, even with the best techniques. These vulnerabilities center on the fact that a stream cipher requires a distinct synchronization point—an identifiable beginning of message. The information following the beginning of a message is subject to simple cryptanalysis or the known plaintext attack.

Chaining ciphers generate changing ciphertext despite the existence of repetitive plaintext within a message, but two messages beginning with identical plaintext will begin with identical ciphertext (until they reach blocks that differ). This is a vulnerability when messages are frequent and short, as in packet encryption; it is less of a vulnerability when messages are very long and nonrepetitive, or when synchronization is infrequent, as in link encryption. In the extreme case of character-at-a-time terminal-to-computer communications over a packet-switched network, where large numbers of messages differ in only one character, individual encryption of packets would result in a simple, predictable, one-for-one substitution of plaintext packets with ciphertext packets.

One way to address this vulnerability is to randomize or *prewhiten* messages by inserting a random block of plaintext at the start of each message before encryption. The receiver discards this first block after decryption. This inserted block does not have to be random or secret: it simply needs to be different each time, and the receiver does not have to know what it is in advance. A simple counter such as a sequence number or time of day is often used. Sequence numbers are a convenient choice when encrypting messages at the transport layer, because transport protocols already have a sequence number in the header of each message that can be included in the encrypted data. You have to be sure, however, that the sequence number is sufficiently wide that it does not repeat often: 8-bit sequence numbers are far too short, and even 16-bit numbers may be inadequate.

Instead of inserting extra data at the start of each message, you can whiten messages by altering the initialization vector for successive messages. Because both the transmitter and the receiver must use the same IV, they must maintain synchronization so that they alter the IV in the same way each time. One way to do this is for the sender to transmit the IV in unencrypted form at the start of each message (the IV need not be secret, as long as it never repeats).

Integrity

An active wiretapping threat is one in which a wiretapper selectively modifies ciphertext in transit so as to spoof the receiver. A wiretapper who cannot read the ciphertext may nonetheless know the format of the transmissions and may know exactly which characters to change in order to cause the desired effect on the plaintext. In a chaining mode, it is not possible for a wiretapper to make a specific change to specific characters in a message: changing one bit in the ciphertext causes an unpredictable change to one or two blocks in the plaintext. While such an effect generally results in destruction of information (denial of service) rather than in selective modification, the fact that destruction is limited to two blocks permits the wiretapper to erase parts of a message selectively—a security threat in some cases.

It is the responsibility of the receiver of the information to protect itself from the adverse effects of selective destruction, using a validation technique such as a checksum inserted by the transmitter. Checksums must be calculated on the plaintext and encrypted along with the rest of the message; otherwise, the wiretapper could simply alter the checksum to compensate for the modifications made. Some types of checksums may not be able to detect tampering, if the wiretapper can change the ciphertext in such a way as to preserve the original checksum. More sophisticated *manipulation detection codes* employ algorithms, such as a cyclic redundancy check (CRC), whose values are more difficult to control by modifying the ciphertext.

A *message authentication code* (MAC) is a cryptographic checksum that is calculated using a chaining mode of encryption and a secret key whose value cannot be predicted without knowing the key. The MAC may consist of little more than the feedback value that emerges after the last block of encryption. A message with an appended MAC can be safely transmitted in unencrypted form without fear of undetected modification. Most encryption techniques, used in conjunction with a MAC, will detect the insertion of false information into a data stream or into the message: without possessing the encryption key the wiretapper cannot generate a decipherable message that passes the MAC check.

Replay is a threat that occurs when the wiretapper records a stream of previously transmitted ciphertext and retransmits the stream at a later time. A serious security problem would arise if, for example, a wiretapper could capture the encrypted login sequence of one user's session and retransmit the sequence at a later time in place of his or her own login sequence. In lines employing link encryption, a potential for replay exists at each synchronization point.

One obvious way to detect replay is to change the key frequently, but this introduces complex synchronization and key distribution problems. Inserting a random block at the start of each message (or after each synchronization point) does not detect replay, because the receiver ignores the random block. The primary way to address replay is to insert a sequence number or time stamp in the message, which the receiver checks before considering the message to be valid. To prevent false rejections, the receiver must account for missing, delayed, out-of-order, or duplicate packets that can occur in a large network. The time stamp or sequence number must of course be protected by encryption or a MAC. This sequence number may be the same one used to whiten packets to prevent cryptanalysis.

Inference

In physical link encryption, a wiretapper sees a steady stream of random bits or characters, whether or not any communication is taking place: the only information the wiretapper may be able to discern is an occasional synchronization signal. In packet encryption, the observer sees individual packets and can discern a number of things: the existence and rate of packets, packet lengths, and unencrypted packet header information (such as source and destination addresses).

Other than flooding the network with dummy packets to confuse the wiretapper, there are no good solutions to the traffic analysis problem. Fortunately, in most environments an eavesdropper cannot gain anything useful from such information, and the threat can usually be ignored. In only a few high-security environments is there a concern that traffic patterns on a network might reveal sensitive information.

The lack of concern about traffic analysis is often justified on the grounds that the transmitter is not trying to communicate with the wiretapper. This seems a reasonable assumption, since the transmitter is the "good guy" who is responsible for the data being communicated; but as we have observed time and again in earlier chapters of this book, we often have to contend with the Trojan horse threat (a topic of chapter 7). The encryption device or protocol entity performing encryption is of course trusted not to disclose information intentionally, but the application software in the host outside the box or above that layer (which is where the data originates) is not. Any of the items in a packet header observable to a wiretapper is a potential covert channel (see, in particular, section 7.2.1), if it can be modulated by the application and observed by a wiretapper. The Trojan horse in the application, being forced to communicate through the trusted encryption layer, cannot directly contact the wiretapper but may have direct or indirect control over packet lengths, destination addresses, and (in the extreme) data link synchronization signals (Padlipsky, Snow, and Karger 1978).

Packet headers and lengths provide a major path for covert channels because so much of the information is directly under the control of the application. You can minimize the Trojan horse threat by encrypting as much of the packet as possible, but heroic efforts are not worthwhile, because some information will always remain unencrypted. If you are willing to accept reduced flexibility, you can control the range of values of header fields (for example, by allowing the application to select from only a small fixed set of destination addresses) and pad all packets to the same length prior to encryption; but even these measures only reduce the bandwidth of the covert channel, without eliminating it. On a local-area network with a rate of several hundred packets per second, even 1 bit of information per packet results in a high-bandwidth covert channel.

We shall discuss the importance of the covert channel further in section 13.5.

Authentication

Authentication—knowing whom you are talking to—means making sure that the entity with which you are communicating is not masquerading as someone else by lying about its identity (by altering the source address that is contained somewhere in its messages). In a sense, authentication is an automatic feature of encryption; if you assume that nobody else knows the encryption key, the ability to communicate with another entity implies possession of the key and, therefore, proper authentication. Authentication does not require encryption if the remote entity's messages are protected by a MAC. While, in theory, you could use a MAC to protect only the source address of a message, and not the data, it is unsafe to provide authentication without some kind of integrity protection of the entire message, because it does no good to know who originated a message if the message might have been modified en route.[3]

If you share the same key with a number of entities, you have to trust them all to identify themselves accurately, because any one could masquerade as another. For this reason, the safest approach is to use pairwise keys: a separate key for each pair of communicating entities. The pairwise authentication process is closely related to key management (covered in section 13.2.4). We shall discuss some of the general concepts here.

When initializing a communication, two encryption boxes residing outside their host systems can authenticate each other by exchanging handshakes of some type. Since the host trusts its encryption box to

---

3. On the other hand, if your threat is minimal, so that you are worried only about wiretappers masquerading by sending false messages rather than by modifying existing messages, authentication by itself could be useful.

authenticate the remote box, the host software can be sure that it is communicating with software on a specific remote host (or more precisely, with someone attached to the specific remote encryption box). Encryption does nothing to help software in the host to distinguish between different entities (processes or applications) on the remote host: the hosts must trust each other for this higher-level authentication.

Unless you carefully analyze how authentication is used in your system, it is very easy to be misled into believing that you have more protection than you actually do. Authentication is particularly confusing because the authenticated identifier (the network address of an entity) is valid only for the protocol layer at which the authentication occurs. Since each protocol layer potentially has its own addressing mechanism, the authentication of a source address on the protocol header of a lower-layer protocol packet does not necessarily say anything about the authenticity of the address in an embedded (higher-layer) protocol packet.

For example, encryption at the transport layer may allow transport-layer entities to authenticate host addresses appearing in the protocol headers of the transport layer; but unless that authenticated host address is checked by the application-layer protocols, the authentication will be useless. In particular, application-layer protocols such as file transfer and electronic mail employ their own addressing mechanisms that are far removed from transport-layer addresses. While a mapping from electronic mail address to transport address occurs on the transmitting side as a mail message is passed down to lower-layer protocols, the reverse mapping is not done on the receiving end, since the addressing information is already present in the header of the mail. Thus, if you get mail that claims to be from Jones at system Alpha, you might have no assurance that the message came from either Jones or system Alpha because your receiving mail system might not have checked the host name in the mail protocol header against the authenticated host address received by the transport layer.[4] Normally, when there is no encryption (and no authentication), protocols have no reason to double-check these addresses on the receiving end. A similar anomaly is possible at the boundary between the data link and network layers.

---

4. This problem should not be confused with the name-to-address translation problem that we shall discuss in section 13.4.2.

13.2.3 Integrating Packet Encryption into a Protocol Architecture

When two entities first wish to communicate using packet encryption, they must undergo an initialization process whereby they identify each other and negotiate the encryption keys. The handshaking might involve an exchange of information with a *key distribution center* (discussed in section 13.2.4). These exchanges mark the start of a *cryptographic session*. In order to avoid the overhead of reinitializing on every message, the two entities must keep track of this session for a period of time until they decide they have finished communicating. For confidentiality and integrity protection, they may have to keep track of certain additional information for each session—such as sequence numbers, as we discussed earlier.

Since an entity at any protocol layer might simultaneously communicate with a number of remote entities, it must keep track of multiple cryptographic sessions. At the application or transport layer, a cryptographic session directly corresponds to a network session or virtual circuit: the protocol at those layers already keeps track of sessions or circuits, and adding the additional cryptographic session state information is straightforward. At the network or data link layer, where datagrams or frames are used, the concept of a session has to be artificially created because the protocol entities do not normally keep track of whom they are talking to. In some cases the session concept can be introduced transparently to a layer by a cryptographic module that postprocesses the datagrams, but it is better to integrate the concept directly into the protocols. (The thorniest problem with implementing sessions transparently consists of figuring out when to end the session and when to purge the state information.)

The need to maintain the state of a cryptographic session and the need to exchange cryptographic information at the start of a session should make it apparent that, when packet encryption is employed in a given protocol layer, the encryption becomes an integral part of the protocol specification of the layer and is best designed into the protocol from the beginning. Inserting packet encryption into a protocol after the fact usually requires a major redesign of the protocol, because it affects both message formats and sequences of exchanges. For higher-layer protocols, it is impossible to squeeze encryption between two adjacent protocol layers in a transparent manner without severely upsetting the layered architecture and performance.

To a certain extent, it is possible to insert encryption transparently into existing protocols at lower layers. This is most easily and most commonly done at the physical layer (where encryption is performed by a device that transforms individual bits) or at the data link layer (where encryption is based on characters, and there is no concept of a frame). Packet encryption can be inserted transparently at the data link and network layers because it is usually feasible to nest an existing data-link-layer or network-layer datagram inside an encrypting protocol at the same layer, by inserting the encrypting layer underneath the layer to be encrypted. You should be aware, however, that—while nesting approaches are the second most common technique used—they are complex to implement and can adversely affect performance.

13.2.4 Key Management

In order to minimize the risk of exposure in a secret key system, a secret key should only be shared by the two entities that are communicating. Each entity must remember a separate key for each other entity with which it is currently communicating. In practice, however, a group of communicating entities often shares the same key. In such a case, if one of the entities is compromised, the others are, too.

Because keys get "stale" after repeated use (the greater the amount of information encrypted with a given key, the easier cryptanalysis becomes), it is necessary to change keys periodically (an interval called a *cryptoperiod*). Manual rekeying is the most commonly used technique today (both in the government and in industry); by this means, keys are created at a central key distribution center (KDC), and the printed list or magnetic tape of keys is hand-delivered by courier to each site and physically entered into the encryption devices.

Key Distribution Center

Manual key distribution is a major management burden, sufficient to limit the use of encryption to the most sensitive applications. In many applications, key management—and not the cost of encryption hardware—is the reason encryption is not applied. One way to minimize the burden is to employ an automated KDC that distributes the keys over the network on demand. When two systems wish to enter into a cryptographic session, they exchange messages with the KDC, which sends them both a key for that session. When the session is over, the systems discard the key. The KDC generates a new key for each session. If a session between two systems lasts for days or weeks, the systems may want to ask the KDC periodically for a fresh key.

Because the KDC resides on the network just as any other computer system does, interaction with the KDC must be authenticated and, for the most part, encrypted. The key for this authentication is a per-system secret *master key*. Each system must permanently store its own master key: the KDC must maintain a database with the identifiers and master keys of all the network entities. The master keys are changed only rarely because little information is encrypted with them.

But the master keys must still be manually entered into each system initially. There is no secure way to transmit master keys on the network: any such technique would require encrypted communications, which would require a second level of master key in each system. Key hierarchies can be constructed where the keys highest in the hierarchy are changed least often (or never) and the lowest keys are changed frequently (perhaps hourly or daily) and automatically. No matter what the architecture, however, you cannot get around the need to enter a secret master key manually at least once into each system. If you ever change these master keys, the new master keys should also be entered manually, since redistributing master keys over the network based on previous master keys does little to improve security.

The KDC concept has been criticized on many counts—some valid, and some unfounded. One misconception is that KDCs make a network unreliable because they present a single point of failure. This problem is easily solved by using multiple KDCs; the protocol that allows a system to switch to an alternate KDC is not very complex. A bit more complex is a mechanism to distribute the network database to multiple KDCs.

Another unfounded criticism is that large numbers of key distribution messages place an excessive load on the network. In fact, the amount of traffic generated for key distribution at the start of each session is minuscule in comparison to the amount of data traffic for sessions of average length.

A valid criticism of the KDC concept (but usually not a serious problem) points to the extra delay for key distribution at the start of each cryptographic session. The delay can be many times that of a normal session initiation for a virtual circuit, especially if the KDC is remote and the two systems that wish to communicate are on the same local-area network. Most higher-layer (end-to-end) protocols, however, can easily adapt to potentially long delays because they must accommodate communication over long distances. Network and data link layers tend to be unaffected by delays because their protocols do not require acknowledgments.

The most serious valid criticism of the KDC concept addresses the management required for large networks. The KDC is one system on the network that must know the identity (and the master keys) of all other systems. In many networks, it is impractical to require all systems to be centrally registered and administered; furthermore, it may be impossible to identify a central authority that all systems on a network are willing to trust. An approach permitting a hierarchical KDC structure, in which each community of systems has its own KDC, is easier to administer but requires complex protocols.

Public Key Distribution

A *public key distribution* system avoids some (but by no means all) of the management burden of the KDC. Such a system has no central registry to distribute keys. Each operating system creates its own private key, which it keeps secret, and then computes the corresponding public key. The public keys for all systems are stored in a file readable by anyone on the network. Using the RSA algorithm, you encrypt a confidential message to be sent to another system with the recipient's public key. If you receive a message from a system that you can decrypt with its public key, you can be sure that the message came from that system. The public key mechanism thereby provides the same degree of mutual authentication that the secret key mechanism does.

As was noted earlier, public key algorithms are very slow and impractical for many applications. The performance problem is minimized by using the public key algorithm only for key distribution and session initiation, where its benefits are greatest. Once two systems authenticate each other, they exchange a randomly generated secret key for the session and employ a fast secret key algorithm such as DES for all subsequent communications. There is no advantage to using a public key algorithm once a secret key has been established.

The public key distribution technique requires establishment of a central registry of systems that lists the public keys. As in the KDC approach, that registry must be trusted and protected from tampering, since reliable authentication depends on obtaining the correct public key for a system.[5] The registry must authenticate itself to other systems, which implies that each system must know the public key for the reg-

---

5. If a MAC is employed on the individual registry entries so that nodes can authenticate entries as valid, the online server that distributes the registry need not be trusted or protected. Such a MAC must be based on a network-wide public key known to all nodes, whose private key in each case is known only to the trusted entities that create the registry.

istry. But unlike the KDC, the registry need not be kept secret, and no secret information need be shared by systems prior to session initiation. The registry can freely be duplicated, and portions can be copied and stored locally. A new system can even add itself to the network automatically by creating its own private key and sending the public key to the registry. A system can change its private and public key at any time by sending an update message to the registry. Almost all network management is decentralized.

Public key distribution techniques have seen very limited use because they are fairly new (the theory was not developed until the late 1970s, and an intellectual debate continues over their immunity to cryptanalysis) and because hardware is not readily available. The extremely long keys involved (hundreds to thousands of bits) has also limited the techniques' practicality. Nonetheless, because of the greatly simplified key distribution they allow, we may someday see public key techniques predominate over secret key distribution centers—even before encryption itself becomes a routine part of computer communications.

13.3 A NETWORK SECURITY ARCHITECTURE

Secure networks have been studied much less than secure computer systems, and few practical examples of them exist. While it is easy to find pieces of network security solutions (particularly those employing encryption), finding an example of an integrated secure distributed system is much harder. The problem is not in the technology but in the lack of an accepted architecture for a distributed system. It is easy for us to draw a generally accepted picture of a computer system as being composed of hardware, an operating system, and applications (figure 4-1); but distributed systems are much more complex, and no simple picture of such a system has yet emerged. In this section we shall consider just one of many possible ways to characterize a secure distributed system. This section discusses the security problems of distributed systems that are addressed by currently available computer and network security techniques.

Our goal in defining a network security architecture is to draw as much of a parallel as possible between a network architecture and a computer system architecture—employing the same technology wherever possible, and inventing new techniques only where necessary to accommodate the differences between networks and computers. Many of the concepts to which we shall refer are similar to those discussed in chapters 3 and 4.

13.3.1 Network Subjects, Objects, and Access Control

A *secure network* is a set of communications mechanisms that provides to its subjects a specific type of service at a given protocol layer (fig. 13-8). The subjects (users) are the communicating entities that use the secure network, implementing their own protocols to communicate among each other. The nature of these subject-to-subject protocols is of no concern to the trusted network. The network consists of all the elements that make up the protocols, from a given layer down; the internal layers of the secure network are invisible to the subjects. This concept of hiding functions and protocols is consistent with that of a layered protocol model. Exactly what types of subjects (processes, computers, people, and so on) the secure network supports depends on the entities supported by the layer you choose to call your secure network

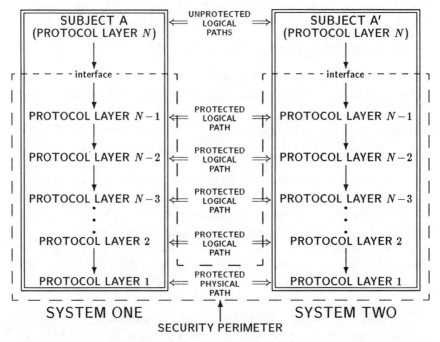

Figure 13-8. A Subject's View of a Secure Network. *Two subjects (peer protocol entities), communicate with each other using services of an underlying secure network. The security perimeter is the interface to those underlying services. The secure network within the perimeter provides services at protocol layer N − 1.*

(table 13.1) and on the security policy that the secure network is to enforce.

We can draw a parallel between the structure shown in figure 13-8 and that of a computer system in which the network is a trusted operating system and the subjects are processes that invoke functions at the interface to the system. Like the trusted operating system, the network manages shared resources and mediates access to those resources by the subjects under its control, in accordance with a security policy. We can also draw a parallel between the internal layering of the secure network and the layering within a secure operating system (see section 11.1 and table 11-1). Of course the details of implementation of the layers inside the secure network are quite different from those of a secure operating system.

The policy enforced by the secure network has the sole goal of determining which pairs of subjects can communicate. Unlike a security policy for a secure computer system, a security policy for a network does not have to deal with objects as permanent information stored in a system. It is possible for the secure network to enforce a security

ISO Layers	Subjects	Objects
5,6,7 (application)	Users	Files Electronic mail ...many others
4 (transport)	**Processes** Applications	Connections Virtual circuits
3 (network)	Hosts Networks	Datagrams Packets
1,2 (data link)	Nodes on end of link Nodes on bus	Frames Datagrams Physical links

Table 13-1. Subjects and Objects in Protocol Layers. *The types of subjects and objects supported by the secure network depend on the layer at which security in the network is implemented. At protocol layers 4 and above, the subjects (users and processes), are the same as those usually supported by a secure operating system.*

policy by directly controlling subject-to-subject access; however, it is usually more convenient to employ the concept of a network object as an intermediary through which two subjects may exchange information. The network object plays the same role played by a file in a computer system that is used for process-to-process communication: one process writes the file, and another reads it. The network security policy, expanded to cover subject-to-object access, then begins to look much like a computer system security policy.

Just as the types of network subjects differ, depending on the protocol layer at which security is implemented, the types of network objects may differ as well. Examples of network objects include messages, frames, datagrams, virtual circuits, and files (table 13.1). Network objects can have widely varying characteristics. Some objects (such as datagrams) are fleeting, existing only between the time they are transmitted by one subject and the time they are received by another. Objects such as physical links are permanent. Virtual circuits may exist for an arbitrary amount of time, from seconds to days. Messages, packets, and datagrams are accessible to only one subject at a time. Virtual circuits and some physical links are simultaneously accessible to a pair of subjects. A LAN bus is accessible to a large number of subjects.

The secure network in figure 13-8 carries out its subject-to-object access control in a manner identical to that employed by a secure operating system. Because the subjects and objects are under full control of the secure network service within each system, access mediation based on discretionary and mandatory security policies is implemented by means of the same techniques as are used in an operating system— and most likely by the same mechanisms as exist within the operating system. For example, subjects may be implemented as processes on a system, and objects may be implemented as memory segments or buffers under the control of memory management mechanisms.

If the trusted network service operates at the transport layer (layer 4), the subjects are processes and the network security policy can be identical to the security policy of the operating system. In other words, the secure operating system and the secure network service work together and present an integrated secure system that enforces a single security policy, whether dealing with network objects or with system objects.

If the trusted network service operates at the data link layer, the network service cannot distinguish between different processes on the same computer and cannot enforce selective access control to the granularity of a process. The security policy enforced by such a network—

where subjects are nodes, and objects are datagrams—bears little relationship to any policy that might be enforced by the operating system running on the nodes.

13.3.2 Network Security Perimeter and Protected Path

As in the case of a secure computer system, we must draw a *security perimeter*—a boundary between trusted and untrusted mechanisms. This security perimeter surrounds everything within the highest protocol layer that constitutes the secure network.

In the discussion that immediately follows, it is assumed that a single security policy is enforced throughout a specific collection of systems on the network at a single protocol layer, in a manner similar to the enforcement of security at a single interface within a computer system. It is further assumed that you have selected a suitable layer based on the security policy you want to enforce and on the types of subjects and objects you want to protect. A network can enforce multiple nested policies—one for each layer—but it is very difficult to devise meaningful nested security policies. We shall talk later about more complex arrangements in which the security policy is not enforced uniformly throughout a network.

In order to maintain the integrity of the security perimeter around a pair of geographically separated systems (as in figure 13-8), you must have a *protected path* between the systems. This path is similar to the trusted path between users and the security kernel (see section 10.4), but in this case the path protects the integrity of communications between two trusted systems rather than between a user and a trusted system. As with the user's trusted path, providing a protected path between systems means ensuring that communications between the systems are physically secure and that all devices and other systems supporting the communications are secure and trusted. The protected path ensures that the entire set of software and hardware within the security perimeter operates as a single coordinated entity, even though the entity is physically distributed. Because the path at the lowest (physical) layer (as shown in the figure) is protected, communication between peer entities in any given layer within the secure network is also protected.

13.3.3 Distributed Secure System

Taken together, a network of several systems—each of which contains a portion of the trusted network service as in figure 13-8, and each of which implements the same security policy—is a *distributed secure system.* The trusted portions of the individual systems interact via secure paths, and the untrusted portions are managed within each system in accordance with the common security policy.

This simplistic view of a secure network, while properly portraying the network from the point of view of subjects in the computer systems, does not represent the way in which the secure network is implemented. We rarely have the luxury of physically enclosing everything throughout the network below a given layer of protocol within the security perimeter. For long-distance communications, for example, software from the transport layer down through the data link layer might be protected within the security perimeter of a single computer system, but the public telephone lines between systems are not protected. In a packet-switched network, the packet switches that route datagrams between the hosts might not be protected.

When physical protection does not extend from end to end (between subjects in different systems), we must replace the physical protection with logical protection through encryption. From outside the security perimeter, the logical view of the secure network remains the same as in figure 13-8; but the architectural view is like the one shown in figure 13-9, where the software and hardware in the lower protocol layers are not trusted. The security policy of the network is enforced only by the intermediate layers within the security perimeter, and security does not depend on correct operation of the untrusted lower layers. Logically, encryption does no more than provide the equivalent of a protected path between the two computer systems at protocol layer 3, making up for the lack of physical protection at layers 2 and 1. Because of this protected path at layer 3, the logical paths between protocols above layer 3 (up to layer $N-1$) are also protected.

Encryption provides a protected path between the two systems in figure 13-9 by ensuring that information transmitted by the trusted network service at layer 3 in one system is received by its peer in the remote system without being observed or altered en route by an outsider. Encryption also provides authentication, ensuring that the two systems are communicating with each other and not with a masquerading system. Encryption does nothing to support the network security policy enforced on the subjects that are above the security perimeter (the insiders with legitimate access to the network services over which each computer system has control). The policy regarding insiders is enforced by conventional computer security controls, as we discussed earlier.

While a security architecture for a network must precisely specify

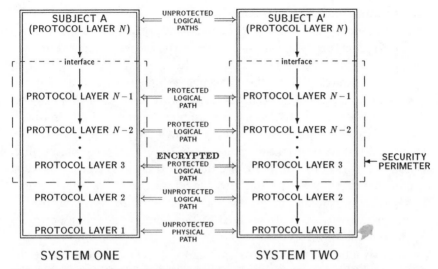

Figure 13-9. Actual View of a Secure Network. *The security perimeter surrounds a portion of the protocol tower in each system. The layers beneath that portion (and everything between the end systems), are untrusted. Encryption between the lowest trusted layers is used to enforce the protected path between the systems.*

the highest protocol layer at which the security policy is to be enforced uniformly throughout the network (the upper limits of the security perimeter), it need not specify a fixed lower limit at which encryption is to be performed. Encryption is only necessary where physical protection of the lower layers cannot be provided between a given pair of systems. Within a local area network, for example, where the systems are physically protected but the wires between the systems are not, encryption might be employed at the data link layer and implemented within the interface units (see figure 13-6). If some of these hosts communicate over a public packet-switched network, where the packet switches are not trusted, encryption must be employed in the network or transport layers to secure the paths to remote systems. Adjacent machines in a computer room connected by a protected physical wire need employ no encryption. Of course, for communications to be possible, both ends of a given protocol layer must employ encryption at the same time.

In addition to compensating for the lack of physical protection of paths between computer systems, encryption can minimize the need to trust some of the network mechanisms within a system. For example, software and hardware that constitute the data link layer need not be trusted if encryption is used at the network layer. The data link layer sees only encrypted data passed to it by the network layer. But realistically, even with encryption, it is difficult to avoid having to trust lower-layer protocols when those layers are implemented in a computer system (as in figure 13-8), because the software in lower-layer protocols usually needs special privileges (for example, to perform I/O). Privileged software can corrupt the operating system and cause a security violation, even if its normal function is only to process encrypted traffic. Using encryption to eliminate the need to trust lower layers is most useful in situations where the lower-layer protocols are implemented in separate physical devices (such as front-end processors or packet switches in figure 13-5). In such cases the devices can remain entirely untrusted and unprotected.

Interestingly, the reverse situation can also occur; in such a case the separate physical front-end device is the only trusted component of a secure network, and the hosts (including each host's operating system) are untrusted. In figure 13-6, for example, the interface units operating at the data link layer may employ encryption to provide a secure data link service to untrusted hosts as subjects.

13.3.4 Mutually Suspicious Systems

Together, the systems in a secure distributed system constitute a *security domain* that operates under a common management and implements a common security policy at a common protocol layer. Each system within the domain is equally responsible for security of the system. Using encryption or physical protection, we can logically isolate the secure distributed system as a whole from other computer systems on the same physical network that are not trusted to be members of the domain. In figure 13-10, a secure distributed system composed of systems A, F, and C exists in one domain. The other systems on the network are not part of that domain.

The existence of the untrusted system E along the physical path between A and F does not necessarily prevent establishment of a protected path between A and F at a suitably high protocol layer. For example, a secure virtual circuit can be established between subjects on A and F with encryption at the transport layer, where E is an intermediate gateway that handles the network layer protocol.

But what if a subject on system A wants to communicate with a peer on system B, where B is not part of the same security domain?

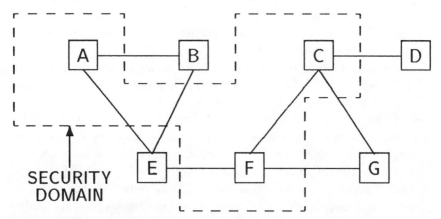

Figure 13-10. Security Domains. *Systems* A, F, *and* C *lie in the same security domain. They can trust each other to enforce the same security policy. Lines represent physical connectivity.*

System *A* must treat *B* as lying outside its security perimeter; the protocol layers within the security perimeter of *A* cannot trust their peer layers on the remote system (fig. 13-11). The entire remote system— and not just the subject at protocol layer *N*—is treated as an untrusted subject, and each protocol layer within the security perimeter of system *A* must be able to communicate with an untrusted peer without compromising its own security or the security policy enforced on the subjects in system *A*.

By allowing an exchange with an untrusted system in figure 13-11, we have built an additional interface into the security perimeter (besides the interface at protocol layer *N*–1 for local subjects). This interface, which is shown as a heavy vertical dashed line in the figure, provides direct access to functions of the secure network that are hidden inside the security perimeter of the distributed system in figure 13-9. Whereas the distributed system's security policy in figure 13-9 deals with subjects and objects at a single protocol layer, an expanded security policy is required for the situation in figure 13-11—one that specifies the types of objects handled by each of the protocol layers within the security perimeter. While these new layers must handle several new types of objects, the security policy need address only one new type of subject: an untrusted remote system. That remote system has multiple interfaces into the perimeter at different layers, but from an access control policy viewpoint it is a single monolithic subject. As far as that policy is concerned, the peer entity inside subject B with which subject A communicates in figure 13-11 is indistinguishable from any other part of the untrusted remote system.

A multiple-protocol-layer security policy is apt to be complex, since it must resolve issues of access by subjects at one level of abstraction to objects at a different level of abstraction. For example, in order to specify what happens when subject A opens a connection at the transport layer to entity A', the policy must account for the fact that the transport-layer objects (messages) are converted to one or more packets or datagrams at the lower layer and are individually transmitted to the remote subject at the data link layer. The remote subject cannot be trusted to reassemble the datagrams into the original message nor to respond appropriately to any of the protocols. Each protocol layer within the security perimeter of system A must protect itself from deception by or malfunction in system B. This requirement is not quite as hard as it seems, since good protocols are usually fairly robust in the face

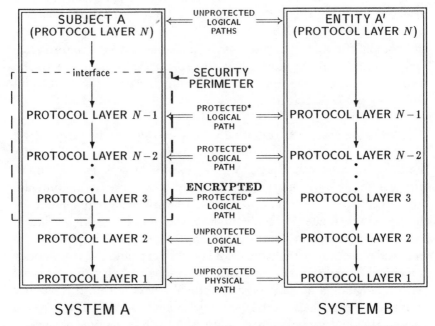

SYSTEM A   SYSTEM B

* Paths are protected as far as interface to protocol layer 3 of SYSTEM B.

Figure 13-11. Mutually Suspicious Computer Systems. *From the point of view of system A, system B is a single untrusted subject. The protocol layers within the trusted portions of system A must remain suspicious of their peers.*

of protocol errors on a remote system. The complexity lies in the definition of the security policy for such interactions.

Encryption is not required to extend the security perimeter at layer 3 in figure 13-11, as it was in figure 13-9, because the security perimeter of system *A* does not extend to system *B*. Encryption or physical protection must nonetheless be employed between the systems, however, in order to create a protected path for confidentiality of communications. Encryption is also needed if the systems want to authenticate each other, for the same reasons that users must have a protected path in order to authenticate themselves to an operating system (see section 10.4). But authentication is only necessary if the security policy requires the remote systems to be individually identified. It is not needed if the policy treats all remote systems alike, giving them all access to exactly the same objects without distinguishing among them.

The discussion here has been from the point of view of a single security domain on the network. A network may contain a number of secure distributed systems—each residing in its own security domain, each implementing a different security policy, and each viewing the systems in the other domains as suspicious. In the extreme, each system on the network may lie in its own domain and not trust the others at all.

13.4 NETWORK SERVERS

A distributed system often consists of a collection of computer systems that trust each other but generally serve their own local users, plus *server systems* that provide various types of services to other systems and users. Because these servers usually maintain data that are shared by a number of other systems, they bear some of the responsibility for enforcing the network security policy.

13.4.1 Authentication and Authorization Servers

Some servers, in effect, help to implement a portion of the security policy. The key distribution center that we discussed previously is an *authentication server:* anyone can use the KDC to determine whether a given message is authentic (was transmitted by a claimed source). A public key distribution center is also an authentication server.

The KDC is also often used as an *authorization server* to decide who can talk to whom, based on a security policy and attributes of systems stored in its database. It can enforce this authorization via selective key distribution—although, in general, an authorization server only provides information and does not directly enforce the authorization.

For example, the public key distribution center cannot enforce anything (because the keys it gives out are public), but it can provide authorization information for others to use.

13.4.2 Name Servers

A *name server* is an entity on the network that provides a way to translate the name of an entity into the network address of the entity. Usually the name is human-readable. Like an authentication server, a name server is a central registry of network entities. Name servers are necessary in large distributed systems whether or not security is an issue, because users cannot be expected to know the network addresses of all the services they use, and because each system on the network cannot store the names of all possible services. The name server allows services to move around on the network, and it can provide the addresses of alternate services if the primary service is not responding. Name servers are usually accessed by distributed applications on a system and not directly by users: the user enters into the local system the name of the service to be accessed (for example, "news wire service"), and the local system then interrogates the name server for the network address in order to make the remote connection to the service.

It is not often realized that the name server needs to be a highly trusted entity, as a name-to-address translation error can render useless all the rest of the network security and authentication controls. Suppose you are logged into your local system and want to send a file to a remote system omega on which you have an account. You enter the command "remote_copy to omega" into your local system, and the remote_ copy program invokes the trusted network service on the local system to send a message to the name server asking, "What is the network address of omega?". The name server returns the value 345678.0987, and your application again invokes the trusted network to establish a connection to that system. The secure network connection is set up, possibly with the aid of an authentication server that assures remote_ copy that it is really talking to 345678.0987, and the file is copied in complete privacy between your local system and that remote system. Of course, you as a user have no idea whether 345678.0987 is really omega: you have to believe the name server. Even if the name server is trusted, you have to trust the programs on your own system to provide the name server with the correct information, as you requested. Thus, for the maximum degree of security, each system needs a protected path to the name server.

Because name servers tend to be involved at the beginnings of sessions and need to be trusted, it is convenient to combine them on the same computer systems with authentication servers. But it is important to understand that the function of name-to-address translation is quite different from the function of authentication.

13.4.3 Other Servers

Distributed systems have a number of other shared services, such as bulk file storage, hardcopy output, and remote interfaces to other networks. Most of these are potentially security-relevant. A file server, for example, might contain files belonging to many different users. Instead of treating the file server as a subject, the trusted network service in the distributed system has to include the file server within the security perimeter, and the services of the file server have to be covered by the security policy. If the file server handles part of the file system for a distributed operating system, the file system is logically part of the operating system.

Techniques have been proposed and implemented in experimental systems where file servers need not be trusted (Rushby and Randell 1983). Such designs rely on encryption and authentication to prevent the file server from mixing files of different users. While the potential for residual covert channels may make the technique unsuitable for some applications, the ability to keep the file server outside the security perimeter is attractive because it reduces the number of special-purpose systems on the network that have to be trusted.

In practice, the use of distributed applications and shared servers (secure or otherwise) is still in its infancy, and few practical results have been obtained by securing such systems. But security is a serious problem in a distributed system—much more so than in operating systems. Perhaps it is not too late to design security into these systems from the beginning, before industry locks itself into fundamentally nonsecure approaches that can never be retrofitted.

13.5 SECURITY KERNEL ON A NETWORK

A distributed system like the one shown in figure 13-8 is really a distributed operating system. If the secure operating system in each system is a security kernel, and you want to enforce the same policy (with the same level of assurance) on the distributed system as you have within the kernel, the security kernels in the individual systems must cooperate in some manner. One way to accomplish this is to allow the kernels to communicate directly with one another, exchanging control information as needed to coordinate the exchange of traffic. This technique requires a set of trusted kernel-to-kernel protocols—and of course a protected path between the kernels. Such *kernel protocols* have very difficult synchronization requirements that must await solutions to still-open research issues.

A much easier technique is to keep the kernels as disjoint as possible, relying on each kernel to enforce subject-to-object access within its own computer system and minimizing the amount of trusted control information that must be exchanged between kernels. It turns out that, for a multilevel security policy, the only trusted control information that needs to be exchanged is the access class of the network objects; the transmitting kernel inserts an access class label on a message based on the access class of the subject that created the message, and the receiving kernel uses that access class to determine who on its own system may read the message. If the trusted network service operates at the transport layer, a label is required only when the virtual circuit is established, and not on each message that is exchanged over that circuit. The kernels must still trust each other to insert and obey the access class labels according to their common policy, but no information other than the labels need be managed or exchanged between the kernels. In particular, the kernels do not have to know the identifiers or attributes of each other's subjects.

In order for the system to label network objects securely, some portion of the network protocols in each kernelized system must be trusted to insert the correct label, and the labeling function must be integrated into the protocol architecture. Such labeling capability is incorporated as an option in the protocol header of the Arpanet's IP datagram at the network layer. Trusted labeling can be provided in various ways without trusting all of the network software that implements these protocols, but in general adding trusted labeling with the same degree of assurance as is possessed by the kernel entails trusting a considerable amount of network software.

The protected path between security kernels is best provided by physical security or link encryption. With packet encryption, unless you can close the high-bandwidth covert channel between an untrusted application and a wiretapper of a line (which is very difficult, as we discussed in section 13.2.2), the secure distributed system has a serious vulnerability that is not present when each kernel-based system is isolated. You need to evaluate this vulnerability in detail, early in the design of the distributed system, because it can be a waste of time and energy to close the covert channels in the isolated systems (to protect yourself against malicious, but authorized users) if you cannot protect yourself against wiretappers (malicious unauthorized users).

When a kernelized system communicates with an untrusted system, the kernel must treat the untrusted system as a single subject that is unable to enforce or provide any reliable labeling. With a multilevel security policy, this means that the untrusted system may communicate with subjects on the kernelized system at only a single access class, which the kernel determines by authenticating the remote system and knowing (from internal tables) the correct access class.

When two kernelized systems communicate, it may occasionally be desirable for one-way communication to occur between a subject at a high access class and a subject at a low access class. The multilevel security policy permits an UNCLASSIFIED process (for example) to create an UNCLASSIFIED datagram, and a SECRET process to read the datagram. In effect, the UNCLASSIFIED process does a write-up to a SECRET process. Because the reverse communication is not possible (the SECRET process cannot send to the UNCLASSIFIED process), the only protocols that will work in a one-way mode are those at the network or data link layers, where two-way handshakes are not required to establish a session or virtual circuit. In practice, few applications call for a pure one-way transmission over a network; the only users of a datagram service are higher-layer full-duplex protocols. Even if the purpose of establishing a virtual circuit is to transmit information in only one direction (for example, to send a file or electronic mail), the virtual circuit protocols are two-way and will not work. Thus, while the security policy may not prohibit one-way communication, there is little reason for a kernel-based network to provide such a service.

13.6 FUTURE OF SECURE DISTRIBUTED SYSTEMS

In contrast to the items discussed in most of the other chapters in this book, the secure distributed system model presented in this chapter is more of a proposal than a description of proven technology. No examples of commercial distributed systems address all dimensions of the computer security problem while concurrently providing a wide range of services for general-purpose applications. The model presented here does show, however, that the architecture of a secure distributed system can be mapped into that of a secure computer system, employing most of the same concepts. The technology and applications of encryption to support the distributed nature of the system are well-understood, although few examples exist of systems that implement the most flexible of the public key management alternatives.

More work is particularly needed in defining an appropriate security model for a distributed system comprising multiple security domains, and in describing and implementing the various types of servers that are needed to support a coherent distributed-system architecture. Because work in the latter area is still in its infancy—even for distributed systems that have no security—we need to exercise caution in defining security architectures that apply to current network implementations but do not generalize to future systems. At the same time, we must balance this cautionary approach with the realization that the use of networks is growing continuously, constantly increasing the vulnerability of the computer systems that use them.

REFERENCES

Davies, D., ed. 1981. *The Security of Data in Networks.* Los Angeles, Cal.: IEEE Computer Society.
  A collection of classic articles and papers on network security, focusing on encryption, with a tutorial introduction; contains a comprehensive annotated bibliography of articles.

Denning, D. E. 1983. *Cryptography and Data Security.* Reading, Mass.: Addison-Wesley.
  A thorough study of cryptographic techniques, access controls, and database security, presented in textbook format with many exercises, examples, and references.

Glahn, P. G. von. 1983. "An Annotated Computer Network Security Bibliography." RADC-TR-83-251. Griffiss AFB, N.Y.: Rome Air Development Center. (Also available through Defense Technical Information Center, Alexandria, Va., DTIC AD-A139578.)
  A massive compilation of 675 annotated references on network and computer security. Although all of the references are unclassified, some may be hard to obtain.

Meyer, C. H., and Matyas, S. M. 1983. *Cryptography: A New Dimension in Computer Data Security.* New York: Wiley-Interscience.
  An up-to-date text on cryptography by leading experts in the field.

National Bureau of Standards. 1977. "Data Encryption Standard." FIPS PUB 46. Gaithersburg, Md.: National Bureau of Standards. Reprinted in *Advances in Computer System Security,* vol. 1, ed. R. Turn, pp. 59–74. Dedham, Mass.: Artech House (1981).
  The DES data encryption standard.

Padlipsky, M. A.; Snow, D. W.; and Karger, P. A. 1978. "Limitations of End-to-End Encryption in Secure Computer Networks." ESD-TR-78-158. Hanscom AFB, Mass.: Air Force Electronic Systems Division. (Also available through Defense Technical Information Center, Alexandria, Va., DTIC AD-A059221.)
  Discusses covert channels that are present when end-to-end encryption is used in a packet-switched network. The conclusions apply to local-area networks as well.

Rivest, R. L.; Shamir, A.; and Adleman, L. 1978. "A Method for Obtaining Digital Signatures and Public Key Cryptosystems. *Communications of the ACM* 21(2):120–26. Reprinted in *The Security of Data in Networks*, ed. D. Davies, pp. 158–64. Los Angeles, Cal.: IEEE Computer Society.
A description of the RSA public key encryption algorithm.

Rushby, J., and Randell, B. 1983. "A Distributed Secure System." *Computer* 16(7):55–67. Reprinted in *Advances in Computer System Security*, vol. 2, ed. R. Turn, pp. 228–40. Dedham, Mass.: Artech House (1984).
A design for a distributed collection of Unix workstations on a local-area network that supports mandatory security controls.

Voydock, V. L., and Kent, S. L. 1983. "Security Mechanisms in High-Level Network Protocols." *Computing Surveys* 15(2):135–71. Reprinted in *Advances in Computer System Security*, vol. 2, ed. R. Turn, pp. 309–46. Dedham, Mass.: Artech House (1984).
A good survey of network security threats and the use of encryption; covers many of the topics discussed in this chapter, and is a good source of further references.

BIBLIOGRAPHY

This bibliography is designed as a supplement to the reference lists concluding various chapters of the text. It is not an exhaustive list of works on computer security, but instead mentions only the primary general books and reports that are up-to-date and will be most useful to you in further study. Preference has been given to sources that incorporate or elaborate on prior work. For a more complete list of literature on a specific topic, and for pointers to original research, see the relevant reference list within the text, and refer to the works cited in those items.

The NTIS and DTIC numbers in many of the entries (here and in the various reference lists) provide a secondary source for the documents through the National Technical Information Service in Springfield, Virginia, and the Defense Technical Information Center in Alexandria, Virginia. Some documents are available only as technical reports directly from the organization that produced them.

GENERAL BOOKS AND PERIODICALS ON COMPUTER SECURITY

Abrams, M. D., and Podell, H. J. 1987. *Tutorial: Computer and Network Security.* IEEE Computer Society Order No. DX756. Los Angeles: IEEE. *A compilation of papers on computer security, with a tutorial introduction, covering a variety of topics. Many of the papers are from journals and conference proceedings referenced elsewhere in this book.*

Computer. 1983. "Computer Security Technology." *Computer* 16(7) (July 1983).

This special issue of Computer *contains a number of computer security articles, many of which are cited in the chapter references.*

Davies, D., ed. 1981. *The Security of Data in Networks.* Los Angeles, Cal.: IEEE Computer Society.

A collection of classic articles and papers on network security, focusing on encryption, with a tutorial introduction; contains a comprehensive annotated bibliography of articles.

Denning, D. E. 1983. *Cryptography and Data Security.* Reading, Mass.: Addison-Wesley.

A thorough study of cryptographic techniques, access controls, and database security, presented in textbook format with many exercises, examples, and references. This book should be on the shelf of every computer security library.

Department of Defense. 1985. *DoD Trusted Computer System Evaluation Criteria.* DOD 5200.28-STD. Washington, D.C.: Department of Defense. (U.S. Government Printing Office number 008-000-00461-7.)

The DoD criteria for evaluating and rating operating systems according to a scale based on security features and assurance. This document discusses many of the computer security concepts covered in this book.

Glahn, P. G. von. 1983. "An Annotated Computer Network Security Bibliography." RADC-TR-83-251. Griffiss AFB, N.Y.: Rome Air Development Center. (Also available through Defense Technical Information Center, Alexandria, Va., DTIC AD-A139578.)

A massive compilation of 675 annotated references on network and computer security. Although all of the references are unclassified, some may be hard to obtain.

IEEE Computer Society. 1987. "Special Issue on Computer Security and Privacy." *IEEE Transactions on Software Engineering* SE-13(2) (February 1987).

A special issue on computer security, with papers on verification, operating systems, and networking.

Lobel, J. 1986. *Foiling the System Breakers: Computer Security and Access Control.* New York: McGraw-Hill.

A discussion of all aspects of computer security and access control— physical and technical—written for a nontechnical audience.

National Computer Security Center. 1987. *Trusted Network Interpretation.* NCSC-TG-005. Ft. George G. Meade, Md.: National Computer Security Center.

An interpretation of the Trusted System Evaluation Criteria *for networks and network components.*

Turn, R., ed. 1981, 1984. *Advances in Computer System Security*. Vols. 1 and 2. Dedham, Mass.: Artech House.
A collection of computer security papers from journals and conferences. Many of the papers listed in the various chapter reference lists are reprinted here.

CONFERENCE PROCEEDINGS

American Institute of Aeronautics and Astronautics, and American Society for Industrial Security. 1985–87. *Aerospace Computer Security Conference: Protecting Intellectual Property in Space*. New York, N.Y.: AIAA.
This conference covers all aspects of computer security—technical and nontechnical—although it is not a primary outlet for technical research on operating systems or verification.

IEEE Computer Society. 1980–88. *Proceedings of the IEEE Symposium on Security and Privacy*. Washington, D.C.: IEEE Computer Society Press.
An annual conference covering topics of computer security, formal techniques, network security, and (occasionally) encryption. It is a primary outlet for reports of current computer security research.

International Federation of Information Processing. 1983–87. *Computer Security:* [various subtitles]. *Proceedings of the IFIP/Sec*. Amsterdam, The Netherlands: Elsevier Science Publishers B.V.
Topics covered include auditing, physical security, risk analysis, contingency planning, computer crime, legal issues, and encryption. There are occasional operating system security papers—usually presenting overviews of recent developments.

National Bureau of Standards. 1978–88. *Proceedings of the National Computer Security Conference*. Gaithersburg, Md.: National Bureau of Standards.
An annual conference, jointly sponsored by the National Computer Security Center and the National Bureau of Standards, covering a mix of technical and nontechnical topics. Oriented toward government needs, the conference emphasizes the Criteria *(Department of Defense 1985).*

SIGSOFT. 1980, 1981, 1985. "Proceedings of VERkshops I, II, and III." In *Software Engineering Notes* (July 1980, July 1981, and August 1985).
This is a small, highly technical conference, sponsored by SIGSOFT (a special interest group of the ACM), held at random intervals; its focus is research on formal verification.

INDEX

Page numbers in *italics* refer to figures; page numbers in **boldface** refer to tables.